Women Watching Television

DATE DUE

APR 2 7 2009		
MAR 2 8		
APR 1 5		

WOMEN WATCHING TELEVISION

Gender, Class, and Generation in the American Television Experience

Andrea L. Press

upp

UNIVERSITY OF PENNSYLVANIA PRESS **Philadelphia**

Copyright © 1991 by the University of Pennsylvania Press
ALL RIGHTS RESERVED
Printed in the United States of America
Third paperback printing 1992

Library of Congress Cataloging-in-Publication Data

Press, Andrea Lee.
  Women watching television : gender, class, and generation in the
American television experience / Andrea L. Press.
    p. cm.
  Includes bibliographical references and index.
  ISBN 0-8122-8169-1. — ISBN 0-8122-1286-X (pbk.)
  1. Women in television—United States.   2. Television and women—
United States.   3. Television audiences—United States.   I. Title.
PN1992.8.W65P74   1991
302.23′082—dc20   90-21274
                                                              CIP

To my mother and the memory of my father;
and to Bruce, for everything, and then some

Contents

Acknowledgments   ix

Introduction   **1**

Part I: Background   **13**

1. Theoretical Framework: Issues of Class, Gender, and Mass Media Reception   15

2. Work, Family, and Social Class in Television Images of Women: Prefeminism, Feminism, and Postfeminism on Prime-Time Television   27

Part II: Women Interpreting Television   **51**

Introduction. Women's Experiences with Television: The Evolution of the Meaning of Television Through the Generations   53

3. Middle-Class Women Discuss Television   63

4. Working-Class Women Discuss Television   97

5. Women Remembering Television: Pre- and Postfeminist Generations   141

Conclusion: Television Reception as a Window on Culture   **171**

Appendix: Methodology   179
Notes   195
Bibliography   213
Index   233

Acknowledgments

I OWE A GREAT DEBT to the many people who helped me complete this book. I wish to thank above all my advisor and chairman at the University of California at Berkeley, and my friend, Todd Gitlin. He provided constructive criticism, even under the pressure of close deadlines, and proved willing to take time out from his own very demanding schedule when I needed it most. He has been extremely understanding and loyal as the original dissertation experienced its inevitable growing pains. Others I worked with at U.C. Berkeley were also unfailingly supportive during the process of researching and writing. Arlie Hochschild and Robin Lakoff provided challenging discussion and laborious criticism of early drafts. Both were able to be at once honest and sympathetic, not an easy combination of qualities for committee members. Robert Bellah offered inspiration and intellectual stimulation, particularly in the early stages of the project. My work for Nancy Chodorow at the Institute of Personality Assessment and Research was also an inspiring experience; I would like to thank her for being an understanding employer and for giving me the opportunity to work with her.

Patricia Smith, my acquisitions editor at the University of Pennsylvania Press, was extremely helpful and encouraging during the darker hours of writing that this book required. I owe her an enormous debt. The comments of the anonymous reviewers solicited by the Press were also extremely helpful.

My fellow students at the University of California at Berkeley were wonderful colleagues, teachers, and critics. I would like to thank Tom Long for creating the Critical Theory study group and for being an excellent teacher and supportive friend. I would especially like to thank all the members of the TV study group—Tom Andre, Jon Cruz, Ron Lembo, Kathy Oberdeck, and Terry Strathman—for their support and intellectual companionship as we began to learn about television together. I also owe thanks to these people at Berkeley and elsewhere—Mandy Aftel, Diane Beeson, Dorothy Brown, Fred Fejes, Elaine Kaplan, Paul Lichterman, James Lull, Elinor Lurie, Diana Saco, Cathy Schwichtenberg, Jennifer Daryl Slack, Averill Thorne, Ken Tucker, Martcia Wade, and Ellen Wartella—for their friendship and intellectual support. Terry Strathman was integrally involved in the writing of chapter 2 and took over preparation of the book's index; she deserves special thanks for this and for her friendship throughout.

For financial support I am indebted to the University of Michigan, the National Institute of Mental Health, the Danforth Foundation, and Soroptimist International for grants enabling me to devote time to writing. Thanks are also due to librarians at the Library of Congress, the University of Michigan, and the University of California at Berkeley, and in particular to the staff of the Department of Communication at the University of Michigan.

Also deserving of thanks, of course, are the women who shared their time and stories with me during the interviews upon which this work is based. Many of them talked unselfishly and openly, and without them, there could have been no project. Jenny Engel, Sue Malakovski, and Judith Drummond were excellent transcribers, and helpful commentators as well. Knowing that I could count on their work eased my mind tremendously.

I owe special thanks to Bruce Williams. He gave unselfishly of his time by willingly reading, criticizing, and improving drafts at every stage of this project. The book is much the better for his attention to it. Without the faith, friendship, intellectual companionship, and everything else he provided, I would never have completed this book.

Ann Arbor, Michigan
April 2, 1990

Introduction

THIS BOOK emerged out of my concern that television in particular and the entertainment mass media in general heavily influence women's identities in our culture. As we enter what some nefariously call the period of postfeminism, it becomes more and more pressing to ask how women in our time use the images and ideas our culture makes available to them as they construct their own identities in the world and as they form their own ideas about what is normal and real outside of themselves. How have individual women's lives and thoughts been influenced by these recent changes and challenges to our cultural consensus about women's identities, roles, and activities? These are the concerns I had in mind when, as I began this study, I asked women to tell me about television.

Women in the Television Age

Women's identity as women—their gender identity—and, concomitantly, the roles women are expected to fulfill within social institutions have been areas of contested terrain in our culture for the past century. Beginning perhaps with Freud's admission of his hopeless confusion regarding the path of development the female personality follows from childhood to adulthood,[1] Western culture has debated the question through the forums of literature, the humanities, and the social sciences.

At the same time, women themselves—rarely afforded a cultural voice of their own—have engaged in ongoing struggles at the social-structural level which have articulated their many areas of dissatisfaction with their social roles and sexual identity, as these have been constituted by Western societies.[2] In fact, women have made substantial progress through political and social movements toward improving social and economic conditions for themselves and toward freeing themselves from the strictures of confining sexual and social identities. For example, women have won the vote; have achieved greater sexual freedom, more widespread use of birth control, and the legalization of abortion; and have taken the first steps toward breaking out of female employment ghettos and receiving equal compensation for equal work in our society.

One of the by-products of these successful reforms has been that our society's reigning conceptions[3] of female gender identity, sexual identity, and socioeconomic roles have been in a state of flux, particularly in the last twenty years given the rapid changes that have occurred during that time.[4] Some of our most basic conceptions have been challenged. For example, the notion that gender roles are "naturally differentiated" has been the subject of heated debate in several disciplines and among feminists themselves.[5]

Women in our culture are currently in a period of transition. The transition taking place is a gradual movement from a period known as feminism's "second wave," that period of intense feminist political activity which marked our society from the mid-1960s through the early 1970s, to a new period marked by a new confusion and a lack of assurance about the relationship between family and society, and women's part in each. "Postfeminism" is a term that has been coined recently to help describe this new state.[6] Generally, it describes a retreat from feminist ideas challenging women's traditional role in the family, an increasing openness toward traditional notions of femininity and feminine roles.

The second wave of feminism[7] which swept through our culture in the sixties and seventies has often been dated from 1963, the publication year of Betty Friedan's first book, *The Feminine Mystique*. *The Feminine Mystique*, incidentally one of the first books to discuss and critique social norms of female identity in conjunction with a critical examination of female images in the popular media, brought in its wake what has been termed a "feminist revolution."[8] Feminists began to discuss—for now there *was* a feminist discourse—possible new identities for women, in terms that were psychological, sociological, economic, and cultural all at once. Change was upon us, and its possibilities seemed limitless.

Dating perhaps from Ronald Reagan's ascent to power in 1980, the hopes and dreams of the women's movement have been seriously threatened as our society's leaders and moods move farther and farther to the right. The Equal Rights Amendment (ERA) was soundly defeated by a sufficient number of state legislatures in 1982.[9] Today, women's right to reproductive freedoms is being challenged by our highest-ranking leaders. Affirmative action programs, a boon to women and minorities seeking entry into the powerful social spheres they have been denied contact with for centuries, are waning in response to our country's mood as well as recent Supreme Court decisions. Some have noted (Nie et al. 1976; Galston 1985) a possible overall shift in public opinion toward the right in our society[10] and, concomitantly, a shift from a feminist to what some term a postfeminist period.

These political events have left those involved with the feminist movement in the nineties preoccupied with a number of difficult questions. Among the most serious of these is the issue of the movement's alleged white middle-class bias during its heyday, and the effects this bias has had on the longevity of the movement's gains and overall tenacity. Are the mass of women truly alienated from the movement, as some have implied? Many current feminist writers, even progenitress

Friedan herself, are writing what can be interpreted by some as anti-feminist tracts. Their attacks are varied. Some accuse the feminist movement of ignoring the family concerns central to so many women (Friedan 1981; Greer 1984; Hewlett 1986). Others accuse the movement of ignoring the plight of poor women and their specific concerns (Sidel 1986).

Still others, in an emerging position labeled by some as a postfeminist point of view, urge feminists to look to prefeminist, essentialist female traditions if they hope to address the concerns of the majority of our society's women (Ruddick 1980; Elshtain 1981 and 1982).[11] The postfeminist perspective questions feminist ideals for women, charging that they primarily appropriate a masculine model of the self. Rather than aspiring unquestioningly toward a masculine image of fulfillment, those arguing in a postfeminist vein urge women to take as their model images rooted in a more traditionally feminine mode. Thus, the prototypical "career woman" ideal is criticized in postfeminist theory and replaced by one that combines career aspirations for women with more familiar, familial goals. Some contend that the latter "woman-in-the-home" theme takes clear precedence over outside achievement for those configuring the postfeminist woman. In any case, the debate over postfeminism at the very least highlights our growing cultural confusion, and dissatisfaction, with the respective places of family and career in the lives of many women.

Some feminists criticize postfeminist thought, saying it will lead us into a period of retrenchment for women and will result in a lessening of the social and political gains and freedoms that many women have experienced in the wake of the feminist movement. Others interpret postfeminist social currents differently, arguing that they allow a new freedom for women, urging as they do an appropriation of the strengths of women's traditional roles in combination with, rather than in place of, more feminist ideals. Whatever the results of this upheaval in our current thinking, women in our culture now stand at an ideological crossroads. How do the mass media represent these developments to women? How do women themselves conceptualize this confusion? Do the mass media have an impact on the way women are responding to these ideological developments?

Our culture's representations of the female gender have changed along with our consensual ideas, in a complicated relationship of response to, and influence upon, our changing cultural notions about female roles and identity. It is representation—and women's continuing interaction with it—that concerns me in this study. Against a background of radically fluctuating ideas about gender identity, shifting representations of gender, and actual concrete changes in the social, economic, and cultural roles both women and men play in our society, I seek to investigate the relationship between the representations women have of themselves—this I define as their "self-image" or "identity"—and one set of representations our culture presents to women of themselves—their images in the mass media, specifically television entertainment shows.

We do not create representations, even representations of ourselves, in the abstract. Representations of gender identity occur within a massive sea of various and conflicting images of gender, many of which are propagated by the mass media. These presentations help to constitute the image-environment within which our adult identities—and our own ability to represent—are developed. Even a cursory examination of one portion of these media images—the images of women in television entertainment—reveals that our culture's contradictory notions about feminine gender identity and female roles are represented in this medium in complex ways. My examination of these images (see chapter 2) reveals that the advent of the feminist movement in the late 1960s coincides with, first, an increase in the number of working women depicted on television and, later, with an increase in the number of women shown both in the family and at work. Contradictions between women's roles in the family and at work, which feminist social scientists and commentators have increasingly noted,[12] are at least glossed over, and often blatantly ignored, in these images.

There are other dimensions of women's lives that are also essentially ignored, or at least masked, in television programming. Whereas feminist analyses highlight the role contradictions between work and family for women and how these have changed over the decades, Marxist analyses emphasize the way in which women's membership in specific social classes must be considered in analyzing their oppression.[13] Eisenstein (1979), Hartmann and Bridges (1979), Weinbaum (1978), and other socialist feminists have long argued that both capitalism (the mode of production) and patriarchy (sometimes defined in parallel fashion as the mode of reproduction; more often considered to mean the system of male domination particular to a given society), that is, the system of class oppression as well as gender oppression, must be considered when one analyzes women's identity and position in complex modern societies.

The mass media in general and television in particular have long been recognized by communication scientists to mask class differences in American society (Adorno 1954; Rubin 1976; Lemon 1978; Jackson-Beeck and Sobal 1980; Sklar 1980; Gould et al. 1981; Novak 1981; Thomas and Callahan 1982), gender oppression (Tedesco 1974; Weibel 1977; Sklar 1980; Mellencamp 1986), and particularly the oppression of working-class women (D'Amico 1974).[14] A significant amount of early communication research in the United States attempted to investigate the television viewing habits of, and television's effect on, members of the working class (Coffin 1955; Geiger and Sokol 1959; Komarovsky 1967; Shostak 1969). More recently in American cultural and communication studies, there has been a conspicuous lack of attention paid to class concerns.

Few researchers, if any, have attempted to investigate television viewing patterns and television's effects specifically on women. of either the working class or the middle class. The American literature, while at times taking seriously Marxist concepts of class in its analysis, has only just begun to pay attention to feminist concerns (see especially Radway 1984b and Long 1986). Little attention has been paid to the particular concerns of working-class women, however.[15] Considerations such as these have led me to focus on a comparison of working-class with middle-class women's interpretations of and responses to television characters and narrative, alongside my examination of generational differences.

British communication studies, particularly the work of the Birmingham School,[16] have fared slightly better, in that at least the importance of studying the cultural experience of women of different classes has been recognized (McRobbie 1978a, 1978b, 1980).[17] The bias of Birmingham School studies of working-class men and women, however, has been the discovery and articulation of working-class subcultures of resistance to the dominant society (McRobbie 1978b; Willis 1978; Hebdige 1979).[18] In these studies, investigation of cultural hegemony—the way the dominant culture orchestrates the consent of those who are dominated within it[19]—is well illustrated in studies that investigate the way working-class subjectivity is colonized in hegemonic interests.

The work of the Birmingham School has been quite useful for the Left in Britain, where the historical tradition of organized working-class resistance is much stronger than in the United States.[20] While Birmingham School studies have in many ways seminally inspired my own project, the defiant spirit with which they discuss British working-class culture is less appropriate when applied to American working-class culture, which has been much less unified historically. Although working-class culture may illuminate working-class resistance to domination in the British context, in the American context the lack of cultural resistance, rather than its incipient presence, and the lack of even the appearance of a rebellious working-class subjectivity, become the important issues when one investigates working-class cultural practices and creations.

Many studies have remarked on the problem of working-class passivity in the United States (Katznelson 1981). It is this prominent issue that implicates the role of the mass media in our society. There has been a fair amount of controversy in media studies concerning the relative activity or passivity of the mass media audience (Katz and Lazarsfeld 1955; Horkheimer and Adorno 1972; Gitlin 1978). In the case of working-class women, however, we have a doubly ignored and doubly oppressed population, and one for whom the Marxist framework which has informed most of these studies has been largely inadequate.[21] Certainly, it is time that their situation vis-à-vis the mass media and the dominant culture more generally be seriously examined.

Preliminary interviews with women showed that, indeed, relationships with and attitudes toward the social institutions of work and family were in a state of flux for many, adding up to a possible "identity crisis" for some and, most important for my purposes here, that concerns of this sort did vary with class as well as age differences. These *differences*, in particular, interested me in this study. Class differences were especially interesting to me because theories about gender, class, and the mass media were so undeveloped in our literature as I began this research.

Among the questions that motivated my theoretical and empirical study were the following. How do women exposed to television images from the time they are young respond to contradictions both in television's portrayal of gender roles and in television's treatment of social class in our society? Are these contradictions assimilated or denied? Perhaps both? Perhaps neither? Do women's self-conceptions correspond to television images, directly or indirectly? Do women perhaps *use* television's images of them in forming their own images of themselves? Do women *identify* with images of women they view on the television screen, and if so, what does identification mean in this context? And finally, is television's *reality* accepted as a *realistic* representation of the social world by female viewers, and if so, what are the consequences of this fact for the issues of female identity in which I am interested? While I have not been able to examine all of these issues, I hope I have at least touched upon them, while focusing in depth on the latter two.

Why Look at Television?

Television is one of our most powerful cultural institutions. In a society in which more people have television sets than indoor plumbing, where children spend more time in front of the television set than in any other activity, few would deny television's symbolic power. Yet decades after the first attempts to research mass media effects, we still know very little about how mass media in general and television in particular influence individuals and social groups. And, while the question of women's particular relationship to television and the mass media has recently sparked much theoretical interest by those interested primarily in analyzing media texts, little empirical research exists to support this body of theory.

My study, with its focus on gender in relation to hegemonic theory, is intended to help refine the debate over the hegemonic functions of television entertainment. Currently there is much debate in the critical literature over the nature of television's impact in our society. Some argue that television and the other mass media help to solidify the domination of certain social class groups over others. I augment this critical tradition by adding a focus on gender domination. Can it be said that television reinforces patriarchal values in our culture? If so, how does television contribute to women's oppression? Either additionally, or alternately, is television in any way implicated when women act to resist their domination in our culture? How does it function to aid this kind of cultural resistance? These are some of the theoretical questions I hope to shed light on with this study.

On a more personal level, television images have been deeply important for me, particularly during the years in which I came of age. I was much exposed and, I fear, much influenced by the plethora of images television offered. Consequently television, more than any other medium, has always been a pervasive presence in my interior life. This personal starting point has sparked my interest in studying the importance of television images in our society, particularly for women at different stages of their life cycle. Of all the mass media, television is possibly the least studied (although this is changing rapidly) and perhaps the most widely consumed in our society. Gronbeck sums up television's overall importance in our social universe of images more convincingly than my own reflections:

> The dream conceived by Vladimir Zworykin, which led to his invention in 1923 of the conomoscope, the "eye" of electronic image-making, has materialized in a sprawling set of interlocking industries worth billions of dollars and employing millions of people. . . . An increase by even 1 percent in a primetime program's viewership represents more people than those who subscribe to *Atlantic Monthly* or *Harper's* magazines. The audience for local news in metropolitan areas dwarfs the readership of the country's largest newspapers. *Thus television is America's only truly "mass" medium.* (Gronbeck 1984:1; emphasis added)

Much of the growing literature about television makes reference to its pervasive presence in our society, and to the far-reaching nature of its importance to our fantasies and, perhaps, to other aspects of our lives as well (Gitlin 1983 and 1986; Allen 1986). My reflections, combined with the growing body of literature noting television's importance and attempting to pinpoint the most effective means of documenting its influence, persuaded me that television images were an appropriate and important focus of study for one interested in the interplay between media texts and conceptions of gender identity.

Preliminary Hypotheses and Procedures

With some exceptions,[22] few studies of media effects and use have concentrated on women's particular experience with mass media, and fewer still have looked at women's responses to television.[23] Yet the field of media effects research is currently in a period of upheaval caused in part by the impact of recent feminist critiques of traditional research methodologies in the social sciences generally. More effects researchers are employing qualitative, interpretive methodologies of study, leading to results of a more interpretive, critical cast than were previously dominant in the field. In this study, I was interested in applying this new methodological tradition—what some would call feminist methodology—to studying women's particular experiences with prime-time entertainment television. By treating the "effects" question more dialogically and openly, and by respecting the subjectivity and activity of those I interviewed, I hoped to contribute to the qualitative work of recent media researchers the feminist theoretical and methodological insights garnered from the experience of interviewing women about television.

I began my preliminary interviews with the suspicion that class differences and generational differences in women's creative responses to television would quickly emerge. On the basis of the small amount of research into class differences in viewers' use of, and response to, the mass media which has been carried out thus far, I expected to find differences between the way working-class and middle-class women judged television to be realistic or unrealistic. Preliminary interviews indicated that, in fact, there were class differences between the way working-class and middle-class women discussed television as realistic. Again, from my reading of the current literature and also my common-sense ideas as to the nature of identification processes, I also expected that women of each class would identify with different television characters, depending upon their class membership, and that the quality of their identification would vary in conjunction with their assessment of television's realism or lack thereof. Again, preliminary interviews indicated that this appeared to be the case, in that class membership influenced both the specific situations in which identification with television characters occurred and the form and quality of the identifications made.

For a number of reasons, I expected that older women would have a different relationship to television from that of younger women. Paradoxically, I expected more fascination with television, though less attachment to it, among older women for whom exposure to television might have come relatively later in their lives than it has for young women who have, almost without exception, grown up alongside television programming. Although television might be a more interesting phenomenon to those who remember its invention and introduction into our culture, for those who actually grew up with it, I expected to find more intimacy in their relationship to it, that ultimately television could be shown to have profoundly influenced their identity and growth, particularly during their early, formative years. Preliminary interviews indicated that this may be the case, and that the content of current television programming was implicated in the ability, or inability, of both age groups to identify with the characters presented. I decided to focus on their respective responses to varying depictions of women's relationship to work and family, since it was these particular qualities of television's women which seemed to provoke characteristic responses from each of the two groups, and since the issue of balancing work and family is central to the current shift in women's identities in our culture.

In the chapters that follow, I illustrate the different responses obtained from my informants in interviews about television. In chapters 3, 4, and 5, I attempt to account for both the generational and the class aspects of these differences in a discussion of the changing depiction of women's class-specific qualities—that is, the material quality of their family lives and their type of paid employment, when applicable—as these are depicted in the content of prime-time television entertainment shows. These chapters are preceded by a theoretical discussion which sets the stage for the empirical studies to follow. In chapter 1, I review the critical theoretical literature about media's cultural effects in some detail, situating my study within it. Chapter 2 selectively and briefly examines the history of depictions of women in television entertainment, concluding with a discussion of recent trends toward postfeminist images in television shows too recent even to be discussed in my interviews. Chapters 3 and 4 focus on the responses of middle-class and working-class women, respectively, and chapter 5 compares women of different generations as they discuss television shows and characters. In the Conclusion, I summarize the theoretical contributions my data offer. The Appendix details the interview process and summarizes some personal details about the women I interviewed.

Part I: Background

Chapter 1

Theoretical Framework: Issues of Class, Gender, and Mass Media Reception

The complexity of television viewing can be best accommodated by applying elements of several paradigms which have recently been used in studying responses to the mass media specifically and culture more generally: "hegemony theory" which has characterized an essentially Gramscian-Althusserian Marxist school of mass media study, the British Cultural Studies tradition,[1] and the more general tradition of British and American feminist cultural studies to which British Cultural Studies has given rise. In the sections that follow, I offer a brief survey of these theoretical traditions, the combination of which has informed the research I present here.

Unlike many currently working in our field, rather than conceptualizing these two modes of response in an either-or fashion, I stress the need to discuss both viewer resistance to our culture's often hegemonic messages and viewer accommodation to these messages as two integral parts of women's responses to entertainment television, both of which come into play for most women in different situations and at different times. It is my hope that the following discussion, in which I explicate my theoretical position more fully, will give the reader a framework which may help in situating and evaluating the research presented here.

Hegemony Theory and Television

Ideology refers generally to the terrain of ideas so centrally constitutive of our worldviews that we fail to notice what they are.[2] The hegemonic perspective asserts that television's meanings play some role in solidifying ideologies in capitalist societies such as the United States (Gerbner 1972; Schudson 1978; Tuchman 1978; Gitlin 1980, 1983; Schiller 1985). Television, which some may analogously describe to be such an integral part of our lives that we also fail to notice it as we might fail to notice a necessary piece of living room or bedroom furniture, provides, in the context of our private experience, a constant stream of social images that impinge upon our view of the world and upon our very definitions of who we are. Television's unobtrusive nature, amplified by its hidden location in the private sphere, may make it effective in the same way ideologies are effective: unconsciously, both structure our conceptions of self and the social world.

The Italian Marxist Antonio Gramsci developed the concept of hegemony to describe the manner through which the ruling class dominates by securing popular consent to its rule.[3] Gramsci adopted the notion of hegemony to give new importance to struggles within the ideological realm of society, claiming that these were as important as physical coercion by the state apparatuses in maintaining popular support for the ruling class (Boggs 1976:17). One writer defines Gramsci's theory of hegemony as "an order in which a certain way of life and thought is dominant, in which one concept of reality is diffused throughout society in all its institutional and private manifestations, informing with its spirit all taste, morality, customs, religious and political principles, and all social relations, particularly in their intellectual and moral connotations" (Williams 1960:587; quoted in Cammett 1967:204). The theory of hegemony for the first time exposed the institutions of the capitalist superstructure—the family, the church, education, and the mass media—to intensive Marxist scrutiny. In the period since Gramsci's writings came to light, these institutions have been examined, with the theoretical tools he helped develop, in light of their function as bolstering and transmitting ideology. This occurs in complex, mediated ways to be sure, but occurs "functionally" nonetheless (Althusser 1971; Boggs 1976; Adamson 1980).

Gramsci used the example of the United States to illustrate what was, in his view, the best instance of a society in which the ruling classes had achieved, throughout their history, almost complete ideological hegemony (Gramsci 1971; Boggs 1976:50–51). In the United States, capitalist development, in the absence of a feudal past, led to the emergence of a new type of individual and a new type of culture, both of which were permeated with capitalist values, in Gramsci's analysis. While Gramsci may have overstated the case, it is important that those analyzing values, beliefs, and ideology in the United States take seriously the possibility of capitalist ideological hegemony and seek to explain either resistance to it or the lack of resistance found among specific groups and individuals within them.

Television, Realism, and Everyday Life

From some perspectives, television can be seen to be a particularly salient instrument of hegemony.[4] Surrounded as many of us are by television in our private lives, its images may come to seem more real to us than our own experiences. At the very least, television images compete with our experience and influence our interpretation of it.

Many writers have commented on the realistic nature of television (Gitlin 1980, 1983; Marc 1989).[5] They note that, in our culture, television has become a part of our daily lives. It is accepted into the flow of our routine, or into our everyday division of labor (Kuhn 1982:25). As a result, television may be unique among media in that its images are strongly positioned to be accepted unconsciously by viewers as presenting images of reality, that is, as painting pictures of our world as it truly exists.

Television is a domestic medium. We watch television primarily in the private space of our homes (unlike films, for example, which have until recently been viewed in public movie theaters). Some researchers connect the way television consumption has increased vis-à-vis films to the historical ascendancy of the private over the public sphere (Williams 1974:28–29) in our culture. As society becomes privatized, the images and ideas we consume in the privacy of our homes become increasingly numerous and influential, particularly with the growth of television as a medium that can bring the outside public world into the privacy of our homes.[6]

In American life, while we pay lip service to the public, for most of us the private is the realm of the real.[7] This reliance on the private realm is particularly salient for women in our society, whose role in the public world is even less legitimated than that of men. Such a pattern of attributing primary importance and reality to the private realm, coupled with our almost universal possession and viewing of television sets, points to the possibility that what television portrays impacts heavily on our views of the world and ourselves (Gerbner 1972). It is possible that we rely on television for images of social reality, which may be skewed, however, in demonstrable, ideologically informed ways. Television helps us to bridge the gap between the public and private realms of our lives and to maintain, in our increasingly fragmented lives, a feeling of connection—however precarious—with the social world, even if this connection is emotive rather than substantive.[8]

Due primarily to its domestic location, television presumes a "family audience" (Ellis 1982; Morley 1986; Lembo 1988) and often, since women spend on average more time in the home than do men, a feminine one (Hobson 1982; Modleski 1982). Probably for these reasons, television content has long been preoccupied with portrayals of the nuclear family.[9] But this preoccupation has taken a particular form. The repetitive series convention of television programming makes television, unlike film, particularly suited to presenting the world as stable and unchanging;[10] the result is that both television content as a whole, and its presumed audience, are depicted in a manner biased toward the stability of the nuclear family.

Television's repetitive series format dictates several other important distinctions between television and more public visual media such as film. The narrative, central to traditional Hollywood narrative film, for example, is incidental to television. Whereas narrative film (like other traditional narrative forms) involves movement of an individual spectator through a problem which is resolved at the narrative's conclusion, television narrative works differently. Problems are never really resolved on series television, since the series must live on. Narrative resolution takes place then at a less fundamental level in television than in film, at the level of individual incidents (e.g., clinches, confrontations, or conversations) that are offered to us each week. It is the dilemma that characterizes the television series, not resolution or closure (Ellis 1982).

Consequently, the individual spectator posited by narrative film is either not posited by television in individual format at all or not attributed the same powerful voyeuristic "gaze" that film structurally imparts to its spectator, according to classical film theory.[11] Television, presuming as it does a family or essentially group audience, focuses its situations primarily around family-like groupings rather than around individuals.

We thus might expect it to be more difficult to make strong identifications with individual television characters than with film characters. As a result, the viewer herself has less power than does the spectator of a narrative film; rarely is there one main, powerful, all-knowing character with whom to identify, but rather merely a series of less powerful, more limited egos as objects for identification (Modleski 1982:91). Feminist theorists (Dinnerstein 1976; Chodorow 1978; Flax 1983) have posited a new "female" model for the individual, arguing that women individuate differently from men, maintaining much closer connections to their mothers, children, and others throughout their lives. In some ways, then, television is uniquely suited to the female viewer, uniquely able to draw women into involvement with itself.

Television's characteristic qualities have given rise to hot debates over its potential social power. While some commentators find television's presence in our interior domestic space threatening and invasive (Ellis 1982), others understand television's domestic presence very differently. Some see precisely this feature of the medium as ensuring its submission, above other media, to the terms of our collective discourse, and therefore to individual discourses when these vary from the collective:

> In going out to cinema we tend to submit to its terms, to become subject to its discourse, but television comes to our discourses. The living room as cultural space means differently to different members of the family. . . . These different meanings of the cultural space of viewing result in different social discourses being brought to bear upon television, and thus in different cultural texts being made out of it. (Fiske 1986:212)

In this argument, television is less totalizing than film because it is more directly subjugated to the terms of our discourse, rather than we to its terms. Others agree, arguing that television's particular appropriation of the traditional narrative actually opens this form up to active, give-and-take participation from the viewing audience (Altman 1986:50). This position emphasizes viewers' abilities to resist television's hegemonic meanings with interpretations of their own. In a particular form, this perspective is articulated in some of the works done by those writing within the British Cultural Studies tradition and by those responsible for the emerging tradition of feminist cultural studies as well. In the sections below, I examine the theoretical tensions between an emphasis on television's hegemonic functions and considerations of viewer resistance, while discussing these traditions more extensively.

The British Cultural Studies Tradition

In Great Britain, theorists associated with the Centre for Contemporary Cultural Studies (CCCS) of the University of Birmingham, sometimes called the Birmingham School (Stuart Hall, Angela McRobbie, Paul Willis, among others), have built upon Gramsci's theory along with Althusserian Marxism to develop a rather distinctive school of qualitative study of media content and cultural influence.[12] Their reliance on both Gramsci and Althusser leads to a tension between a focus on the active subjectivity of the working class, which Gramsci at times stressed, and a belief in the determinative structures of society delineated in the works of Althusser. In general, theorists of the school have used ethnographic and interpretive as well as histori-

cal methodologies to search for evidence of both ideological and political resistance to dominant social ideologies, and the colonization
of this resistance, among oppressed gender, class, ethnic, and other
groups.

Some of those working in the British Cultural Studies tradition have
been interested in actual empirical study of the mass media audience.
Works of the Birmingham School that treat media audiences specifically include Morley's recent work (1980, 1986) and, in part, the earlier
works of Cohen (1973) and Hall et al. (1978). Other Birmingham
works treat the operation of culture within consciousness generally, examining in depth the consciousness of specific social groups (working-
class youths or women, for example) in order to illuminate in general
the ways in which culture does, or does not, determine class, gender, or
group consciousness. Among the best of these works are Willis (1977,
1978) and McRobbie (1978a, 1978b, 1981, 1984).

Qualitative methodologies—the in-depth interview, ethnography,
and participant observation of small groups and small group discussions—have been used almost exclusively by British Cultural Studies
researchers. Such methods have been deemed necessary by members
of the school in order to unmask the apparent resistances they seek.
Recently, Morley in particular has been interested in using ethnography, and ethnographic interviewing, to replace more traditional interviewing styles, allowing the researcher to pay more attention to the
context, rather than merely the content, of informants' remarks (Morley 1981:5; 1986).[13]

There is a tension in Birmingham School work generally in the
operant definition of "culture" which members of the school use.[14] As
Hall describes, Birmingham researchers tend to investigate both consciousness—the realm of ideas—and, in a more anthropological vein,
the social practices of cultural groups. This dual mode of investigation
leads to a contradiction in their theoretical orientation. Their investiga-
tions of consciousness are primarily informed by a Marxist conception
of ideology, which implies that at times the consciousness one investigates is "false," obscuring what is real. Thus Willis (1977), for example,
can conclude his study of working-class schoolboys' consciousness,
Learning to Labor, by making the claim, however indirectly, that the lads
he studied do not fully understand their position as members of the
working class in capitalist society and that, despite the appearance of
resistance, their subjectivity as constituted contributes to their own
oppression as members of this class. This judgment, however, for it is a
judgment of their consciousness, conflicts with the anthropological emphasis in cultural investigation, which urges one to record and under-

stand practices rather than to evaluate them, and particularly urges one to avoid labeling specific forms of consciousness and levels of understanding as "false" or "true."

Such dualities of thought have kept Birmingham researchers, in some respects, ambivalent. They are interested in identifying and describing the practices of subcultures in capitalist society in an anthropological mode; yet their descriptions are always set within a critical Marxist framework, which would lead them to place negative judgments on many of these subcultures. Their respect for the oppression of those they study, however, and their unwillingness to privilege their own position as intellectuals capable of seeing the truth,[15] leaves them many times unwilling to make such judgments and at times seeming to glorify the subjective forms of resistance practiced by oppressed groups, even when these are ineffective. Yet overall, members of the school have a distinct and subtle goal, which they often achieve rather elegantly in their work: to show how active consciousness also contributes to domination in capitalist societies (MacCabe 1986; Willis 1978 is particularly elegant as he achieves this aim). The work of the school has been pioneering for those interested in studying culture and consciousness within capitalist society.

British Cultural Studies as a framework, in accordance with its Marxist heritage, has privileged the concept of social class as a basic category of social analysis. The Cultural Studies paradigm has been used, therefore, primarily to articulate working-class experience with, and appropriation of, dominant cultural forms in capitalist society, again because their Marxist heritage leads Birmingham School researchers to search for resistance by those dominated in society. One of the school's primary terms of analysis, the "subculture," frames cultural use as almost inherently oppositional to the status quo. Cultural groups are categorized as to whether they possess this critical perspective, or lack it. There has also been more of a focus on public groups which are formed according to social class-related criteria, on people who live, work, or go to school together, than there is on the family or the individual as a unit of analysis. In part, this is because the masculinist bias of the school has led its members to concentrate on male expressions of resistance, which are often public, overt, and more easily studied than the characteristically privatized female forms.[16]

The Cultural Studies framework is strongest in its ability to illuminate class-specific responses to mass culture characteristic of the working class, particularly working-class men, but it has not been widely used to investigate the experiences of members of other classes, even in the same society. Gender differences have been particularly difficult for this framework to analyze, therefore, primarily because the genders relate in very different fashions to the subcultural groups that form the basic units of analysis in Cultural Studies. Long (1989) eloquently discusses three main points of feminists' critiques of British Cultural Studies: their public bias, the primacy of class, and the assumption that resistance is rationally expressed. Feminists working in the Cultural Studies tradition have challenged each of these features which dominate most of the school's work. These challenges have led the feminist Cultural Studies researchers in new, somewhat unorthodox directions, spawning a significant body of feminist Cultural Studies in both Britain and the United States.[17]

One of the products of this feminist reaction is Angela McRobbie's remarkable work (1978a, 1978b, 1980, 1982, 1984).[18] In an early piece (1978b), McRobbie notes the virtual absence in the youth culture literature of any discussion pertaining to women.[19] One reason for this, she notes, is the difficulty the observer normally has in gaining access to girls and to female groups. Girls generally spend much more time in private places, such as their homes, or the homes of friends and other family members, than do boys. Girls' groups tend to be smaller—the best-friend dyad is predominant—and again, to gather more often in nonpublic places. Even more important, McRobbie senses that girls' groups exhibit a greater degree of hostility toward the outside questioner than males have shown, perhaps because of the more private, intimate focus of the female social world.

All of these factors contribute to the difficulties the researcher interested in women's cultural experience must face. McRobbie found herself forced to rely more on in-depth interviews (my main tool here as well) and less on participant observation techniques than did Willis in his study of males.[20] Confronting all of these limitations, McRobbie nevertheless produces a fascinating document of the cultural world inhabited by working-class girls. She posits the possibility of a "culture of femininity" which is passed on from mothers to daughters, the content of which differs significantly from the dominant male culture. Interesting for my purposes here is the fact that McRobbie pays close attention to her subjects' creative appropriation of mass media meanings as she describes the content of the "culture of femininity" she has discovered.

McRobbie well notes the masculinist bias of the British Cultural Studies tradition.[21] Effectively, she challenges their privileging of class as the most important culturally organizing category, introducing the variable of gender as at least as important. The integration of these two variables, gender and class, therefore, becomes a major concern for McRobbie and others in her tradition.[22]

Women's Culture and Gender-Based Theories of Media Reception: New Developments in Feminist Cultural Studies

British Cultural Studies articulates the specificity of working-class culture and gives us the theoretical tools with which to begin studying this phenomena, at least insofar as it occurs among male members of the working class. But in order to flesh out the notion of gender-specific culture and cultural processes, which will also be important in my analysis here, we must extend McRobbie's critique of Birmingham School work to some of the insights of American feminism. In its focus on individual development and processes, American feminism[23] adds to the Cultural Studies' class emphasis a deeper understanding of conscious and unconscious processes governing individual thoughts and behaviors. Viewing, so often practiced by individuals alone in private settings,[24] must be analyzed in part through attention to these aspects of the process.

Feminist Cultural Studies as practiced in the United States has borrowed the American feminist emphasis on individual psychology but has applied this primarily to the analysis of texts (in the tradition of American cultural studies; see note 1 to this chapter). Psychoanalytic theory has figured prominently in the works of this group, particularly in the area of feminist film theory, but again, there have been few attempts to apply this theory to the empirical study of reception processes in actual people.[25]

Radway's (1984b) innovative ethnographic study of female romance readers has helped to pave the way toward a new methodology for studying the female audience. With a background in literary criticism, Radway drew not only from social science research but also from the growing reader-response tradition in literary study as she conceived and executed her study.[26] She identified a group of romance readers in the Midwest and conducted in-depth interviews, group interviews, and surveys with these women in order to investigate the meaning of romance reading for them. Radway employs a feminist interpretation of romance reading, suggesting that the reading activity itself serves the function of claiming personal time for women who might otherwise have very little time to themselves. Radway (1984b:187) also believes that women identify with the active, independent qualities of the romantic heroines they preferred.

Radway's study, with its provocative conclusions, raises many questions. One is particularly left wondering about the tensions between the patriarchal and the feminist aspects of romance content, in conjunction with the possible function of the activity of reading itself.[27] As in the work of the Birmingham School, there is a tension in Radway's book between her desire to respect and simply record the cultural practices of the women she studied, and her feminist political commitments which give her some grounds for making negative judgments regarding the content and ultimate consequences of romance reading.[28]

Radway's sample is predominately middle-class.[29] One cannot help wondering how her readers' discussions of romances were shaded by their class position. Would working-class women have identified so strongly with the female heroines the middle-class women preferred? Or, given that working-class women might have chosen a different set of heroines with different qualities as their favorites, would identification with these fictional characters have been as primary a process for working-class women at all? Radway's study leaves these class-specific questions unanswered, making it difficult to determine whether her findings are generalizable to *all* women, or apply only to this class-specific group.

Radway does offer an interesting discussion of the ambivalent attitude her informants display toward the reality of the romantic stories they read.[30] While almost all of Radway's informants deny that romantic stories are "realistic," and assert that they do not expect their own lives to resemble the lives of romantic heroines, at the same time they insist that romances often instruct them about history and geography, broadening their experience and knowledge of the world. Radway concludes that, at the very least, women display an ambivalent attitude toward the reality of the stories they read. She consequently remains ambivalent in theorizing the real impact of romances: in some respects they are liberating, encouraging women to find their own, independent identity, while in other respects they conservatively encourage women to conform to the dictates of their traditional roles as wives, mothers, and nurturers of men and children.

The women may in fact believe the stories are only fantasies on one level at the very same time that they take other aspects of them to be real and therefore apply information learned about the fictional world to the events and occurrences of theirs. If they do so utilize some fictional propositions, it may well be the case that the readers also unconsciously take others having to do with the nature of the heroine's fate as generally applicable to the lives of real women. In that case, no matter what the women intend their act of reading to say about their roles as wives and mothers, the ideological force of the reading experience could, finally, be a conservative one. In reading about a woman who manages to find her identity through the care of a nurturant protector and sexual partner, the Smithton readers might well be teaching themselves to believe in the worth of such a route to fulfillment and encouraging the hope that such a route might yet open up for them as it once did for the heroine. (Radway 1984b:187)

Radway relates her informants' belief in the reality of romantic characters and stories to their more general acceptance of the reality of the romantic world created by the romance narrative itself (1984b:186–208). Romance novels, she demonstrates, combine the elements of both myth and novel. They offer a plot that promises to detail the adventures of a unique, individual woman but that actually tells a story which has been told many times before and proceeds in a fashion extremely predictable to its readers, although they are not always aware of these elements of repetition (Radway 1984b:207–208). In this sense, as Radway notes, the narrative conveys the message that in some respects, despite individual differences, women are all the same, that they should and must conform to a generically "female" role, reinforcing our society's traditional sexual division of labor (1984b:208). Thus Radway finds that, although women readers may assert their independence with the act of romance reading, the content of romances actually undermines their independence by affirming that the destiny of all women consists in their filling fundamentally identical social roles.

By focusing on romance novels, Radway chose a cultural product specifically directed at, and consumed by, a female audience. Her study paves the way for the possibility of discussing those aspects of women's reception of culture that are specific to their position in society, a position that has been in great flux in recent years, making generalizations all the more problematic. Although focused on middle-class women, Radway's work helps us add to the British Cultural Studies' emphasis on class a deeper understanding of the meaning of gender for women's reception of culture. Other recent American works,[31] in particular Long's (1986, 1987) studies of women's reading groups and the interpretation of books, have helped to extend further the theoretical terms and empirical dimensions of Radway's study, delineating the specific issues involved in women's cultural reception and describing the forms women's reception takes in American society. Among their other concerns, these works address women's responses to popular understandings and representations of feminist ideas deriving from the women's liberation movement and the fluidity of women's social positions it helped initiate.

The intersection of class and gender cultures forms the backdrop for my analysis of women's discussions of television. Although the universe of prime-time television entertainment is of course much broader than that of the romance novels Radway studied and much less narrowly directed toward women, there are some similarities between the assumptions about the reality of that universe made by both romance readers and television viewers alike. Here my study benefits from analyses of television content informed by hegemonic cultural theory (Gitlin 1980, 1983). Regarding audience response, my discussion of differences between women of different social classes adds a new dimension to the analysis Radway presents; this aspect of my study benefits directly from British Cultural Studies works. There are distinctions among women in the degree to which they judge and expect television to be realistic and in the standards they apply to that judgment. There are also social class and generational distinctions concerning women's ability to identify with characters they view and in the form such identifications take. (Do women identify with individual characters? With working women or family women? With family or work situations and groups rather than single characters themselves?) I not only encounter the issue of women's responses to feminism but also must confront women's responses to popular understandings and representations of social class relations, class positions, and social mobility in the United States. Each of these factors comes into play in the comparisons I draw.

In constructing my study and in actually interpreting informants' responses to television, therefore, I draw on both the psychological and the textual dimensions characterizing American cultural and gender studies, as well as the British Cultural Studies' emphasis on social class. I respond to the tension between hegemonic analyses of texts and reception, and the emphasis on audience resistance, which one finds to differing degrees and in distinct configurations in each of these traditions. What follows is an attempt to construct an alternative to the dichotomies characterizing current debates in the mass media literature between those who, on the one hand, might argue that all television works to strengthen hegemonic values in its viewers and those who, on the other hand, argue that resistance to domination is always a part of the viewing experience. It is my hope that this work will make it easier to understand and conceptualize television's impact not only on the groups I have specifically studied but on us all.

Chapter 2
Work, Family, and Social Class in Television Images of Women: Prefeminism, Feminism, and Postfeminism on Prime-Time Television*

Television's presentation of women has changed considerably over the course of its history.[1] Particularly when we consider the relationship of television women to family and work, we can see marked changes in the type of female character most often seen over time. As the shape of the American family has changed with the rising divorce rate and increased acceptance of alternative family forms, and as more and more women, many of them mothers, have entered the paid labor force, television's depiction of the workplace and the family, and of women's relationship to each, has altered significantly as well.

Changes in television images have not always paralleled actual changes in society. Particularly with regard to the depiction of women, we can see how social ideologies mediate between changes in the real world, the images that become available on television, and viewers' choices of television images to watch. Many of us assume that viewers' choices reflect changes that have occurred in the real world, but this is not always the case. We can point to certain themes of discrepancy between real-world changes and the television images people choose at corresponding moments in history.

Like other forms both of art and mass culture, popular television images represent certain social groups, issues, and institutions systematically and repetitively in a manner that often reflects the position of these groups within our society's hierarchical power structure. In the case of women, some have argued that popular television narratives minimize the problems contemporary American women face as they attempt to carve out new identities for themselves as individuals in the face of social realities and expectations which have altered radically and rapidly. Studies find that television portrayals of women fail to represent the pressures of work and family, finding and paying for child care, balancing home and job responsibilities and stretching the family budget, which many women experience in their lives. On television, all single mothers are middle-class or wealthier and almost half of all families are at least upper-middle-class; there are no poor families. This contrasts with our society, in which 69 percent of all homes headed by women are poor, and the annual median income for a family with two working parents is just over $30,000. Also, more than half of all television children in single-parent families live with their fathers, who experience few financial difficulties in being a single parent; in society, on the other hand, 90 percent of all children in single-parent families live with their mothers, whose average annual income is under $9,000.[2]

Popular television, of course, cannot be said to reflect society, nor should this be its role. Popular television *does* reflect a desire to simplify terrains of ideological confusion and contradiction within our society. Some argue (Taylor 1989) that television provides us with fantasy-level solutions to some of our most pressing social problems, particularly those relating to the disintegration of our families and the growing instability of our private lives. Other commentators stress the ways television misrepresents our most common social and personal problems, thus proliferating representations of our lives which are systematically distorted in ways that reflect the dominant ideologies in our culture (Gitlin 1980, 1983).

Without taking a conclusive stance on this issue (although I instinctively desire greater overt recognition by television of women's problems in both the family and the workplace and feel critical of television when this recognition is lacking), I nevertheless maintain that it is sociologically interesting to pinpoint precisely those places in which television representation departs most widely and systematically from reality, insofar as the latter is possible to ascertain. I leave it to the women I have interviewed, however, to address, as audience members, competing theories as to television's proper role in our society. In this chapter, I discuss some of the ways in which television has changed in representing women, work, family, and their interrelationships, and I place this discussion in the context of actual changes women's lives have undergone in the decades of the television age. I hope that this discussion of television's treatment of women, though necessarily abbreviated and unavoidably partial, will help to illuminate women's discussions of these images, to which I will turn in Part II.

Prefeminist Family Television

Prefeminist fiction television had no shortage of women who were active, insightful, and personally courageous. And indeed there was frequently the suggestion in early programming that women's lives were colored by an injustice that came to their sex. But here, different from later television narratives, there is a sharp dichotomy between women's social roles *as women* and the divergent path they would have to traverse were they to escape their destiny as women and become fully articulated human beings. For the most part, on early television women are depicted primarily *as women*. Rarely (if ever) are early television women shown to be mature, independent individuals. Family women in particular are shown to be women whose existence is closely bound up with, and by, others in their family group, particularly their male partners. In addition, family women on early television are consistently pictured almost exclusively in the domestic or private realm; rarely do they legitimately venture into the male, public world of work. And, unlike the male individuals peopling these shows, early television women are often depicted in inextricable solidarity with one another.

The extremely popular middle-class situation comedy *I Love Lucy* illustrates well these typical qualities of women on early television. But *I Love Lucy*, like other shows on early television, features a subtext of resistance to many of these conventions. Many plots revolve around Lucy's struggle to escape her circumscribed housewife role and enter the glamorous world of show business in which her husband works. In a typical plot of the show, Lucy (Lucille Ball) manipulates and schemes (her "scheming" character is often referred to in the course of the series) to get a part in some production in which her husband Ricky (Desi Arnaz) is involved.[3] Through trickery and deceit, Lucy again and again *almost* achieves her aim—show-biz fame and glory are almost hers. Yet inevitably Lucy is humbled—and "domesticated"—in the end. Her schemes fail, usually falling to pieces in a comic denouement, and she ends up where according to the show's overt value structure she belongs—right back in the bosom of her nuclear family, usually crying with relief at being welcomed back by Ricky and spared the fully disastrous consequences of her mischief.

Most *I Love Lucy* plots would be inconceivable without Lucy's best friend and sidekick, Ethel Mertz (Vivian Vance). By adding Ethel, the conflict is moved into the realm of gender versus gender, men versus women, as opposed to being simply a matter of husband versus wife. The two are shown constantly together, plotting and executing Lucy's schemes. The usual theme of these plots concerns the women's rebellion against either the expectations or the rules laid down by their husbands, Ricky and Fred (William Frawley).

One way *I Love Lucy* can be read, underneath its comic structure, is as a chronicle of the deep friendship and joint struggle of two women, both of whom are oppressed by the structures of patriarchy (in this case, the middle-class family).[4] Lucy and Ethel are entrapped by the "feminine mystique" Friedan (1963) described for women of their approximate generation. Their overriding dissatisfaction—and the unifying thrust of their struggles—is with their lack of power, in society and in their own families vis-à-vis their husbands. Ricky and Fred seek to confine their wives to the domestic, or private, realm and to the reproduction of that realm. It is in their interests to be sure that they have some place to come home to; should Lucy live out her fantasy of working in the public world, or having her own public life, her family's private life will be deeply threatened, as Ricky suspects. This is the primary source of the struggles between the men and women on the show.

While the men try to protect their private lives by confining their wives, Lucy and Ethel resist. Together they live, create, and recreate a subculture of resistance against the dominant patriarchy as they attempt, usually in vain, to subvert the norms characterizing the dominant culture, which their husbands' desires and beliefs represent.[5] They confide in each other and generally help each other to subvert the desires of the men in their lives, whose interests are so different from, and so often in conflict with, their own. Lucy and Ethel as a duo engage in a very active sort of resistance against men, a resistance that ironically, in its continual failure, reproduces both their femininity and domesticity.

In some respects, we might see this duo as serving a vicarious wish-fulfillment function for the women watching the show, who might wish for a partner in crime, for the opportunity to engage in more active forms of resistance themselves, or even for their husbands to come and rescue them and return them to the home. Feminist film and media theorists (Arbuthnot and Seneca 1982; Lesage 1982; Press 1986) have proposed that female film viewers can derive pleasure from apparently hegemonic films through readings which emphasize a feminist subtext (or "pre-text"), chronicling feminist resistance, often through close connections to one another, to the patriarchal hegemony pictured in the main text of the film. Such subtexts of resistance can be inscribed within narrative structures themselves, through characters embodying purposefully contradictory qualities, and with the use of filmic techniques such as lighting, shot angles, characters' use of space, their look, their stance, and their use of touch, all techniques operating alongside the overt narrative of the film (Arbuthnot and Seneca 1982). Theorists argue that women identify with these underlying subtexts, thus enjoying films which on the surface seem unlikely to appeal to women and to have little positive to say about them and little to offer them. Television texts like the *I Love Lucy* show may be pleasurable to female viewers for similar reasons. Viewers may consciously or unconsciously discern, and identify with, a subtext of female bonding and resistance to patriarchal values in the show (I discuss viewer response to *I Love Lucy* in some detail in chapters 3 and 4).

In many of the respects I have articulated, Lucy and Ethel resemble Alice (Audrey Meadows) and Trixie (Joyce Randolph) of *The Honeymooners,* a popular working-class situation comedy of television's earliest days. Alice is a working-class housewife who, though serious, unlike the zanily comic Lucy, shares many qualities with the Lucy character. Except for a limited number of episodes, Alice also does not work outside the home, making her entirely dependent on her husband's paycheck for her own survival. She also must put the needs of her family before those of herself. Alice and best friend Trixie (like Lucy and Ethel, the two live in the same building) resemble Lucy and Ethel in their vocal opposition to their husbands Ralph (Jackie Gleason) and Norton (Art Carney).

Unlike the middle-class Lucy, however, Alice's horizons are shown to be limited in ways that are fairly typical of the American working-class family.[6] Her husband is a bus driver. She truly does "go without" in ways that television's middle-class characters do not. Unlike Lucy and Ethel, who live in well-kept and decorated houses or apartments, Alice lives in a bare, stark, two-room apartment that looks out on a depressing urban jungle. She has few modern appliances (we know this not only from the appearance of the set, but also because she makes repeated reference to this fact throughout series episodes). Money is tight in her household, much tighter than in the middle-class series of these years (although money, while not nearly as tight, is also a source of struggle between Lucy and Ricky). Many plots revolve around Ralph's desire to spend money on some personal item or other, and the havoc this causes in the household budget. Alice repeatedly restrains him from these impulses. Between the two of them, she is the voice of authority, sense, and reason.

Honeymooners episodes typically close when Ralph, having been struggling with and chastised throughout by Alice, recognizes that she has been right all along. His closing line "Baby, you're the greatest!" restores her to the morally superior position in the couple, since it is usually offered in recognition of the accuracy of her judgment with regard to some sort of disagreement between the two. The phrase is particularly restorative since Ralph's other trademark line, "To the moon, Alice!" is also offered weekly as an attempt to suppress her resistance and to write off her advice in no uncertain terms. *The Honeymooners* pictures the struggle between the sexes, and the myth of female power, in early television's most blatant form.

Alice's friend Trixie is the wife of Ralph's buddy Ed Norton. Trixie and Ed have a less volatile relationship than do Alice and Ralph, Ed being much more easy-going than is hard-headed Ralph. Alice and Trixie share many activities and pleasures but rarely conspire or scheme as do Lucy and Ethel. They do not have to; Alice is so powerful a character that she is able to stand up to Ralph on her own. Ironically, on this show it is Ralph and Norton who conspire, not infrequently against Alice, and in a strange reversal it is Ralph who needs allies in his attempt to subvert the voice of reason which Alice represents.

In one very interesting *Honeymooners* episode, for example, Ralph is laid off, temporarily, from his job as a bus driver. It makes no sense for him to find another job, as these layoffs have occurred before and are temporary. Over Ralph's objections, Alice decides she will go to work in the interim, and she lands a job as a typist. Ralph is embarrassed that she is working and becomes jealous as she talks about the other people in her office, who are all men. When Alice's boss wants her to work one weekend, Ralph insists that the two of them work in his apartment. At this point, Alice confesses to Ralph that to get the job, she told her boss she is single and that she lives with Ralph her brother. Upon meeting her boss and watching them work together, Ralph becomes increasingly jealous. During their work session, Ralph discovers he will be rehired, and at that moment he violently throws Alice's boss out of the house. Alice is both angry and flattered at Ralph's violent jealousy. Like him, she is glad to return to their customary roles and seems compensated for her lack of autonomy and worldly power by her power in the family. This episode illustrates the necessity of maintaining a traditional division of labor in the family in early situation comedies.[7]

Lucy and Alice differ as characters in important respects. Alice, the real boss in her family, is a powerful figure. In fact, much of the show's humor turns on Ralph's incompetent, arrogant, and bumbling personality. The Kramden family is a working-class matriarchy. Husband and wife are not shown to be making family decisions collectively, nor is the family truly governed by Ralph, much as he considers himself the family head. The case of *The Honeymooners* illustrates mass media's tendency, continued in the modern-day working-class shows, to romanticize working-class women by exaggerating their power and the respect they are given in society and especially in the family.

Mama, another early working-class comedy, features a less contentious central couple, but Mama is clearly in control of family affairs and finances. More discreet in the exercise of matriarchal power, Mama is always able to bring her family around to seeing that her way is the right way. Each episode opens with the respectful, nostalgic "I remember Mama. . . ." In fact, these working-class shows used conditions of working-class life as comedic fuel—the dependence on arbitrary bosses, the constant scarcity of money—but the long-term damage that these conditions inflict on families was never shown. The generation of tensions from lack of autonomy and material scarcity disappeared by the closing credits. The situation-comedy genre depends on maintaining our belief in the indestructibility and perpetuity of the family, which must stay together if we are to view it week after week. Alice is the morally superior and powerful one, and in the end, Ralph's childlike resistance is always domesticated.

In contrast to Alice, Lucy occupies the more childlike image; she is similar to Ralph in this respect.[8] Like Ralph, her resistance proves trivial in the end. The middle-class Ricardo family, no more egalitarian than the Kramden's, is, unlike the Kramden's, patriarchal. In almost all episodes, Ricky has the final word. Lucy is left beaten and grateful to be so sensibly governed by her husband.

Where images of women in *I Love Lucy* and *The Honeymooners* converge is in the representation of the leading women's friendships and solidarity with one another. The teams of Lucy and Ethel, Alice and Trixie have little if any discord within them. Women's unflinching unity with each other, alongside their conflict with men, is the natural order of affairs. Neither show casts any doubt upon women's implicit understanding and primal unity with one another. At the same time, the heterosexual nuclear family is just as unquestioned a state of affairs, fraught as it is with internal dissension and contradictions. No matter how hostile are intergender relations, and they are most often noticeably hostile, the viewer knows that in the end they will never break apart the family: all will be successfully resolved, the unity of the family restored (and the show's perpetuity assured) by the show's end.

Of course, not all shows of the prefeminist period depicted dissatisfied family women. Many middle-class family shows—*Father Knows Best, The Danny Thomas Show, Leave It to Beaver,* and *The Dick van Dyke Show,* for example—featured relatively satisfied family women in prototypically happy families. Rebellious females were featured on *The Donna Reed Show* and by the working women on *The Gale Storm Show, Oh, Susannah!, Our Miss Brooks,* and *Hazel.* These popular early working-women's shows featured single women often mischievously searching for husbands on the boss's time, or thwarting their often rather irrational, authoritarian bosses in other respects. On early television, the theme of women's rebellion was common enough overall to deserve mention as one of the most prominent of this era of programming.

The two working-class family shows I have discussed, *The Honeymooners* and *Mama,* present important contrasts to television's early middle-class family shows. In the middle-class shows family authority either lay primarily with the husband (especially in the case of shows featuring "dingbat" women such as *I Love Lucy, Burns and Allen, December Bride,* and *I Married Joan*), or was achieved through a somewhat egalitarian negotiation between both members of the couple (in the suburban family shows such as *The Danny Thomas Show, The Dick van Dyke Show, The Donna Reed Show,* and *Father Knows Best*). Working-class families, in contrast, are shown to be governed by strong, decisive females (Alice in *The Honeymooners* or Mama in *Mama*). While a certain amount of tension and struggle between the sexes is shown in both middle-class and working-class family images, these are generally resolved according to the lines of the dominant authority characterizing each class representation.

This contrast between images of the working-class and middle-class family raises some interesting questions regarding the ideological dimensions of television images of class, of women, and of the relationship between the two. Most basically, the working class is grossly underrepresented on early television family shows.[9] This is a problem that continues in television's later years. Even more interesting, working-class family structure is stereotyped in a way that displays specific prejudices about sex roles in working-class versus middle-class marriages. The working-class family is seen as "matriarchal" as opposed to the "patriarchal" or "egalitarian" marriages portrayed in the middle-class families. This is interesting since in reality working-class women have even less power than do middle-class women in their marriages, as they do in society, because they have fewer alternatives to their domestic role.[10] As this chapter will repeatedly illustrate, working-class life, and the working-class woman's experience in particular, is glorified on popular television.

"Feminist" Television

Different television genres have taken up different social tasks and followed different developmental histories. Even in the era of "recombinant" programming—that is, where television shows customarily reproduce and repackage the qualities of other, successful shows—we need to distinguish the role of women in the situation comedy from the representation of women in drama. If we have focused on the situation comedy thus far, it is no accident. Early television was dominated by variety shows and dramatic anthologies. With the exception of *The Martha Raye Show* (variety) and *The Loretta Young Show* (drama) the most popular shows were hosted by men. As dramatic programs with continuing casts and situations replaced the anthologies in the late fifties and early sixties, women became even more peripheral. Women played only supporting roles in the westerns that supplanted the anthologies in the ratings—as the "love interest," or as the "innocent imperiled." Only in situation comedies did women provide an active center. Women (and the working class) were ghettoized in the world of canned (and live) laughter.

The second-wave feminist movement of the late sixties and early seventies coincided with and helped to produce a marked change in the television images of women across genres. Where women's exit from the snug bonds of domesticity had been a cause for amusement, as in the situation comedies, or a source of danger, as in the dramas, women were now seen with increasing legitimacy outside the home. By the late seventies and early eighties, it was no longer unusual to see images of strong women working in nontraditional positions. I have tentatively called some of these representations "feminist" because they stress women's activities in the public, rather than the domestic, realm. I realize that this is an oversimplification of the term and that it magnifies what was often a very thin social content; nevertheless, it is useful in describing what turned out to be a short era in the history of television's portrayal of women.

In the action-adventure genre, the success of *Charlie's Angels* showed that women could hold audience attention in active roles traditionally reserved for men. It also showed that success could be the composite of quite diverse "viewing pleasures." The *Angels* were both active and attractive; their collaboration and command could appeal to feminist sensibilities; their glamour and sex appeal could also appeal to decidedly nonfeminist sensibilities, including the action genre's historically male audience. The three glamorous detectives, after all, worked in the service of the unseen (and clearly authoritative) Charlie.

> Throughout the run, the Angels got in and out of jeopardy while relying on Charlie, their unseen detective boss, to bail them out. It was probably no small part of the show's appeal to men that Charlie was heard but never seen. Male authority was invisible, and the "girls" kept free of romance. Charlie's ambassador on the scene was the sexless Bosley, eunuch to Charlie's harem. In the male viewer's fantasy, he could *be* Charlie, ever supervising, ever needed, ever returned-to monopolist of Angels. (Gitlin 1983:73)

As Todd Gitlin remarks, the Angels are both independent career women while remaining distinct sex objects. In a sense, they promised women it was possible to have the best of both worlds at the same time, to be sexy (for men) while engaged in exciting work (for themselves, but also for men's admiration). Such dual messages were carried by many representations of women during television's "feminist" era.

Hill Street Blues also had three women in central roles, but its "dirty realism" was far removed from the glossy, sunny fantasy world of *Charlie's Angels,* and its representation of women was more complex. Joyce Davenport (Veronica Hamel) was the hard-nosed, no-nonsense public defender, portrayed as relentlessly professional, intelligent, ambitious—and beautiful. Although her relationship to police captain Frank Furillo provides dramatic heat, her often difficult and dangerous role as a public defender is never subordinated to her "private" relationship. Indeed, the conflict between her public role as advocate of the accused and his public role as the "top cop" often leads to discord between the sheets. Joyce is shown as glamorous but uncompromised by her sexuality. Joyce's working-class counterpart, patrol officer Lucy Bates, is equally committed to her work, but both her person and her work role are articulated as less than glamorous. While Joyce Davenport, as public defender, must hold herself "above and apart" from the corruption she finds, survival for officer Bates is premised on solidarity with her fellow (male) officers. She must be one of the boys.

For both of these women the public-private split is suspended because their "work-families" are—at least potentially—their sources of emotional support and intimacy. The only woman on the show who is negatively characterized is Faye Furillo (Barbara Bosson), Furillo's wife/ex-wife, and this is because she is *not* a part of public (i.e., police/male) life but is, as a traditional wife and mother, absorbed with private, familial (and hence, narrow and "silly") problems. To the degree that she becomes engaged in public (police) activities over the course of the show, her character is redeemed from total "silliness." *Hill Street Blues*, then, divides up the issues for women: glamorous/unglamorous, middle-class professional/working-class public servant, single/married, public/private. Only the police world has legitimacy, but to the extent that women enter this world they can share in that legitimacy.

The situation comedy also works through the tensions of women's new situation through the formula of what Ella Taylor has described as "work-families." In *The Mary Tyler Moore Show,* for example, most plots revolve around Mary's colleagues at work, who form a sort of "pseudo-family" which Taylor argues serves metaphorically as an antidote to both the actual coldness and impersonality of our increasingly bureaucratized workplaces and the growing instability of associations in our private lives. Though single and searching for a husband, Mary is not really lonely, because her workplace associates fill in quite effectively as substitute family. Mary seems to have the problems many single women have, but the most serious of those problems—the horrible loneliness many experience and the financial instability due to women's often unequal treatment at work and to their frequent status as single parents—are minimized in Mary's life.

Turning to working-class representations of the work-family, the show *Alice* is the most successful of the era. *Alice* is the story of the widowed mother of a twelve-year-old son. Alice (Linda Lavin), an aspiring singer, found interim work as a waitress in Mel's Diner. Alice worked there along with Flo (Polly Holiday), a loud and crusty woman, and Vera (Beth Howland), young, naive, and quiet. Many episodes revolve around the relationship of the three waitresses to lovable but grumpy old Mel (Vic Tayback). Mel's bark is loud but underneath he has a heart of gold, supposedly. The women are continually trying to avert his anger at them for different things that they do. Other themes treated on the show include the women's family lives, their experiences on the dating scene, and their relationships to Alice's son, Tommy. In all, however, the boss-worker themes and the workplace-family images predominate, making this an unusual work-centered show for prime-time television in that the workplace it depicts is so decidedly working-class.

Alice's female characters come across as essentially strong, and although actual workplace tensions are minimized for dramatic purposes, the show does present some politically important issues to the prime-time audience. Yet in many respects, again, the plight of the single woman—in this case, the working-class single mother—is minimized. Alice is not really lonely because the inhabitants of Mel's Diner fill in as family members. Women's responses to *Alice* provide a good illustration of the way working-class women search for realism on television and do not feel that they find it in representations of their own situation. I discuss this issue in more detail in chapter 4.

Television's moment of feminism was brief (and equivocal) indeed. If we mean by "feminism" the fairly explicit representation of women's interests as *collective* interests (rooted in gender), rather than the articulation of the rights or abilities of particular women as individuals, then feminism is practically nonexistent in television programming of the seventies and eighties. Even some of the most acknowledged feminist shows—*Mary Tyler Moore*, for example, or *Cagney and Lacey*—emphasize, in the tradition of our dominant liberal/utilitarian ideology (Blum 1982 and Press 1986),[11] women's success as isolated individuals rather than as members of a collective group. Postfeminism is television reassuming its more traditional family element after only the briefest flirtation with feminist representations.[12]

Postfeminist Era Television

Since the heyday of the second-wave feminist movement, television images have changed once more, again partly in directions that can be alarming from some feminist perspectives. There is a trend for women to be shown back in the home and for shows to espouse what may be termed postfeminist values, which are often those values concerning women's proper roles regarding work and family that were traditional in the fifties. This is the era of postfeminist television.

Postfeminist television retains some of the aspects characterizing feminist era television, but repackages them with a twist. For the most part, women are attributed some version of a work identity, however superficial, along with their family role but not at the expense of a family role. On postfeminist television, women's family role is normally emphasized; or if it is not, this very fact commands a great deal of narrative attention in the television show. The trend on postfeminist television is to take women out of the workplace-family and put them back in the home, in a revitalization of traditional family values that melds with a superficial acceptance of feminist perspectives concerning women and work. Concomitantly, the theme of women's collective resistance to these families is not nearly as prominent as it was in many prefeminist family shows. Perhaps now that we can no longer take the family for granted, television cannot afford to be so cavalier in offering multiple, comic depictions of women's dissatisfactions and rebellions.

Of course, the term "postfeminist" is itself ambiguous, and often connotes contradictory meanings. Brought to the attention of the public by Betty Friedan in 1981, postfeminism has been used by feminists to mean the recognition that the women's liberation movement of the late sixties and early seventies no longer presents a unified front, that the particular circumstances of race and class are not merely "add-ons" to the central circumstance of being a woman, and that we are in a period where the "fact" of power is felt everywhere, but where the sometimes oversimplified attributions of power, whether to men, "the big bosses," or the Tri-Lateral Commission, no longer seem to offer such immediate and intelligible hoped-for redress.

But postfeminism is often taken to mean something else too—something felt quite bitterly by women who have identified with the women's liberation movement; this sense of its meaning is the closest to mine here. Postfeminism has been used to describe the mindset of a generation of women who have come of age after the heyday of the women's liberation movement and reaped the benefits of the social reforms and changed attitudes that the movement gained—often at the cost of upset and humiliation to the women who fought for them—but who categorically refuse to call themselves feminists, and who cling to symbols of women's traditionally "special" status (these include men opening doors for women and other signs of chivalry).

Ironically, the mass media, primarily television and film, if not the sole determinant of this antifeminist trend among young women, have been a leading cause or at least a leading source of these ideas in our culture. Media representation of this version of postfeminism has occurred in three major forms. First, negative images of the women's movement have proliferated in the major media; their pejorative and caricaturized presentation of "strident feminists" (Tuchman et al. 1978; Baehr 1980; van Zoonen 1988) has become a cliché in both nonfiction and fiction television. The media have provided the environment for this by their symbolic annihilation of feminism from its beginning. Strident feminists are usually seen as loners or disconnected souls. Women as participants in a movement simply are not represented.

Simultaneous with the symbolic annihilation of the women's movement, and again ironically, many of the critical issues that the women's liberation movement raised were incorporated into television narrative. But these issues were raised in a particular, mass-mediated form. The second way television has "posted" feminism has been the tendency to personalize or individualize solutions to the problems of women. This tendency furthers media annihilation of the women's movement, encouraging as it does the lack of any group identity for women. In television, a woman might experience a problem because she is a woman, but she would solve the problem because she is a competent or even superior individual. The solution might occur to her in interaction with others, but in the end it is *private* insight and personal courage—not public or collective action—that offer her a way out. That television would come to this solution in the representation of women's issues, given the deep cultural legacy of utilitarian individualism, is not at all surprising. Fiction and nonfiction television alike are clearly more able to represent politics as a function of personality than as a product of social structure or collective action. It is perhaps ironic that such "collective" productions as are television products take such an individualist bent.

Finally, because of the mass media's commercial packaging, whatever thin slices of feminism might survive in the finished media product are sandwiched between thicker slices of commercial femininity. Stridently feminist women—Maude, for example—rare images even in feminism's heyday, have all but disappeared from current programming, to be replaced by more "balanced" images. Largely, these include extremely "feminine" professional women characters, characters such as Clair Huxtable on the *Cosby Show* (called by one commentator "superwoman incarnate; she embodies a feminine mystique for the 1980s and is rarely seen working or even discussing her work" [Taylor 1989:159]), Murphy Brown on *Murphy Brown, L.A. Law*'s professionals, or the lead characters on *Designing Women*. Femininity traditionally conceived, including traditional images of both glamour and/or maternalism, has made a return on network portrayals (it was never absent but did recede during the feminist stage) and determinedly accompanies all potentially unconventional, feminist images.

Network controversy over *Cagney and Lacey* is a good illustration of the networks' commitment to commercial femininity even when producing a show with explicitly feminist themes and values. *Cagney and Lacey* is a cop show centering around the adventures of two women police officers, Christine Cagney (Sharon Gless) and Mary Beth Lacey (Tyne Daly). It is a rather conventional cop show except for the fact that the two are women; their sex leads them to combat problems not normally raised in male police shows such as sexism, their relationships to their fellow officers, reactions of others to their unorthodox work, problems with unemployed husbands, the problems of working mothers, and a series of other issues related to women's lives, even though these crises are often posed as the problems of individuals rather than of women as a collective group (Taylor 1989:159).

From the series' beginning in the spring of 1982, CBS found its leading characters lacking in requisite feminine attributes. When ratings were poor, the networks blamed the show's feminism: "'Th[e Cagney and Lacey characters] were too harshly women's lib,' said an unnamed CBS executive in *TV Guide*, 'too tough, too hard, and not feminine. The American public doesn't respond to the bra burners, the fighters, the women who insist on calling manhole covers peoplehole covers,' he continued. 'I perceived them as dykes'" (quoted in Brooks and Marsh 1985:136). The network forced recasting of Cagney, then played by Meg Foster, by an actress they termed more feminine and glamorous, Sharon Gless. When the ratings remained poor in the 1982–83 season and the series was cancelled, there was a great deal of outcry and attention paid to the innovative character of the show. Viewers began to tune in to its reruns that summer, to see what the fuss was about. The show won an Emmy the next fall and, surprisingly, CBS renewed *Cagney and Lacey* in the spring of 1984.

Murphy Brown is another interesting case. In this instance, the lead character Murphy Brown is a woman who in many ways is extremely feminist, in that she is shown to be a professional woman, autonomous almost to an extreme. But what makes this representation more post-feminist than feminist is the attention paid, and fun poked, at precisely these qualities of her character. Murphy is almost too cool, too calm, too competent, and the show continually reminds one that these characteristics are quite humorous in a woman, or at least are striking enough to make those in her company uncomfortable.

Murphy Brown presents us with a series of interesting postfeminist themes. In one episode, for example, Murphy's investigative reporting is responsible for freeing a falsely condemned criminal. He becomes friendly with her and the office staff, because he has no work skills and cannot find employment. When Murphy's secretary quits, the office manager persuades Murphy to let him hire the ex-con as the replacement. He does a dreadful job, wreaking havoc throughout the whole office. Of course, no one shows his or her annoyance directly to him except Murphy, and the rest go out of their way to excuse her harsh behavior to him (although they clearly agree she is in the right) with jokes about how no one takes her severe words seriously and he should just laugh at it, including jokes about it being the "wrong time of the month." Eventually, all agree he should be fired. Because the man is so friendly, however, no one wants to be the one to fire him. They all look to Murphy, knowing that she will be the only one tough enough to be able to dismiss the employee. Just as she is about to do so, he praises her so much that even she cannot go through with it. She then spearheads efforts to find him another job. Indirectly, she succeeds, and he reluctantly leaves the office.

What is particularly interesting about this episode is that the narrative considers it extremely funny that Murphy is the only one in the office hard enough to dismiss a nice employee, and that her "harsh" personality becomes the focus of so much of the show's humor. Were a man in her role, one suspects that the humor would have to be focused entirely differently (at least the "time-of-the-month" jokes would be out). *Murphy Brown* highlights our culture's continuing and perhaps growing discomfort with women with stereotypically feminist personalities and roles.

The *Cagney and Lacey* incident, as well as *Murphy Brown*'s plots and main character, illustrate the complicated interplay between public views about feminism and feminist representation, public expression of those views, and network perceptions of public opinion and responses to those perceptions. The creators of network television images straddle a wobbly fence as they assess how best to appeal to the largest segment of the public while offending as few as possible, when treating issues that have become as controversial as feminism in our society (Tuchman et al. 1978; Gitlin 1983).

Postfeminist Family Television

Turning to some examples of postfeminist family television, one finds that, while class differences in the representation of family women remain, the theme of women's unity with other women has dropped out of the situation-comedy arena, or at least is markedly de-emphasized when compared with prefeminist family programming. This development is quite distressing when one considers that it occurs in the wake of the feminist movement. While the working-class Roseanne and the middle-class Clair Huxtable present different images in many respects, they are similarly different from earlier television family women in that neither bonds with other women in opposition to their families or husbands. Instead, both of these family women work outside the home. Work, and women's relationship to it, now substitute for the unity with other women that marked television's earlier representations. What are the consequences of this development for media's treatment of the feminist movement, and for media's adoption of the themes of postfeminism? A closer look at some of the television shows of this period will illuminate this issue.

Network television seems incapable of ignoring the pull toward traditional femininity in representing middle-class women *except* in the case of working-class shows, which at times seem capable of escaping these conventions.[13] On *Roseanne,* comedienne Roseanne Barr (who exercises an unusual degree of control over the show's content)[14] breaks sharply with television's tendency to emphasize traditionally feminine qualities in portraying women. Overweight, sloppy, unkempt, uncouth, not at all traditionally "feminine," the character Roseanne fights with her husband, yells at her kids, complains to her boss, bonds noticeably with other working women, and generally thwarts our expectations of proper female behavior.

Yet in some respects, Roseanne's image is yet another form of media's romanticized working-class matriarch. Roseanne is shown to be in control of her family. Although her relationship to her husband, Dan (John Goodman), is much less discordant than Alice's relationship to Ralph, when conflicts do emerge Roseanne is usually proven correct. In fact, one of the most interesting features of *Roseanne* is the image of Dan, which is somewhat of a breakthrough image—although certainly an idealization—for working-class males. According to the strictures of the postfeminist working-woman family, Dan is much nicer, more sensitive, and more communicative than Ralph Kramden, Archie Bunker, or television's other earlier working-class males. Dan's character con-tributes to a marked idealization of the marriage relationship in this family, and this idealization shows us how superfluous and unnecessary Roseanne's bonding with other women would be.[15]

Roseanne marks a new era in television's representation of work. The ill-paid, dull, repetitive, demeaning aspects of working-class labor are remarkably well-presented on this show. Roseanne herself is often shown at her job, and at work she is shown to have fairly close relation-ships with her fellow workers, almost all, accurately for these low-paid fields, women. In some respects, however, the depiction of deep-seated conflict in the workplace on this show is balanced by a thorough idealization of working-class family life. While her forced overtime and long working hours are shown, their impact on home life is dimin-ished: these conditions are not too much of a problem for her because husband and kids all pitch in. When Roseanne comes home from work, she often just collapses, leaving husband and kids to fend for them-selves (*Roseanne* features perhaps the only truly messy house on televi-sion).

As feminists have noted (Hochschild 1989), most working-class women do not experience quite this same utopian family situation. While it would be wonderful for them if the family all pitched in and tolerated the demands of their working hours, the majority of working-class women face a "double-shift" of duties, meaning that when they return home from work, they must cook dinner, clean up the kitchen and the rest of the house, make lunches, do the grocery shopping, take children to the doctor and to activities, and other chores, all with relatively little help from most of their husbands. Many women are worn out and do not have the encouragement of their families to help them through the rigors of their day.

Roseanne offers an interesting split in the representations of family and work, corresponding to earlier themes in television's portrayals of the working class which I have discussed. While the show offers an idealized portrayal of family life and relationships, it is more critical and attempts to be more realistic in its depiction of the workplace situation. This pattern is consistent with postfeminist ideology. Post-feminist thought retains from the feminist movement its ability to confront some of the important issues for women in the workplace; but postfeminism differs from feminism in that it retreats from all criticism of the family. Postfeminist thought seems threatened by any less-than-idyllic pictures of the nuclear family. Traditional family life is inexplica-bly idealized alongside stereotypically feminist, liberated women in the postfeminist world.

The following *Roseanne* episode illustrates the show's extremely progressive, and feminist, depiction of women at work and of women's camaraderie over work issues, as well as its idealization of family life. On this episode, Roseanne is shown at work in the plastic-spoon factory. As Roseanne and her coworkers toil away, they are told by an obnoxious, unsympathetic supervisor that there is to be mandatory overtime that evening until they make their quota. Apparently, there had been a great deal of mandatory overtime for the women recently, and they were extremely tired, as well as pressured by the demands the overtime was making on their families. We see the women, Roseanne in particular, struggle with their supervisor over the need for overtime; they lose the struggle and are forced to work late.

Roseanne returns home exhausted, cannot deal with her noisy household, and asks her husband for permission to go out for a few hours, which he cheerfully gives. She then ends up in a late-night coffee shop, comparing notes on her life with the waitress. The waitress is an older woman, widowed, and they end up discussing how much she misses her husband and how she hates her job. Refreshed by this moment of camaraderie, Roseanne returns home to fall asleep, exhausted, next to her husband.

In this episode, Roseanne does in fact connect with other women, at work and in the coffee shop. At work, she and her coworkers are united in their attempt to resist their unreasonable, unrelenting supervisor, but at home, all is harmony and happiness with her husband. This is confirmed by her discussion with the coffee shop waitress, whose only regret is to miss her husband, who had made her life of toil worthwhile. *Roseanne* does retain a feminist critique of work, and an impressive one for prime-time television, but it places this feminist critique alongside a vision of the family which, in my view, depicts men's support for women in an idealized manner and undercuts many of the feminist movement's criticisms of the family. The show is postfeminist in that it combines these two visions.

The remarkably successful *Cosby Show* offers us yet another example of postfeminist television, this time focused on the middle class. *Cosby* features quite a different sort of female image from that shown on *Roseanne*. An attempt to reclaim the black family in the wake of storms of publicity about its demise,[16] the Huxtables are a remarkably peaceful, congenial, happy, and prototypically upper-middle-class "normal" family. Clair Huxtable (Phylicia Rischaad), Dr. Heathcliff Huxtable's wife on the show, is depicted as both wife and mother, as well as a successful lawyer. The Huxtable family appears to run quite smoothly, as does Clair's personal and professional life. Conflicts between Clair's roles are minimized, although for real women today such role conflicts prohibit, in most instances, the fulfillment of both to their own satisfaction. Clair Huxtable's role on the *Cosby Show* illustrates well the hegemonic view that families need not change to accommodate working wives and mothers. On the *Cosby Show* conflicts for the working woman barely exist; they are avoided in part by showing attorney Clair primarily at home, occupied with family rather than work-related tasks, in postures traditional to the stay-at-home wives and mothers idealized in the fifties. The husband-wife relationship is consequently perceived to be free from the pull of Clair's professional obligations.

As with Roseanne's husband, Clair's husband Cliff Huxtable (Bill Cosby) is also an idealized family man. Several television critics have found it noteworthy that on *Cosby*, both Clair and her husband seem to have a great deal of leisure time to spend on the most trivial family problems, despite the fact that both occupy prestigious professional positions.[17] Although he is an affluent, successful pediatrician, the Huxtable character is intimately involved in running his family's home life as well, finding the time to teach his children the day-to-day lessons of growing up. In this respect, Cliff Huxtable continues television's tradition of middle-class patriarchy. While he and Clair are shown to have a fairly egalitarian relationship, Cliff is pictured as being home more than she is: Dad's word goes, then, simply because he is home more often. This eighties version of patriarchy justifies male rule with an ironic twist of traditional gender roles (on *Leave It to Beaver* and *Father Knows Best*, the threat of Dad's judgment even in his absence— "wait 'till your father gets home!"—was the surefire way for stay-at-home mothers to ensure instant obedience).

Clair is seen to bond with other women even less than Roseanne, who has women friends when she is at work. In fact, an interesting difference between the two shows is that the working-class Roseanne is often shown at work, whereas Clair's professional workplace remains invisible to us. Although Roseanne does bond with women at work, neither she nor Clair is shown conspiring with other women against her husband as do prefeminist television characters. Perhaps we can no longer take the family for granted in postfeminist times; knowing its vulnerabilities, is it too threatening for media to continue to picture this fragile unity under constant, gender-related onslaught? Postfeminism signifies a cease-fire in yesteryear's battle between the sexes.

Although the characters of Dan and Cliff differ in many respects, both are almost perfect "family men." They help with children, do some housework, and generally spend a great deal of time with their families. Both are unfailingly supportive of the demands of their wives' postfeminist job/career. In postfeminist television, the ideal man has replaced the prefeminist ideal family woman we knew and loved in the fifties. Unfortunately, postfeminist television idealizes the family at the expense of more feminist insight into women's struggles within it.[18]

In sum, current television offers us a relatively feminist view of women in the workplace. Both working-class and middle-class women are shown to be workers, and they have jobs in which television women of an earlier era would not have been shown. At times, women are seen to bond with other women at work in feminist-type struggles against authorities in the workplace. Yet television's progressive images of work are counterbalanced by its postfeminist images of the family, which idealize the traditional nuclear family widely criticized by the feminist movement. While television's family women once bonded with other women in common resistance to male authority within their families, this type of female bonding has all but disappeared from current family images. Instead, paradoxically, television offers us a conglomerate ideology, which I call postfeminism, advocating newer work roles for women but also presenting an uncritical picture of older, more traditional family values.

Postscript: Female Bonding on Postfeminist "Postfamily" Television

Alternative family forms are increasingly finding a forum in the situation comedies on television. It is interesting that old-style female bonding continues in this forum. While images of female solidarity are scarce in family television of the postfeminist era, they seem more permissable in "postfamily" television, or shows that depict women living (as do increasing numbers of single, divorced, widowed, and single-parent women) in alternative forms of the traditional nuclear family.

One interesting example of alternative family television is the successful CBS series *Kate and Allie,* which first aired in 1984. Kate and Allie are two divorcées who have been friends since high school. In an effort to save money and provide mutual emotional support, they decided to share an apartment in New York. Together with their three young children, Kate and Allie live as a sort of postfeminist family, pooling their resources to create a smooth-running household. Although both are female, the two represent alternate ends of the traditional sex role continuum. Kate is a glamorous, contemporary career woman, while Allie is an old-fashioned, proper, industrious housewife. Stories revolve around the problems of adjusting to communal life, raising children in the city, and Allie's tortured love life (Brooks and Marsh 1985:442). One season, Allie remarried. But she sees her spouse only on weekends, enabling the close relationship between Kate and Allie to continue with only minimal interference even by the marriage. Other shows in this vein include *Golden Girls,* a show depicting older women living together as a family group, and the newer *Designing Women,* which focuses on a group of young women who work together. The perils and joys of female bonding figure centrally in typical plots of each of these series.

As with the idealized men in more conventional families of this television era, these female-centered alternative families can be read on one level as an idealized solution to the problems of loneliness, overwork, and inadequate resources which many single women face. Yet Taylor neatly sums up some of the major problems, from a feminist perspective, of these representations. Their potential for creating alternative visions, as she describes,

is undercut or diluted by the level of generality, the cheery politics of social adjustment, with which family change is endorsed even in shows that experiment self-consciously with gender and family roles. With few exceptions the family comedies of the 1980s are less genuinely adversarial than those of the early 1970s. . . . With the sting of divorce, family poverty, and other problems removed, single parenthood and stepparenting turn into a romp, a permanent pajama party. Even [with] *Kate and Allie* . . . the television narrative hedges its bets by nodding in the direction of radical changes in family form and structure without taking them seriously.

Similarly, the vigorous airing of women's concerns observed in the prime-time feminism of the 1970s has been attenuated or transformed. (1989:158–159)

While many of the family shows of the 1980s glorify female bonding and alternative family forms, this potentially radical perspective is undercut by their continued trivialization of the obstacles real women would face if actually attempting to achieve these goals. As Taylor notes, single parenthood and its pressures are transformed into fun, one long pajama party; this is hardly the affirmation women who are struggling and in need deserve from our culture.

Conclusion

In sum, there are important differences between images of women and the family shown in early prefeminist situation comedies and those shown in later programming periods. Later images indicate the influence of postfeminist ideology on the mass media and on our culture more generally. Most significantly, postfeminist images of women highlight a traditional nuclear family, in which women perform a traditionally feminine nurturing role. In addition to their role in this traditional family, postfeminist women as depicted in the media also work for wages in the paid labor force, in both middle-class professional positions and occasionally in working-class jobs.

Postfeminist images display almost no conflict between the sexes within the family. In this respect, they differ sharply from prefeminist family images, which on television often focused plots and characters around such intersexual conflict. Prefeminist women were often shown in warlike alliance with their female friends against their husbands, a plot standard which has all but dropped out of current programming. Certain themes in the portrayal of the working-class have remained the same: the working-class matriarchal figure can be found in both periods, and certain aspects of the work situation are rather honestly displayed, particularly as compared with depictions (or the lack of them) of middle-class work. Yet differences in the overall image of the nuclear family between the two periods are glaring.

The growing pervasiveness of postfeminist ideology in our culture, as indicated by its increasing presence in the mass media, is a phenomenon that demands attention from all those interested in women's troubled status in our society's workplaces as well as in our families. Postfeminist thought sanctions current treatment of women in the workplace and holds forth the traditional nuclear family as a societal ideal. Both professional and nonprofessional women, working-class and a middle-class, still experience a variety of forms of discrimination in their respective workplaces which television's current representations not only fail to confront but, indeed, effectively help to mask. Television's female professionals are not shown facing the kinds of discrimination that women in the upper echelons of our professions continue to face.[19] Nor are they shown experiencing the harsh demands of housework in addition to their working lives, as current sociologists document (Hochschild 1989). If they are—as in the shows *Cagney and Lacey* or the newer *thirtysomething*, for example—this dilemma is turned into a criticism of women's decision (or need) to work, rather than the critique of a system that demands women choose work or family exclusively or pay a heavy price for having both. Nonprofessional working women, while also experiencing these dual pressures, face even more crippling discrimination in a workplace which, even in the wake of feminist political efforts, continues to deny them not only equal pay and opportunities for promotion but even equivalent pay for jobs of comparable worth to those typically occupied by men (Kessler-Harris 1989; Blum 1990). By ignoring almost entirely the issues that are centrally important in structuring the real lives of working women, television can only be seen to help glorify and support a status quo that is in many ways oppressive for women. Television's unwillingness to confront, admit, and address so many troublesome aspects of women's situation in our society is unfortunately one of the strongest forces ensuring that it is perpetuated.

The mass media in general and television in particular are central in constructing and shaping postfeminist ideology in our culture. A powerful domestic medium, in both its content and its location in the heart of our domestic lives, fiction television comments upon and helps to shape our experience of, and ideas about, the form our private lives should take. Televisual domesticity merges with our own; if not always accepted, its ideas must be confronted, either consciously or unconsciously, as we seek to make meaningful our increasingly fragmented domestic experience in this postfeminist—some would say postmodern—age. How this confrontation occurs is the subject of the rest of this book. In Part II, I move from this cursory examination of television itself to the discussions of it offered by women of different social classes and ages during my interviews with them.

I would like to give special thanks to Terry Strathman for giving generously of her time and ideas during the writing and rewriting of this chapter.

Part II: Women Interpreting Television

Women's Experiences with Television: The Evolution of the Meaning of Television Through the Generations

Television technology qualifies as a social institution precisely because it helps organize ways of seeing, living, acting, believing, and behaving (Williams 1974). Viewers experience the technology of television in a social context, a context that changes historically and varies according to the demographic groups involved. We are only beginning to understand how these contextual variations influence the way television is experienced and understood in our society. In this introductory section, I begin by offering my own interpretations of the historical development of television content and then undertake a general exploration of some of the historical and class-specific variations in women's experiences with television which were brought up during my interviews. This general discussion will set the stage for the more focused comparisons between interpretations of television by women of different social classes and age groups.

As an institution, television means different things to older and younger women. For older women, television can be experienced as a technological invention that disturbed and permanently altered previous social patterns.[1] One older woman, Amy, talks about life before television in this way:

We had a pingpong table in the basement and we had all kinds of friends in. And we had a pingpong tournament nearly every night. . . . Well, you know, there's no TV to watch. And when you're active, you do things like that. And then we didn't have anything else to do, so we started a hiking club and every Sunday we walked five miles. And in the wintertime or when it was cold we rented a cabin and then one couple was the host. And then we sang around the campfire. . . . We made our own entertainment. And we did that for years. (Amy)

This same woman discusses her reaction to the introduction of television. She owned her first set in 1951. Although her first response when asked about television is "we thought it was marvelous," she continues by complaining about the ways in which television changed her life and her socializing patterns:

The thing I think we resented the most is that nobody wanted to visit anymore or they didn't want to play games. . . . In fact, it changed our social habits, because if you were going to go to somebody's house and all you were going to do is sit there and they kept saying shush! [the television's on], what's the reason to go?

Interviewer: You mean you'd try to visit people and they'd be watching television?

Well, they'd want to. And if you're just gonna sit and watch, you may just as well stay [home]. Why bother to get ready and go somewhere if you're just gonna [sit]. And that was my reaction to [television].

Interviewer: So it really had a major impact?

Oh, yes. See, I've been in the bowling world since '39 and the people who used to get together and spend their time in bars afterwards. . . . Now everybody's rushing home.

Interviewer: To see television.

Well, you know, they have a favorite show. (Amy)

For Amy, at least, television had a significant—and in her view, not entirely positive—impact in changing her socializing patterns. The introduction of television cut down on her social interactions with her friends and neighbors. Amy's interpretation of this is that television made everyone much more isolated and made leisure a more private process: rather than caring about the group, people's social lives now focused on their own private experience at home. Instead of desiring a social environment during their leisure hours, as was once the case, everyone rushes home to view their favorite television programs.

Another woman brings up the point, somewhat surprising in light of current arguments about television and the privatization of American culture, that in its earliest days, experiencing television was actually a social event. The first on her block to own a television set, Janet relates the way in which television dictated patterns of socializing in her community:

> We were the only ones who had TV. Before we were married I won a big radio-record player console in a drawing in a music store. . . . Somehow, I was able to go down and trade in this big monster thing for the first TV, and this is 1951. And nobody in the family had TV; nobody in the block had TV. Nobody in our apartment building had TV. And it was actually very large—this 21-inch black-and-white table model—Adler—and it sat on the card table in the corner of our living room. And it was the only piece of furniture in the room. Every Saturday night I had friends . . . Saturday night was Sid Caesar and Imogene Coca shows. And the *Jackie Gleason Show*, those two hours I recall. It was always an hour here. . . . And we had potluck supper and we sat around our utility room and watched TV every Saturday. (Janet)

And another woman recounts similar experiences:

> We had the first television. Miltie's, oh, Uncle Miltie was the big, that was the one show. An absolute must where all the neighbors came flopping in. They didn't have television sets. You set up your living room like a theater, with chairs; you could be having dinner yet, not even finished, and they were ready just sitting on their chairs waiting for the show to start. Funny that I, you know, this brings back so many memories I'm trying to recall that I don't think the thoughts have crossed my mind in years like that. (Estelle)

Apparently, when television was first introduced, the relative scarcity and novelty of sets led a collective form of experience to predominate in early television viewing. Privatized viewing patterns took some time to develop.

Other women recall their social lives before the ascendance of television, noting that the habit of watching television regularly and customarily in private took years to develop in our society, but that when it did, it completely transformed their leisure behaviors:

> See, we weren't like today. Oh no. We came home, if we didn't go out, we watched TV if we were home, but we went out a lot. We had a lot of friends. People weren't stuck in their house with TV like they are today. (Marilyn)

And

> It wasn't like today. We didn't stay home to see shows deliberately like people do today. (Seline)

These women all equate the advent of television with a privatization of leisure, seeing television as an institution that detracts from one's interaction with others.

Younger women, however, who have come of age with television, are much less likely to equate television with privatization. On the contrary, television for them is an integral part both of their connection to their culture and, in some cases, of their family's collective experience. Several young women (all working-class) mention their fond memories of their family coming together over television. Working-class families especially seemed to celebrate the television experience:

> Our family would watch a lot, in the evening, together during the week, the school year. I would say half the time it was on during dinner . . . and after dinner, we'd get together and watch television. I never watched TV by myself. We'd always really watch a lot of stuff together. (Pamela)

Similarly, another woman remarks:

> Our family used to get together and watch, especially if it was a big movie. The whole family was together, we had popcorn and we all huddled around the TV.
>
> Interviewer: Did you ever get your own TV?
>
> Uh, uh, it wasn't that kind of family [laughs]. (Kim)

Kim has fond memories of watching television together with her family and of how the experience of watching was actually intertwined with the intimacy she experienced through her family connection:

> Interviewer: Would you talk a lot during the shows, say, "Wasn't that stupid," or "That was funny"?
>
> Yeah, probably little comments like, "I wouldn't have done that. He shouldn't have done that. He knows better than that. Why did he do that?" Or, "I know what's going to happen next, I bet such and such is going to happen." Not really talk a whole lot, but comments like that.

Another woman, Debbie, a middle-class woman whose parents did attempt to limit her television watching, also openly celebrates the experiences she has had watching television together with her family,

> Yeah, it was [more fun to watch with her brother] because—I mean, by ourselves, there's not really anyone to say, "Wasn't that funny?" or to laugh and then look at someone else and see if they're laughing. . . . I thought that was funny, and if I was alone there was absolutely no one to look at or say, "Wasn't that funny?" (Debbie)

Young women vary on issues such as whether or not they watched television at friends' houses, or primarily in their own homes, some saying they rarely if ever watched at friends' houses, some saying they did so often. Yet their basic attitude that television-watching is a collective experience, and their experience of watching television with some or most other members of one's family, though not universal in my interviews with young women, are strong themes in their discussions of television in their childhoods. With both class groups these memories varied depending upon whether they came from intact families or were children of divorce. Nostalgia for these group experiences was common with children of divorce.

I do not have a single instance in my interview data of a working-class woman remembering actual efforts or even any comments by a working-class mother or father aimed at limiting television consumption. Some, on the contrary, felt encouraged by their parents to watch television:

> My whole family watches television. Maybe they thought it was good for us all to watch it, I don't know. (Pamela)

This comment coincides with working-class women's desire to learn from television, which I discusss in chapter 4, and contrasts sharply with the comments of young middle-class women, who more often than not mention their parents' attempts to limit their television viewing as children.

Working-class women, however, were not the only women who used the television-watching experience as an occasion to come together as a family and as a source for group discussion and common ground. Young middle-class women also mention forming bonds specifically centered on common television-watching experiences with those outside their families. Vivian, a middle-class woman, describes how common interest in a television show formed the basis for a new friendship:

It's a bond, now, there's a guy who was in my class that I started talking to. And, I don't know how it came up, but he mentioned *All My Children* once, and I said, "Oh! *All My Children.*" And then he said, "Oh, do you know what happened," I mean . . . so now, if I see it, I can run up to him and go, "Guess what." It's really fun, because it's something you can share, relate with someone about. About what happened. And . . . it's never very analytical. I mean, we've analyzed before on our own level, but most people—when we talk about it— and usually we don't analyze the show, we just say, oh, well, they did this, and they did that. Never very conscious, it's more like just gossip. (Vivian)

She also describes the bond it provides between her and those who are already her close friends:

I was gone this summer, and I came back and said, "Oh, what happened on *All My Children,*" and they [her roommates and friends] couldn't wait to tell me what happened, because all these things had gone on.

Of course, since in this instance a college student is discussing a soap opera, this is in some respects a special case involving a television subculture which is sometimes formed by groups of young people around soap operas or other products of mass culture (Lemish 1985; Fiske 1986). Yet it is interesting that Vivian was quite socially involved, a young woman with many friends. Her comments contrasted sharply with those of several more socially alienated or isolated young middle-class women, who tended to eschew altogether television and all the values related to its consumption. This suggests that television may be correlated for at least some young women with peer-group involvement.

Television as a Cultural Frame of Reference

The relationship between television and peer-group involvement for younger women is highlighted by the experiences of some women, all middle-class, whose parents severely limited the amount of television they could watch as children. Several young middle-class women I interviewed speak of such efforts. For three, these efforts were indeed successful, and it is particularly interesting that all three describe themselves as "loners," and that two out of the three express some resentment at their parents for forcibly excluding them from what has become an important common cultural reference for their peers.

One such woman, Kristine, was severely limited in the amount of television she was permitted to watch all during her youth. Her parents restricted her television watching to one day a week, two hours a day: "We could choose either Friday or Saturday from 7 to 9 P.M., that was it." Certain television shows, she claims, which are an integral part of her peers' sphere of cultural reference, have no meaning for her. Kristine experiences this as a definite and, sometimes, a sad absence: "I think *Happy Days* seemed to have had a great influence on people. And it was in the middle of the week and I never saw it. . . . There's a whole . . . mass part of TV that I never watched—I didn't grow up on cartoons."

Kristine's history with television makes her feel, in part, an outsider in her own generation. At times she yearned for, as she terms it, a "TV background"—to help her fit in:

> Why I . . . went out with surfers when I lived in La Jolla, is 'cause I wanted to be—I wanted to be a WASP, stupid, not [intelligent] . . . the whole way in which my parents brought me up was so sort of eccentric, that I really wanted to conform. *And I wanted to have a TV background.* . . . when I was in high school I wanted all of that. [Emphasis added]

Here, she connects her lack of television experience with other aspects of her identity as an outsider—being Jewish, for example, and being an intelligent woman. She describes in detail trying to act dumb to gain a surfer-boyfriend and a more insider status, like most other girls in her La Jolla high school. A television vocabulary is equated in her discourse with the insider identity she craved.

Another young woman, Terry, experienced similar feelings when her parents heavily restricted her television watching. In Terry's case, her family had no television at all until she reached the age of twelve, because her mother strongly disapproved of television. (Once the family did buy a set, her father proved to be an avid watcher!) Like Kristine, Terry alludes to feelings of being outside the television culture of her peers:

> I hated it [not having television]. I wanted it. My grandparents used to bring it for Christmas for a treat. [It was hard] with all the kids at school watching. Now, in a way I resent it because it seems like a lot of the older programming was so much better than it is now and than it was later. I wish I had it as a reference more than anything. (Terry)

Terry's greatest regret at lacking experience with television concerns losing the frame of reference that television offers to her generation.

Television provides a common culture, as is perceived most acutely by those who lack it.

Both Kristine's and Terry's parents wanted to be sure that their children became readers, and this accounts in part for their restrictive measures. For both women, the strategy seems to have worked; both mention that they read a great deal, as did their parents while they were growing up, and that today they rarely turn on the television because, as Kristine puts it, "I still don't have it [television] ingrained in me. . . . When they [her friends and peers] talk that's just part of them. And it's not [for me]."

However, both Kristine and Terry are distinctly marked by their particular histories of television restriction. They speak of furtively sneaking around to watch television, staying long hours at their friends' or grandparents' homes so that they can watch, stretching good-nights with their parents so that they could watch a bit of the television that was on in their parents' room:

> When I watch movies a lot of times, my head starts turning and I watch out of the corner of my eye because my parents would sometimes be up and watch something on [educational television]—a lot of times it was *Monty Python*. And my brother and I would go in to say goodnight to them and we would just talk for a long time to them and out of the corner of our eyes would be watching the TV. (Kristine)

Their creative search for ways to subvert parental restrictions has an almost desperate quality to it, a quality of using mass culture to defy parental authority aimed at, in these daughters' perceptions, turning them into creatures alien to their own culture.

Kristine feels that in some ways her parents' restrictions made television into much more of a treat, a more sought-after curiosity, than it might otherwise have been for her:

> I don't think that they [her parents] . . . managed very well. Because what it did was . . . it made TV be really valuable. I mean, TV was just this great thing. And what's funny is that it still worked out better because . . . even if I went over to a friend's house to sleep over . . . they would turn on the TV and I would just sit there. I was completely hypnotized 'cause for me it was magic . . . [the heavy emphasis on reading in my childhood made television seem even more] magical, 'cause you just turn off. You just—you don't do anything. (Kristine)

While Kristine probably watches less television, and reads more, because of this experience, her resentment over the method of its en-

forcement persists. For Terry, her mother's refusal to purchase a television set during her childhood spawned strong feelings of resentment
and, in her view, confounded her identification as a cultural outsider to
her peer group that, as with Kristine, has persisted into adult life.
When she spoke with me, Terry was extremely critical of modern
society, which can, of course, be a desirable characteristic in a young
woman but can also be accompanied by a painful degree of alienation.

Another woman (Jennifer) mentions that she read much and
watched little television in her youth, but this seems to have occurred
more because of parental example than because explicit limits were set.
Jennifer also identifies herself as a cultural outsider, mentioning often
television stars her friends might have adored but which, she would
proudly relate, had no effect on her. Jennifer seems more comfortable
with her outsider status than does either Terry or Kristine, perhaps
perceiving it to be a matter of choice rather than coercion.

Other middle-class women also discuss their parents' attempts to
limit television or, for example, to make it a reward for successfully
completed chores or good behavior. Most of these attempts seem relatively unsuccessful as compared with Kristine's and Terry's rather extreme cases, and modest attempts at television limitation do not seem
to be accompanied by the feeling of alienation and lack of common
reference to which these examples of extreme limitation gave rise.

For young women, then, experience with television assumes quite a
different meaning from that of our culture's older women. For older
women, television, when introduced, was a curiosity, a technological
wonder. As one woman states, when television was new, "we watched it
until the thing went off every night" (Amy). The idea that television
was a force to be limited, that exposure to it might be harmful, took
years to develop in our culture. However, television indeed intruded
into the social patterns that existed before its appearance. It gradually
led to a more privatized style of leisure and the loss of outside contact
for families and, ultimately, for individuals, which some older women
note with regret.

Young women, in contrast, grew up for the most part with television
in their homes. Television watching is often an occasion for family
gathering and can be associated with times of family togetherness, of
unity. Contrary to the recollections of older women, television for
younger women is often associated with social contact, both with family
and with peers. This is poignantly highlighted by the painful alienation
from peer-group culture experienced by women who grew up with
little or no television. Rather than a force of fragmentation, television
for young women is often seen as an institution that works in the
interests of social cohesion for both family and peers. In chapter 5 I

discuss generational differences in women's interpretations of television that may in part result from these different experiences. But first, in the next two chapters, I describe interpretations of television characteristic of members of different social classes.

Chapter 3

Middle-Class Women Discuss Television

In this chapter, I discuss the dominant themes that emerge when middle-class women talk about television. I attempt to paint a picture of what the television-watching experience is like for them, and in particular, how it may be distinctive for women of the middle class, given the elements of their particular cultural situation. Using women's own words rather extensively communicates, I hope, the flavor of their discussion. This chapter sets the stage for the comparison I make between middle-class and working-class women in the next chapter.

There have been several studies of American middle-class women's reception of cultural products other than television. In particular, Radway (1984b) and Long (1986) have each examined white middle-class women's reception of books, Radway focusing on romance novel readers and Long looking at women's reading groups. That both of these studies have focused on women implies that a background notion of "women's culture," or at least the idea that women receive cultural products in a distinct way, has informed these works. In fact, both Long and Radway discuss the relative powerlessness of even middle-class women in our society and root their concept of women's culture in a search for women's resistance to the dominant culture given the fact of their exclusion from it.

Current social scientists have documented the continuing ways even middle-class women are discriminated against, denied power, and forced to perform particular forms of work in our society (Arendell 1986; Hewlett 1986; Hochschild 1989). While women have entered the paid labor force in increasing numbers, more often than not they occupy female ghettos and earn significantly less than men (Blum 1990). In most middle-class (and working-class) families, women continue to be responsible for the bulk of domestic as well as emotional labor (Chodorow 1978; Hochschild 1983, 1989), resulting in an unequal distribution of labor between men and women, with a disproportionate burden falling on women. Even women with full-time paid jobs usually do most of the housework and childcare required by the family, performing what some have termed a "double shift," and the trend toward longer work weeks for women seems to be rising rather than waning (Hochschild 1989).

Chodorow (1978) and others (Dinnerstein 1977; Benjamin 1977, 1978; Balbus 1980; Flax 1983) have argued that women's exclusion from the dominant culture, along with certain tasks they have customarily performed in society, have given rise to a distinctive way of looking at the world. In particular, the strong history of women's emotional labor in the family has given rise to distinctive skills and strengths women in our culture possess disproportionately vis-à-vis men. Chodorow argues that the fact that women are mothers, and in a psychoanalytic sense both learn to be mothers from their own mothers and teach their daughters to be mothers, gives them the capacity to relate to others more closely, makes close relationships one of the foci of their lives, and essentially gives them a sort of "female culture," or at least a set of priorities and modes of being, such as nurturance, supportiveness, and creativity, which are passed down through generations of women. Critics of this thesis have argued that it is more readily applicable to middle-class, white, Western women than to others, which makes it particularly interesting for our purposes here.[1] Some current feminists argue that these psychological and concomitant cultural strengths give women a capacity for a uniquely critical perspective on the dominant culture, which is created and determined largely by the men who hold positions of power within it and are responsible for reproducing it and which bears strongly the mark of male values such as hierarchy and competition.[2]

Both Radway and Long invoke these current feminist theories in their discussions of women readers. Long finds that members of her reading groups are able to use characters in books as part of a process by which they strengthen those aspects of the female self that come into direct opposition to the dominant male culture. Radway similarly finds women identifying with independent yet nurturant heroines. In addition, Radway finds that female romance readers use the act of reading itself to assert time for themselves against the often draining demands of their families. Further, in their reading women derive emotional sustenance from their identification with and vicarious relations to fictional characters, sustenance women continually give to their families but rarely have given to them. In several dimensions, then, Radway's romance readers are able to use their cultural consumption to resist the status quo.

In addition to these gender-specific qualities of women's cultural reception, both Long and Radway find evidence of peculiarly middle-class beliefs governing their informants' discussions of books. In particular, Long finds that in their resistance to cultural authority, the members of women's reading groups stress middle-class notions of individualism and bring little historical or cultural context to their reading.[3] For example, congruent with the American middle-class view of the world, the women tend to focus in discussing novels on individual characters, and to keep their discussions at the level of personality rather than moving to a more potentially subversive and penetrating level of political or social-structural criticism. In some respects, their focus on and identification with individual characters helps them to strengthen the female aspects of their own selves;[4] but in other respects, such readings de-politicize their understanding of and approach to books.

Long also finds that her informants believe books should be, and generally are, a reflection of reality, or in other words that her middle-class respondents show a "tenacious adherence to a vaguely defined 'realism,'" which again blunts the potentially critical aspects of their reading experience. This belief in the realism of the text obscures the constructed nature, and the source, of the written text, leaving unquestioned the rules of narrative and genre and the limits of representation itself (Long 1986:609).[5] Radway too finds that judgments of the potential realism of both characters and events are important determinants of readers' likes and dislikes with regard to romance novels, although she finds that women make a distinction between historical and geographical facts, which they expect to be realistic, and character depiction, which they do not necessarily expect to be realistic, despite the fact that women often identify with the novel's main character. Women generally read romances rather than watching television, for example, in part because they find aspects of romance books informative about the historical and geographical world (Radway 1984b:112). Women judge romantic characters and the events in romance novels to be somewhat less representative of real life yet are often able to identify even with characters they see as unrealistic. In fact, women's ability to identify emotionally with such characters, or in Radway's words, women's ability to "recognize something of themselves in her feelings and responses . . . insures that the experience [of reading] will be an affectively significant one" (1984b:98).[6]

Middle-class women's discussions of television resemble some of these findings about their reception of books but also differ in important ways. In many cases, middle-class viewers, like middle-class read-ers, identify with, strongly like or dislike specific television characters, and discuss these characters in detail, even characters who they may consider to be unrealistic or who they view in the context of a show they find to be unrealistic. In this, they resemble Radway's romance readers and Long's reading group members and contrast with working-class women's speech about television, which as I discuss later follows a "class-specific" pattern of generally invoking television's middle-class ambiance rather than focusing on specific characters and their own involvement with them.

Many middle-class women identify with television characters even though they do not expect television itself to be very realistic. In the latter respect, my respondents' attitudes toward television differ some-what from Long's and Radway's respondents' attitudes toward books. Middle-class television viewers do not expect to learn facts about the real world from television, nor do they seem to expect to see very realistic characters portrayed. Despite their judgment that the medium as a whole is unrealistic, they often find that they are able to mentally work through personal and moral issues in watching and discussing television women. They in part resemble Radway's readers who judge romance characters to be unrealistic but find that they identify with them nevertheless. Even these readers, however, expected to learn some facts about the historical and geographical world from romance novels. Middle-class television viewers do not delineate the boundaries of fiction in entertainment television in this manner.

Since many of my middle-class informants are more focused on specific television women, in particular on their personal, relational qualities and their roles in both family and work, I find that their in-volvement with television is characterized by "gender-specific" themes. Like Long, I find that middle-class women viewers often resist the dominant culture in the sense that they use television characters as "part of a process that revalorizes aspects of the female self—such as nurturance, or female sexuality—devalued by our culture" (Long 1986:610). They are interested in television women's relationships to their families, to other women, and to work, and often bring in their own similar experiences, especially dilemmas pertaining to women's roles in each of these spheres, by discussing the particularities of the characters.

In the discussion that follows, I illustrate these general points and focus on describing the form of middle-class women's involvement with television. First, I discuss the personal involvement with television females that many of my middle-class informants exhibit, particularly regarding dilemmas about women's roles in relationships, the family generally, and at work. I then look closely, again, at the sort of "ideal women" that television, at different stages, has offered to us, and briefly discuss how these ideals have changed through television history in the context of how women relate differently to the various ideals that coexist on television today. I discuss ideals with respect to women's roles at work and in family, general modes of interaction with others, and female sexuality. Next, I define the sense in which many middle-class women juxtapose discussions of television and realism. Finally, I discuss the precise type of language most middle-class women use in discussing television, noting their distance from and cynicism about the medium itself, commenting on the relationship between these aspects of their responses and their level of involvement with television's female characters, and noting the difference between their language and that of working-class women. This last comparison introduces my discussion of working-class women talking about television in the next chapter.[7]

Middle-Class Women and Gender-Specific Themes

Middle-class women tend to bring up interpersonal themes in the course of discussing television. By "interpersonal" themes, I mean subjects that serve to highlight women's position *as women* within relationships, the family, and/or the working world. Women sometimes use their discussions to clarify or air the problematic interrelationship of these spheres in their lives. Such subjects at times come up in the course of women's recognition of some aspect themselves, either similar situations they have been in, or feelings they have had, particularly as, in the course of their discussions with me, women have recalled television characters who were particularly compelling for them. In this sense, I speak of middle-class women as invoking gender-specific themes, or themes involving their gender roles in family, interpersonal relationships, and at work in their discussions of television.

One middle-class woman's discussion of the prime-time soap opera *Dynasty* illustrates this point. Rachael, a great fan of *Dynasty,* uses her discussion of various plots and characters on the show to vent her feelings about the way relationships in the family ought to proceed and about how people ought to act with their closest relations. She is particularly interested in the marital relationship between Blake and Krystle. It became clear in the course of the interview that this relationship and the problems the two have faced reminded her of her own relationship with her husband and of certain problems they have faced together. Rachael specifically comments on the quality of the communication between the two, an issue she has found to be particularly central and often problematic in her marriage. She is very critical of the way in which characters on *Dynasty* communicate or fail to communicate with each other. She herself has found that open communication has been necessary to preserve the quality of her marriage. It irritates Rachael that neither Blake nor particularly Krystle seems aware of this fact.

One set of *Dynasty* episodes that Rachael invokes involves a plotline wherein Blake and Krystle both receive pictures showing the other in compromising positions with a member of the opposite sex. Blake immediately confronts Krystle with the pictures he received that showed her apparently kissing the man she worked with. For several episodes he argues and torments her, demanding to know the meaning of these pictures. Meanwhile, Krystle has received similar pictures of Blake that showed him in apparently compromising positions with a female friend. All through Blake's cross-examination of her, however, Krystle refuses to reveal that she had received similar pictures.

Rachael is quite impatient with Krystle for her passive response to Blake's harangues. She has these comments to make on the situation:

> Krystle doesn't really give him any . . . I mean, with those pictures. Why didn't she tell him that she had gotten similar pictures? But no, she had to wait. I would have yelled at him so many times! She's just—I don't like her at all. She's a wimp! (Rachael)

Further, regarding Blake and Krystle's marriage, she says:

> I think she ought to talk more to him. She hasn't even talked to him. I mean, they haven't yelled about it. They haven't gotten it all out. So I hate to see the marriage fall apart without trying to talk about it first because—I guess they're both innocent, from what we've seen on TV, it looks like they're both innocent. They don't face the reality that it's only hurting their marriage for them not to talk. They're both holding things back that would ease the whole situation if they only talked about them. (Rachael)

And more generally, she remarks:

> Well, see, I have this general gripe. My general gripe is none of them really speak their mind. They're always sort of being asked to speak their mind and a lot of times they don't. And you don't admire that. Because they don't realize that it's only hurting themselves. (Rachael)

Rachael castigates both Blake and Krystle for not "speaking their mind," or for their lack of open communication. As it turns out, this issue is quite alive for Rachael in her personal life as well as primary in her discussion of *Dynasty*. The argument Rachael makes regarding Blake and Krystle's marriage and the desirable level of communication in relationships more generally is paralleled by her later discussion of the important function of communication in her own marriage. As she sees it, her own function, like Krystle's, is to bring issues out into the open that her husband, left to his own devices, would never discuss.

> Okay. My husband's somewhat like that. He'll say—rather than bring it up, "I'm going to protect you by not bringing something up. I'm going to hold it in and I'm going to try and cope with it." And I object to that because I feel that—especially in a relationship, especially in a marriage—you want to air out all these things because what's gonna happen is you bring up these resentments. They're gonna sometime have to be aired out anyway. So I try to get him to tell me every little thing that bothers him—that I know bothers him. Because I know it's going to come back to me at some time later on anyway. And so he doesn't need to feel the need to protect me because it's going to be harmful in the long run. (Rachael)

Her critique of Krystle's inability or unwillingness to bring up difficult issues with Blake and her focus on this issue is based on Rachael's beliefs about her own role relative to communication in her marriage. Rachael is sparked by her discussion of Krystle and Blake's problem communicating to allude, elsewhere in her interview, to actual problems that she and her husband were presently experiencing and to their current lack of communication, noting that she and her husband "haven't done a whole lot of talking" recently since she had been inordinately busy in school of late.

As romance reading functions for many of Radway's readers, so too the act of television watching can be used as a mechanism of self-assertion in close relationships. Since television watching is an activity that often occurs in conjunction with one or several others in the family, in either a joint family living room or a den, or for women, in bedrooms they may share with husbands, the act of negotiating what show to watch, or when to watch television at all, can be a fairly tricky power negotiation. Women sometimes bring up the issue of this negotiation in conjunction with discussing shows they particularly like or those they dislike which others in the family may want to watch.

In this case, Rachael, who has mentioned that she and her husband have communication problems, describes the implications of the very act of watching *Dynasty* for her relationship with her husband. She explains that watching *Dynasty* is her "vice," and connects this description to the fact that her addiction to *Dynasty* often leads her to explicitly preempt something her husband wants to watch on television that night:

> That is something I do really for me, that it feels very selfish. Because sometimes John wants to watch something on Wednesday nights but he can't because I have to watch *Dynasty*. I won't even let him record it [*Dynasty*] because I have to watch it when it's on. (Rachael)

Rachael's watching of *Dynasty*, therefore, is a part of the relationship between her husband and herself, a mechanism through which she asserts herself with him, perhaps in the absence of more direct communication.[8] The tone of Rachael's discussion of *Dynasty* implies that she sees *Dynasty*, and the lessons in relating or communicating it evokes for her, as directed particularly at her own viewing, and not at her husband. Her description of the watching scenario indicates that her husband is virtually chased out of the television area while *Dynasty* is on (relative newlyweds, they have only one television, in the living room). The impression is that Rachael enters a very personal world when *Dynasty* is on, one which gives her the opportunity and the space to reflect, through her responses to the fictional characters' dilemmas, upon aspects of her personal life that may be troubling or puzzling to her. Perhaps *Dynasty* offers her this opportunity for solitary reflection since her husband is so uninterested in its subject matter and declines to watch the show. In any case, Rachael's responses to this show, her interpretations of it, the incidents she chooses to focus on, and the conditions under which she must arrange to watch it are all integrally tied to aspects of her intimate relationship with her husband.

Ellen, another middle-class woman, interprets and experiences *Dallas* similarly to the way Rachael interprets *Dynasty*. Ellen's observations about the character of Pam on *Dallas*, for example, bear some similarity to Rachael's observations about Krystle. Like Rachael in her critique of Krystle, Ellen is critical of Pam's inability to communicate her feelings frankly, in this case, to express her love for her ex-husband Bobby:

> I think Pam is another weak character. I don't think she's got a lot of guts. You know, it's like you decide you're still in love with your ex-husband and you don't manage to tell him, she's now agreed to marry someone that she's not really in love with because she feels guilty. She's allowed her idiot sister to manipulate her for stupid

purposes. It's never going to work out. There's no way in the world she's ever going to get Bobby, which I think is just plain stupid, and she's gotten involved with the most dangerous person in town. You know, she's made an ally of J.R. Pam probably never should have married Bobby in the first place. I don't care how much she loved him. (Ellen)

Ellen's description of Pam resonates similarly with accounts of her own personal experience also discussed in her interview. She, too, through an account of her divorce and her second marriage, has stressed the need to keep the channels of communication open in marriage and relationships, to "speak your feelings" honestly and sincerely. The communication theme is a key one both in her discussions of Pam's fictional situation and in relating and explaining incidents in her own life.[9]

At other times, Ellen compares herself even more directly with television characters, noting the similarities between characteristics of her personal self-in-relation and those of the characters she watches.[10] Ellen's critical discussion of the *Dallas* character Lucy illustrates this tendency to evaluate characters according to the similarity or difference between their actions and attitudes and her own:

No, I don't like Lucy. Well, you know, Lucy does dumb things that I never would have done. And I can't respect them because they were her choice. She married someone who wanted to be independent and make it on his own, and she made that very hard for him, and she didn't value what was important to him in life, and she was so stupid that she couldn't see what she was doing to someone else. (Ellen)

Ellen's more favorable evaluation of the character Miss Ellie, whom she considers a sort of ideal that she herself could never realize, follows a similar pattern. She likes Miss Ellie, because she would like to possess the personal qualities Miss Ellie possesses. She feels she does not possess these qualities and never could, however. Miss Ellie is more of a normative ideal (as Lucy is an object of normative criticism) than she is a realistic object of identification, however, since Ellen sees her qualities as virtually unobtainable. Her remarks on Miss Ellie's character are intertwined with references to her own.

In general, I like Miss Ellie. I could never be like that. She holds a lot back. There's a lot of things between her and her husband that she didn't say, and she didn't stick up for things, and a lot of times she let things go on. She did because she wasn't taking control. She's given up a lot of power that she had voluntarily, but, you know, she's like some of those other characters that I like, she does what she wants with her life. Her life is the way she wants it to be. She's an ethical person. A lot of these people that I've liked, they've had values that show their concern for other people, and they balance what they wanted against what other people needed. They weren't just out for their own ends. And they managed to live their lives in a way that didn't cost other people. Most of the characters that I really like on the shows have managed to have a balance between what they want and what other people want, and their responsibilities. (Ellen)

Like Rachael, Ellen's discussions of television characters are intensely personal ones, intimately focused on the characters' relationships and on the relative morality or immorality of their conduct with other people. Both women have developed their opinions about these characters to a rather detailed level. In fact, similar to the way Long's readers focused their discussions of novels, much of their discussion of television shows themselves consists of such in-depth character analysis.

Ellen is remarkably conscious of the personal nature of her involvement with the characters she discusses here. She explicitly conjectures that television characters may actually serve as substitute relationships for her, filling in gaps so often left by her actual relationships:

I enjoy being entertained a lot more than I enjoy a lot of my real relationships. And I find it a real refuge to have those parts of my life, because I consider those shows—especially those continuing stories—a part of my life. They're something that I feel involved in. I don't think they're really relationships, but they probably function the same way that fantasies do, because they allow you to do all these things without having to do anything, and I find that those parts of my life are a lot more satisfying, because they're intended to be satisfying. And the other parts of my life which just—you know, the real world, which just goes the way it wants to go and can be very frustrating, and you don't get really good resolution of problems, they sort of dribble on forever. (Ellen)

Here Ellen brings up her feeling that problems in real life often seem unresolved, to "dribble on forever," in the context of relating how much more satisfying it is for her to watch television, the implication being that on television problems are at least fictively resolved. Ironically, however, the continuing soap opera, on which problems by definition are rarely resolved, is the television genre she most enjoys. In some cases, as she indicates, Ellen's television experience may be more satisfying than real personal life experiences of the same order.

Ellen's level of consciousness about her relationship to television characters vis-à-vis her relationship to those in real life, if not the pattern of these relationships, is unusual for women of either class in my study. But the pattern of her responses, in which her discussions of television focus primarily on specific characters and their qualities, and in which her affective relationship to television focuses on identification with these characters, is not atypical. Other middle-class women also construct their remarks on television in this vein.

Television and the Negotiation of Women's Morality

Stacey, another middle-class woman, has lately decided to stay at home full-time with her small child. Having worked full-time as a teacher and at other jobs, this decision is a new one for her, and she is experiencing some conflict over it, as evidenced by the fact that she has attempted part-time work but gave it up because she felt that her child was seriously disturbed by her absence. As she describes it, her conflicts are heightened by the fact that she herself was brought up by a maid while her mother went to law school and then worked full-time as an attorney. She is attempting, she told me, to do a more effective job of child-rearing than her mother did, although her return to the home flies in the face of the feminist assumptions prevalent in our culture and in the media generally.

Stacey focuses her discussion of *Dynasty* around the specific conflicts between work and family that Krystle had been experiencing just prior to the time of her interview. Krystle, having recently given birth to her first child, Kristina, had just gone back to work on a horse farm, having felt that simply remaining home to care for her child was insufficiently stimulating and fulfilling. Stacey has this to say about Krystle's situation, a situation that resonates with her own, but which she has chosen to resolve very differently:

Lately, she [Krystle] hasn't been too good. I mean, that horse is really starting to . . . [laughs] I don't know about it. I don't think it's right. I really don't. I guess that—with her baby, I feel that she's taking time away from her child that she shouldn't to go spend with her horse.

Interviewer: So you agree with Blake when he said, "Your place is here, with Kristina!"

Yes. Yes, I do. And I believe that she's entitled to have outside interests, but from what you see on the television, it seems the horse is taking a primary role that I don't think is right. If she spent as much time with Kristina as she did with the horse, you know, and she spent as much time with the horse as she spent with Kristina, I would say it's fine. But I don't think that the time allotted to each is appropriate.

Interviewer: Even though she can afford all the help she needs?

Exactly. I think nobody can take the place of the mother in the home. (Stacey)

Here Stacey offers what is a clear negative moral judgment of Krystle's behavior, a course of action she contrasts markedly to her own. She goes on to delegitimate further Krystle's decision to go back to work by linking it to adulterous desires for her partner Reese:

Interviewer: Why do you think Krystle has gone back to work?

Why? I don't know. I guess I've never given it much thought. I guess that maybe she's attracted because, well, isn't what's-his-name, Reese, there? I guess that there's a bond there that existed before her and Blake were ever involved and maybe she feels young and beautiful being around him, versus *being an old mother with kids at home* [emphasis added]. (Stacey)

Her description of Krystle and her actions is fraught with moral judgments. Krystle has made the wrong choices, giving in to vanity while neglecting her family responsibilities and her child's needs.

Nevertheless, these issues require continual negotiation in Stacey's life. That Krystle's dilemma reminds Stacey of her own conflicts and choices is clear as she continues:

An identity crisis, really! Even the beautiful Linda Evans feels it sometimes. You know, I think everybody once in a while would like to shun their mother garments and go out and be a swinging single for a night. But I think it would take one night and you'd be so happy to be home. At least I would. (Stacey)

The conflicting images in these statements interpreting Krystle's actions—from being an "old mother with a kid at home" who is "shunning her mother garments," versus the feeling of being in the end "so happy to be home"—indicate that for Stacey, *Dynasty* does indeed resonate with conflicts and choices she has faced in her own life.

Discussion and interpretation of the show serves as a forum upon which she plays out or tests her ideas, particularly those wrought with some uncertainty or conflict. Criticizing Krystle's choices and finding support for her criticisms in her interpretation of fictive events on *Dynasty* seem at times to be attempts to justify and bolster Stacey's own decisions.

In this instance, Stacey is conflicted over some of the difficult consequences of her moral conviction that a mother ought to stay home with her children. In her case, giving up her work to stay home and, thus, giving up the autonomy her work gave her, the money and the sense of an outside identity, has been difficult. The *Dynasty* plotlines that resonated with her own life choices are particularly salient in her discussions with me.

The theme of choice between work and family is one that emerges in a different form in discussions between middle-class and working-class women. Working-class women seem less preoccupied with choice and more focused on immediate survival issues, with many women talking about how they are going to "get by," making plans for their own further education, job training, and that of their husbands. One woman talks about finding someone (a man) to "take care" of her and her daughter (Marie). Another woman mentions her conviction that, although she was sure she would always work, she would put her family first once she was married, and had no conflicts about doing so (Linda). No working-class women I interviewed perceived the "choice" issue in quite the same conflicted way that some middle-class women do. Perhaps consequently, this theme rarely emerges in working-class women's discussions of television. Such personal issues, focusing on female identity, are understandably less of a preoccupation for working-class women than for women of the middle class.

Television's Ideal Women: A Class-Specific Appeal?

Since they focus their discussions so closely on individual television characters and on comparing themselves with these characters, particularly with regard to their roles as women in our society, it is interesting to look at some of the television characters middle-class women most admire and their reasons for admiring them. Particularly striking are several instances in which middle-class women use explicitly feminist imagery to describe characters working-class women criticize specifically for their lack of independence or other qualities working-class women found praiseworthy. As will become clearer in the next chapter, middle-class women often admire television characters about whom working-class women find much to criticize. While television offers middle-class women some characters to whom they feel positively attached, working-class women find such characters to be far more sparse. This situation is perhaps responsible for working-class women's more distant response to most of the television characters they watch.

The prefeminist character Lucy of the *I Love Lucy* show serves as a good example of a figure middle-class women admire. Several middle-class women use decidedly feminist language to describe what a strong woman they consider Lucy to be:

> She was this housewife, she was struggling to—I guess to be—she wanted to do something which her husband was doing, and he'd never let her do it. . . . But she also was strong in a certain way, because she was the star of the show, she had the power to make everything funny, and to keep the story going, and to—I mean, it was *I Love Lucy*, it wasn't I Love Ricky or Ethel, or anyone else, but she had the strength of her personality. She was more dominant than anybody else, but yet she also struggled in her life. To do something. (Sarah)

This woman finds Lucy strong as an individual, someone whose personality essentially dominates over others in her family and the show. Other women express similar sentiments, calling Lucy "dominant."

> I was always aware that she was very, very, she was the dominant force in the family, in the show. I was looking forward to seeing her show. (Alisa)

One woman finds Lucy's lightheartedness and irreverence for society liberating, particularly compared with some of the experiences she has had herself as a woman in society:

> She stimulated a kind of gaiety, a kind of freeness, like you could really be crazy, even though society was teaching you some ways you had to be, even my own mother taught me. . . . Well, Lucy was so outrageous, she made you think you could do *anything*, you could act crazy. And she, I mean, she had to act crazy 'cause society didn't let her do things through the normal channels. Her husband wouldn't let her, but she found a way. (Terry)

These middle-class women comment upon Lucy's strength in an admiring way. She was the one who kept everything going on the show, the one who subverted the limits of "normal channels" and became, for these women at least, a symbol of freedom from both her husband and the larger society. In a sense, Lucille Ball's status outside the internal language of the show as *star* of the show gets built into these women's evaluations of her.[11] As star, Ball gets top billing, is central to all plots and most scenes, and is responsible for most of the narrative movement in the show. She possesses most of the strong personal qualities these women attribute to Lucy's character on the show. Other middle-class women comment more overtly on Lucille Ball's skill as an actress, a skill that seems to increase their pleasure in watching the show.

Overall, it is interesting that middle-class women, in looking back on the Lucy character, actually remark on her feminist qualities. Few, if any, scholarly surface readings of the show have interpreted either the *I Love Lucy* show or other early television family shows as paeans to or even precursors of feminism.[12] In addition, as I discuss further below, working-class women do not share this middle-class interpretation of the Lucy character. Rather than finding Lucy to be a feminist figure, working-class women comment negatively on her manipulative use of "feminine wiles" to get what she wants, her silliness and her craziness, and do not see her character as feminist or even more generally as very positive or admirable. That middle-class women pick up on the power within the family which Lucy appropriates from her husband and on her attempts to gain more social power, generally by finding work outside the home (which for Lucy involves not doing what her husband wants her to do), is itself interesting. Their comments strengthen my thesis that middle-class women in particular focus on television's portrayal of what are specifically women's issues, in this case, women's power or lack of it in the family and in society, even when alternative interpretations of characters and events dominate both the literature and the interpretations of other groups.

A further example of middle-class women's self-conscious, positive identifications with what they see as feminist aspects of television females occurs in their almost uniformly laudatory response to two shows that portrayed independent, single "career" women in the 1970s, *That Girl* and *The Mary Tyler Moore Show*, shows of what I have earlier called television's "feminist" period. Middle-class women are overwhelmingly positive in their discussions of these shows, indicating specific identification with the leading characters of each. Apparently, the popularly "feminist" qualities of the leading characters in these shows, which include the facts that they work (actually, pursue careers), live alone, feel free to pursue relationships with men, and are seemingly independent in certain respects, captured middle-class women's imaginations at the time these shows were on, particularly for young women imagining and making plans for their future lives, or for women planning out the relationship between work and family.

Women admire both leading characters Ann Marie and Mary Richards for their independence, attractiveness, jobs, boyfriends, and living situations. Comments on *That Girl,* in which Marlo Thomas plays leading character Ann Marie, a would-be actress, include the following praises from three very feminist, self-possessed women:

> Interviewer: What did you think of Marlo Thomas in *That Girl?*
>
> I thought she was great. You know. Yeah, she had her own apartment and she was independent. She didn't have a job or anything. She had a nice boyfriend. She was happy. (Nadine)

Another remark:

> I liked *That Girl* because, I don't know why, just because she was somewhat independent and used to tell her boyfriend off once in a while. And she had her own apartment. And I always wanted to grow up and just move away from my parents and everything. And . . . I was pretty rebellious. (Terry)

Another woman comments:

> I liked *That Girl.* I thought that Marlo Thomas and—I can remember now, at one point, wanting to be like her, in some way. She was also pretty and she had this nice boyfriend. (Sarah)

Lead character Ann Marie is praised for her independence, good looks, and generally glamorous lifestyle. It is interesting that in these descriptions, qualities that could be termed "feminist," such as independence, are juxtaposed with more traditional female qualities like attractiveness and glamour. Viewing her today, Ann Marie hardly looks like a feminist figure, with her constant dependence on either boyfriend Donald or "Daddy." Yet apparently, this is how she was received by at least some women viewers. Television's version of feminism in the *That Girl* period consists in a particular intertwining of new and traditional female qualities which seems to have particularly appealed to some women, satisfying both newly inculcated feminist desires and the attempt to live up to aspects of an older female ideal.

Respondents make similar comments about *The Mary Tyler Moore Show,* where women find that a woman can be "popular," a traditionally admired attribute, as well as independent, occasionally alone, and successful:

I remember in high school really thinking that I wanted to grow up and be like Mary Tyler Moore. Like, I remember consciously thinking that just 'cause Mary Tyler Moore was, you know, real independent. She didn't have dates on Saturday night but she was still popular. Really, she was still a nice person, you know. She wasn't ugly or anything. (Nadine)

Another remarks:

I remember admiring Mary Tyler Moore when I was younger, thinking that she was really, not admiring completely everything that she did herself, but just thinking, she seems to be very successful and she lives in an interesting place and had an interesting job. And I thought that was really good. (Lori)

These middle-class women note aspects of the career woman's lifestyle depicted in *The Mary Tyler Moore Show* that caught their imagination sufficiently that even years later they remember admiring these attributes. Their comments are especially interesting given that these somewhat similar remarks come from very different women. Nadine is a rather conventional, seemingly confident, woman in professional training. In the course of my interview with her, I had the impression that she had not been as popular as she would have liked in high school and that this might be one reason she admired characters like Mary, who was popular as well as independent. Lori, on the other hand, was a more rebellious figure. Dressed in punk fashions, with extremely short hair, Lori gave the impression of feeling "above" conventional life, conventional associations, and conventional people. Her admiration for Mary Richards was somewhat surprising in this light. Lori makes this remark as she is telling me that Mary Richards is, for her, an exceptional television character in that she is one of the only ones she identified with. She implies that, even though she found most of television to be extremely unreal, "apart from the real world," "entertainment," the Mary character was so real she could not help identifying with her and being influenced by her (although the influence of this conventional character on Lori's nature was not immediately apparent).

Working-class women rarely mention admiration for or identification with these characters, or do so only with qualifications. Understandably, they may have found it more difficult to identify with these middle-class characters than did middle-class women. None mentioned *The Mary Tyler Moore Show* as having been a favorite, although several noted that they actively disliked Mary Tyler Moore and had not enjoyed the show. Because the two shows picture essentially middle-class images, working-class viewers understandably may find the shows more unrealistic and difficult to identify with. Middle-class women, in contrast, have little trouble identifying with these particular images, which apparently strike a responsive chord among young middle-class women with their all-too-rare images of middle-class female autonomy.[13]

One more current female image, an image I have termed "postfeminist," to which women of both classes respond positively is the character Clair Huxtable on the *Cosby Show.*[14] Clair Huxtable is depicted as both wife and mother and a successful lawyer. The Huxtable family runs quite smoothly, as does Clair's personal and professional life. Conflicts between Clair's roles are minimized, although for real women today such conflicts prohibit, in most instances, the fulfillment of both. Feminists have recently commented on the fact that, while popular conceptions of women's right to enter the paid labor force have changed, traditional assumptions about the family form have been much slower to evolve. As a result, many women find themselves trapped by the demands of both job and family. In neither sphere have demands on women's time been altered to accommodate their dual role.[15]

Clair Huxtable's role on the *Cosby Show* illustrates well the hegemonic view that families need not change to accommodate working wives and mothers. On the *Cosby Show* conflicts for the working woman barely exist; they are avoided in part by showing attorney Clair primarily at home, occupied with family rather than work-related tasks, in postures traditional to the stay-at-home wives and mothers idealized in the fifties. The husband-wife relationship is consequently perceived to be free from the pull of Clair's professional obligations. Several television critics have also found it noteworthy that on *Cosby,* both Clair and her husband seem to have a great deal of leisure time to spend on the most trivial family problems, despite the fact that both occupy prestigious professional positions.[16] Women of both classes enjoy the image of Clair Huxtable, in accord with their enjoyment of the Huxtable family generally.

Emily of the *Bob Newhart Show,*[17] another modern working-wife image, inspires similar praise when she is brought up; two middle-class women mention her positively. They admiringly note her intelligence, poise, and independence. These women, independent and career-oriented themselves, particularly comment favorably on her relationship to husband Bob, which they find a pleasant example of a relatively egalitarian modern marriage, one in which both partners maintain a certain degree of autonomy (one woman says "she [Emily] tells him to leave her alone when he's bugging her" [Nadine]).

Middle-class women, then, seem susceptible to television's prototypically feminist woman. They watch, notice, and remark on television women with attributes that have come to be stereotypically feminist in our culture, primarily autonomous women with their own careers. Middle-class women also cast some of television's prefeminist women, Lucy for example, in surprisingly feminist terms, given the popular conceptions of these images. Postfeminist television women of the eighties—women like Clair Huxtable, for example, who "has it all," or the intelligent and educated Emily Hartley—are also admired by middle-class respondents.

Overall, middle-class women's comments about television women indicate that they experience conflict from their adherence, on the one hand, to a culturally "feminist" ideal that stresses independence and career success for women and, on the other hand, to an older (and also newer) ideal that praises more traditional female qualities and urges women to find happiness through family (e.g., relationships with men and children). These two ideals are combined in some postfeminist images of women that have recently appeared on television, some of which provoke admiring responses from middle-class women. As of the time this study was conducted, however, these images are too few to enable judgments as to women's continuing response to them.

Representations of Female Sexuality and Television's Female Ideal

Televised images of, and references to, female sexuality inspire some interesting differences in response from women of different classes. Working-class women are much more critical of stereotypical television depictions of "sexiness" than are the middle-class women I interviewed. They also mention pejoratively television's portrayal of women's helplessness or, in their terms, women's "use of feminine wiles" to manipulate men. Middle-class women, on the other hand, seem either not to notice this manipulativeness or to label it differently, in less pejorative terms, at times even connecting these qualities to what they label "feminist strength." In addition, middle-class women seem less offended by, or more in tune with, television's conventional representation of stereotypically sexy women; the same representations were criticized by some working-class women for their lack of reality.

Middle-class women in fact seem to respond quite positively to some of television's stereotypically sexy women. Consider women's responses to the two young female characters on the show *Gilligan's Island,* for example. *Gilligan's Island* involves a group of castaways marooned on a desert island. Among this group are two young women, Ginger (Tina

Louise) and Mary Ann (Dawn Wells). Ginger is portrayed to be an overt sex symbol in a comic way, a Hollywood movie star before the ship-wreck; Mary Ann is shown to be attractive but much more naive and innocent. Ginger dresses ostentatiously, wearing high heels and eve-ning gowns; Mary Ann is more simple, often wearing plain shorts and so on.

Many women mention that this is a show they had often watched. When I asked for women's reactions to these two characters, working-class women seemed a bit put off by Ginger the sexpot, whereas middle-class women were much more at ease with this image, seeming almost to enjoy it. Sarah, for example, describes the two in this way:

> I wanted to be like Ginger. I thought she was the sexy one, and she got all the attention. Mary Ann was nice but she was sort of boring. (Sarah)

A Freudian might call this remark a displacement of Sarah's desire for the attention she had wished for but had not received from her father (Sarah's parents had been divorced and she felt very distant from her father, whom she found to hold sexist attitudes toward women). An-other middle-class woman describes the two of them affectionately:

> They were interesting. Ginger was real glamorous, and was real re-moved, because she was in the Hollywood scene, and Mary Ann was all—from Kansas, and she was real wholesome, and real sweet. . . . And yet, they were all pretty appealing.

> Interviewer: Did you ever fantasize being like Ginger?

> Well, not Ginger, but I remember watching Miss America and think-ing, oh, I want to be Miss America someday. And going into the bathroom after the show and making my acceptance speech. And thinking, gosh, this is really fun. But it was fun to be glamorous. We used to play dress-up and make-up a lot. (Vivian)

While Vivian did not overtly fantasize being like Ginger, mention of this character recalled her own fantasies of being similarly glamorous. In fact, Vivian was preoccupied with fashion and the presentation of self. In a punk-fashion way, she was quite glamorous and seemed to enjoy this aspect of her femininity without feeling that it detracted from her abilities and more practical attributes.

Some of the working-class women with whom I spoke have, in con-trast to these responses, vaguely hostile reactions to the character of Ginger. They exhibited some discomfort or hostility when confronted with the overtly glamorous, movie-star image of womanhood, while middle-class women admitted to admiring it and aspiring toward it. Whereas working-class women label such images "unreal" and find them impossible to identify with or relate to, these qualities seem less of a problem for middle-class women. Is it, then, every little American girl who fantasizes being like Miss America; or do only middle-class girls have this fantasy?

I have mentioned above cases in which middle-class women also seem to find certain television women feminist, in a favorable sense, whom working-class women see as neither feminist nor admirable. Different attitudes toward female sexuality may in part cause this difference. Again, the Lucy character serves as a good example. While middle-class women label Lucy a strong woman, someone who knows how to get what she wants and keeps trying to do so, many working-class women criticize Lucy, finding that she resorts to "feminine wiles" to get what she wants, often flirting and flattering men. These responses indicate differing attitudes toward female sexuality in women of different classes. Middle-class women seem comfortable with overt displays of sexuality, and even with manipulative uses of it in power relationships.

Middle-class women, then, seem more favorably disposed toward a media-defined image of the glamorous, sexy female ideal than are working-class women. Working-class women seem better able to keep their distance from, and to criticize as unreal, this particular ideal of female sexuality, as they similarly keep their distance from the media-defined feminist women of the seventies and even the assertive housewife Lucy. I label that aspect of television's ideal which seems to affect middle-class women more broadly a "gender-specific" ideal. Middle-class women seem to notice and to be able to identify with and even to appreciate television images that give them often conflicting ideals for women: the assertive housewife, the independent feminist, and the sexy glamour-girl. As discussed in more detail in the next chapter, working-class women both attend to less and criticize more these multifarious female ideals television offers.

Realism and Middle-Class Women

Middle-class women are very likely, more so than working-class women, to express the belief that television generally is not a very realistic medium. They both expect and desire something of television other than being confronted with realistic images when watching it. Some women simply respond to my questions about television with overall disclaimers about television in general: "I don't think I really took television all that seriously" (Terry), or "TV is a joke, a big advertisement" (Kristine).

These women seem somewhat puzzled overall by my focused interest in television. Both Terry and Kristine are in fact rather unconventional women who do not understand why television viewers—or academics studying it—would take television seriously. Both felt that television had been only a minor influence in their lives and seemed unable to imagine any other scenario, indeed to seem slightly disgusted by the idea that television may have been important to them.

Others remark more directly and specifically on television's lack of realism. Rachael's comments concerning *Dynasty*, a show to which she claims she is "addicted" and which she obviously enjoys, are representative:

> I take it with a grain of salt, I really do. I mean, [my husband] says, "I don't want to watch that! That's filthy!" But I laugh at it. I really do. I laugh at it. I know that nothing like that could ever really happen. (Rachael)

Some middle-class women, in fact, mention that they like shows *because* they are unrealistic, as in Ellen's case, when she explains why she likes to watch *Love Boat:* "Oh, because, it's so romantic and unrealistic and it just looks like everybody's always having such a good time!" Ellen is a woman who has searched desperately for, and feels that in her several relationships and with her handicapped child she has found precious little of, the sort of romantic and domestic happiness she alludes to here. Her ideal is alive and well, however, especially on television.

A good example of the different flavor of remarks offered by women of each class is the contrast between middle-class and working-class women's remarks on *Cosby*. Middle-class women tend to focus their discussions on different aspects of television content than do working-class women. While both classes' comments on *Cosby* respond to its idealized portrayal of the family, they focus on different aspects of the show and its characters. While working-class women comment more on the family's economic success, as I discuss at length in the chapter below, middle-class women tend to respond more to the family-oriented aspects of the *Cosby Show*, perceiving the show as depicting an idealized family but enjoying this portrayal and identifying with it in a very personal and emotional sense, despite its lack of realism:

> What I feel is unrealistic sometimes is the way they [the Huxtable family] relate to each other. They're wonderful. It's the kind of

family like you'd want to live in, you know. They listen to you. That's what I like about it. I like the family unity. And even though they have their differences sometimes, they work them out. It's a, it's a nice way. (Ellen)

Alisa, another middle-class woman, mentions the episode of the show on which the entire family celebrated the anniversary of Cliff Huxtable's parents as being a particular favorite of hers. She very emotionally recounts how she enjoyed the image of family unity and happiness the show presented:

I enjoyed the show where they celebrated his parents' anniversary . . . and they did the big show at the end, they were all singing. I really enjoyed this one. Because they went to the trouble of doing this for them and it was very creative. His parents were just like my grandmother. . . . If I just sent my grandmother a photograph or if I just sent her a letter, my grandmother would be the happiest person in the world. Just the thought that they went to all this trouble, they were really thrilled about it. (Alisa)

Other middle-class women mentioned specifically enjoying the love portrayed between Cliff and his wife, Clair, again emphasizing the idealistic aspects of this portrayal:

[I like] the closeness that they seem to show to each other and respect, I guess, too, for what they're doing. (Holli)

Another remarks:

Oh, I think they love each other. And they kid a lot and they're both real smart. It's not him fixing them all up, I mean she settles some of the problems. . . . They show them a lot together just by themselves, I mean, they may just be dancing or sitting on the couch. You know, it's kind of toward the end of the show every night and a lot of times it's just the two of them together. And it looks like stuff, you know, you're so happy that they're by themselves and have some time by themselves. (Brooke)

Both Holli and Brooke, like Alisa, are essentially conservative and family-oriented in their personal lives. Brooke, who is married, has a rather traditional division of labor in her marriage. Both Holli and Alisa talk about marriage in terms that combine their desire to work with their very strong desire to have children and a happy family life;

each mentions taking time off from her career to take care of children. It is not difficult to see why the relationships pictured on *Cosby* would appeal to these women.

Middle-class women, then, while noticing the lack of realism on the show, become involved in the familial relationships portrayed and identify with persons and situations, despite a perception and judgment of unreality. In their comments, middle-class women easily move back and forth between their own experience and descriptions of the television characters and situations that directly inspire particular memories and that often add up to an overall feeling of personal relatedness, which is not quite present in working-class women's remarks.

One can sense television's hegemonic impact at work here also, as middle-class women are drawn into admiring and identifying with televised portrayals of families characterized by idealized interfamily relationships, as well as a lack of even the middle-class financial woes most families experience. The form this impact takes is subtly distinct for the middle class, however, and in some ways even more insidious than the way television operates for the working class. Middle-class women focus on the components of television's individuals and on the form of their relationships with others. Potentially, despite their disclaimers of television's lack of realism, they are even more likely than working-class women to absorb television's subtle dictates about how to be a person, in particular how to be a woman. In this realm, television content often relays to middle-class women patriarchally hegemonic messages. It is alarming that postfeminist television in particular helps encourage middle-class women to yearn for a configuration of personal and emotional satisfactions that are unlikely to be achieved by more than a favored few.

Some middle-class women seem to desire more realism in their viewing experience, either denigrating television for being something other than realistic or stating a preference for film over television, giving the reason that in film, characters are more finely and realistically drawn than they can be on television series, given the limitations of prime-time conventions (see Gitlin 1979):

> I know it's because they have such short scenes [on television]. And I find that very insulting. Because life is not one person [who] walks in the door, talks for two seconds, and then the person walks out. The scenes are all about twenty seconds long. And it's a big joke to think that this person enters and exits within twenty seconds. I guess that's my gripe about the show [*Dynasty*], is because it doesn't really show— like movies do. The reason that I think I like movies is because

characters are more developed. You see them communicating for longer periods of time. You get—you feel like you know them better because you have more to judge than just short little one- or two-word scenes. (Rachael)

Evelyn, an older woman, feels she learned a great deal about her children and their generation from the movies they attended together:

Then I began to see those movies because I realized that I had better relate to what my children were into or surrounded by. Just that simple. [About *The Graduate*:] And I never thought it was possible, but obviously a thing like that can happen. And that's what I'd think; I had better face reality. If that's what's going on, you better find out about it. (Evelyn)

Note that both of these women mention turning to the medium of film for more realistic character portrayals and for information about the real world. They seem to put television, however, into another entertainment category; they seek entertainment from television, not education about the real world. Evelyn, in particular, while mentioning that she enjoys realistic films, nevertheless maintains that she would rather not see too many real-life problems on television. There is also a moral edge to Evelyn's remarks, a feeling that television should not show images that are morally compromising (she raised two children and was very strict about limiting the time and content of their television watching). Evelyn mentions the drug crisis in particular as something she would rather not see on television: "Now that our children are all grown up, we don't want to see this all over again on TV—I know I don't. I worry about my grandchildren as it is. So I don't have to have it flaunted at me" (Evelyn).

Overall, middle-class women do not stress the search for realism in making their television viewing choices. At times when working-class women might criticize television, or speak with disgust of its lack of realism, middle-class women might focus on particular television characters they like or may read shows comically or satirically, even those that were not necessarily meant in such a vein, and derive enjoyment from television in these alternate ways.

Distance, Judgment, and Cynicism: Middle-Class and Working-Class Language about Television

In accord with their expectation that television will not be realistic, some middle-class women display a noticeable cynicism toward television images that litters their comments about television and is noticeably lacking in my working-class informants. Middle-class women's speech about television is sprinkled with references to the fact that they "never took television seriously," that even though they may have enjoyed certain shows or characters, they never considered them to be realistic. In fact, many repeatedly maintain that they like certain shows and characters *because* they are unrealistic. Some found dramatic television shows to be pretentious in their claim to be real, while others read such shows to be comic, even when it seems no comedy was intended.

Some of my standard questions provoked peals of laughter from middle-class informants. For example, one woman gave these responses to questions about a lead character in the soap opera, *All My Children:*[18]

Interviewer: What stories on the show did you like the most?

I like Erica.

Interviewer: Why?

'Cause she's a bitch.

Interviewer: Would you like to be like Erica?

Yeah, I want to grow up to be like Erica. No, Erica's just funny 'cause she's always doing bitchy things.

Interviewer: So, do you think Erica is a bad person?

She's supposed to be a bad person. But she's the most interesting, one of the most interesting characters on the show, 'cause she's not, you know, 'cause she does have some life in her. She's supposed to be bad, but that's why I like her.

Interviewer: Well, do you think she's bad?

Do I. . . ? How do you make judgment on Erica? Yes, Erica is bad. She's bad, she's bad! (Nadine)

Or another woman describes her response to the characters on the same show:

Interviewer: Which characters on the show do you like?

On *All My Children?* I don't like any of them, really, they're just— they're just fun to watch. I like Opal, because she's just so tacky, and she's funny. I mean, she's—she kind of frustrates me when I watch her, because she's so, such a fool in a lot of ways. (Vivian)

Again, this woman does not take the question of liking entirely seriously, as the woman above did not or could not take the task of judging the character of Erica entirely seriously.

The women above approach television from a more distanced vantage point than do many of the working-class women I interviewed. Compare their accounts with the following descriptions of Opal, culled from working-class transcripts, such as this:

Interviewer: What did you think of Opal?

She's so dingy. I don't like her. She's tacky, no taste. (Linda)

Another responded similarly:

Interviewer: Do you like Opal?

Opal? No, I don't like Opal. I didn't like Opal. They changed her character somewhat with time, but no. Opal sent her young, virgin daughter out to work in a sleazy bar to make money because she was too lazy to do it, and told her going to school wasn't important. You know, she should be a model. And her values weren't the best thing. (Marie)

Compare these comments about Erica:

Erica's a snob. Erica's your typical snob . . . just wants to do everything for herself and doesn't care about what she does to other people. Nosy, wants to get her nose into everybody else's business. That's about it. (Linda)

Or as Kim remarks:

Interviewer: Now is Erica someone you like?

No. I don't like her. I enjoy watching her, but I don't like her. (Kim)

Class differences are also apparent when one compares working-class women's descriptions of the character Jenny on *All My Children*. For example:

Interviewer: How would you describe Jenny?

Oh, very sweet and caring. You know, just a pretty, really nice person. (Linda)

Another working-class woman comments:

> Interviewer: Who were some of your favorite characters?
>
> All of them, yeah. All of them. Kim Delaney, the one that played Jenny.
>
> Interviewer: You liked Jenny?
>
> Yeah.
>
> Interviewer: What was she like?
>
> God! What a sweetheart! She was so sweet, so kind, so naive, you know? Like a churchgirl, you know, just so *good!* (Marie)

In contrast, a middle-class woman remarks:

> Interviewer: Do you like Jenny?
>
> Yeah, I think she's nice, but she's sort of a wimp. She doesn't—well, everybody on those shows—on all television shows, seem like that, is that, they can never make their own decisions. She can't make her own decisions. (Vivian)

The differences between the working-class and middle-class responses to these characters, though sometimes subtle, overall indicate a resistance on the part of middle-class women to offering a literal response to questions about television characters. Working-class women, when asked whether they like or dislike certain characters, for the most part give straightforward and direct responses, rather than answers smacking of the cynicism or sarcasm that attaches to many middle-class responses.

Women's comments on the prime-time soap *Dynasty* serve as further illustration of this class distinction. Consider, for example, the following comments made by working-class women about characters and incidents on *Dynasty:*

> Interviewer: Whom do you like on *Dynasty?*
>
> Krystle. I like Krystle.
>
> Interviewer: What do you think of Alexis?
>
> She's arrogant and she's real snobby and [would] do anything to better herself. [Would] walk on anyone and she doesn't care if she disgraces them. Definitely not like me.

Interviewer: But you identify more with Krystle?

Yeah. And I think Fallon is changing more to be a nicer person too. She's changing into a much nicer, sweeter person. (Linda)

Another woman talks of *Dynasty* in this way:

Who do I like? Oh . . . Krystle's just wonderful! And Alexis is just— just horrid! She's just a mean lady. She's . . . I don't know. I feel that she carries that through even, you know, when she's not that charac- ter. It's just her. She's—she just isn't the least bit—nice. What can I say? Krystle just is so warm and loving, and Alexis just always seems to be cold and calculating and looking out for what's best for Alexis, even though many times, you know, it almost costs her children.

And she continues:

I don't think Krystle is like that. Krystle is always looking out for the good of everybody else. Everybody comes to her to discuss problems. You know? Deep emotional sorts of things. Where Alexis, nobody trusts. If you did fill her in on something, she'd use it against you eventually. (Nancy)

Both of these women take the meanings offered by the show itself literally, at their face value. There is no irony or critique in their talk. When asked whether Krystle functions as a role model, both unhesi- tantly reply that she does. Linda responds:

Krystle is very sweet and caring. You know, just a pretty, really nice person.

Interviewer: Perfect, a perfect woman?

Yeah, maybe, you know.

Interviewer: Is that kind of your ideal of what you'd like to be?

Oh yeah, I would, sure, like to be like that, but nobody's perfect.

And Nancy remarks:

Interviewer: Do you feel Krystle is a good role model for women? Would you like to be like her?

Oh, *sure!* I mean, to look beautiful all the time! I mean, it's an unrealistic existence, but it—it's neat. You know, I'm kind of like up there with a goal, an unrealistic goal. What she does in her life is good. (Nancy)

Another working-class woman offers the following:

I don't care for—what's her name?—Alexis. Can't stand her. Can't stand her sister's books either. There's something that goes against me. I don't know why truthfully. Now which is his wife? The blonde? I like her. (Marilyn)

All offer little or no critique of the good/bad split in images of women present in any surface reading of the show's text. Contrast these responses with the following replies culled from middle-class transcripts:

Interviewer: Which of the women [on *Dynasty*] do you like?

Alexis. Because she's fun, you know, she's amusing. She's like—they make her out to be this real evil woman. But she's, you know, she's real independent. She goes after what she wants and she's a bitch. (Nadine)

This woman goes on to describe her reaction to the character of Krystle:

I really can't stand what's-her-name—Linda Evans. Krystle—ugh! She is such a bad actress and just really—well, they all are but . . . She's real one-dimensional, just like, "Oh, Blake!"

Another middle-class woman mirrors her views:

I hate—I don't like Krystle. Well, I don't hate her. But I don't like her. Because too many scenes I've seen her on her knees or in a similar manner [sneers] talking to Blake like he is "the" person of the world and she has to show all respect for him. I don't like her. She doesn't speak back to him, . . . (Rachael)

When asked about Alexis, Rachael replies that it is the unreality of the character's juxtaposition of perfect success with perfect evil that bothers her:

Alexis—well . . . no one could be like an Alexis. Or maybe there are women like Alexis, but they couldn't have things go right for them all the time like she does, I don't think. I guess part—I kind of feel like if you do things like that, you're really going to get it some day.

Both of these women seem to have rather emotional responses to the show. They give relatively long, involved answers when asked for their responses to particular characters and go on to describe particular scenes and plotlines and their reactions to them. Yet, unlike the working-class women cited above, both deny that any of the characters function as role models. The first woman quoted simply says no when asked whether she identifies with any of the *Dynasty* characters. She goes on to describe an episode of the show with a great deal of comic distance:

> Someone just took Fallon's baby. They're trying to figure out who. And the ex-wife Alexis is gonna try and marry that guy she almost killed having sex with him [laughter]—Colby. Oh, it was great! They tried to convince you that they're having such strenuous sex that this guy had a heart attack. So they had like fifteen minutes of cavorting with all this music and stuff. Then all of a sudden he goes gasp! gasp! [laughter]. . . . I can't freaking . . . and Alexis gets really pissed and she starts slapping him across the face and going, "You can't die, you can't die, you asshole! We have to get even with Blake! We want revenge!" And she's slapping him. And you think he's dead, but then it turns out he's in this oxygen tent. So she's gonna marry him and somehow they're gonna get revenge on Blake. And then, they just found out that Blake has this long-lost son that was kidnapped when he was a little baby and this guy's gonna come in from Montana and claim to be the Carrington son because the other one just left the series. And what else? Oh, and Claudia's gone bonkers. They thought she had the baby last week but it turned out she just had a doll. (Nadine)

Notice that as she is describing a scene which was obviously meant to have a great deal of dramatic impact (Colby having a heart attack), this woman is quite detached from the surface level of the show's meaning. Rather, she is in touch with what she perceives to be a comic undercurrent of the show. The sense of Nadine's remarks is that she finds it hilarious that an elderly man was shown having a heart attack while having sex with Alexis.

What identification processes, if any, are occurring for this woman are unclear. Whether on some level the comic pleasure she takes in Alexis's character, which she exhibits in the first set of quotes above, derives from an identification with her, is difficult to determine. If this identification does take place, it is not on a conscious level. This woman is an ambitious professional woman and does share certain qualities with the character of Alexis, so an unconscious identification between the two is certainly a possible source of at least some of her pleasure.

A literal interpretation of the narrative, however, is not what Nadine seeks from *Dynasty*. In fact, middle-class women often claim to like shows very much, while at the same time making cynical remarks about them. In one particularly blatant example, a woman discusses her enjoyment in watching *Ironside*, a detective show starring Raymond Burr:

> Interviewer: What shows do you remember liking?
>
> Oh, the guy in the wheelchair—*Ironside*. I used to think they were funny, especially when they had drug episodes, 'cause I thought they were, I didn't believe . . . I thought they were fabricated. Let's see . . .
>
> Interviewer: Did you have experience with drugs in school?
>
> Mmm . . . not in school, but I'd smoked pot a few times. I'd even taken acid once when I was twelve from my cousin that I knew. So, you know, she'd talked to me, she was kind of my idol and she talked to me a lot about it, I think, and so I was quite skeptical of these *Ironside* plots.
>
> Interviewer: So, you heard what drugs were really like with her and tried to experience them a little bit so when you saw them on TV you were struck by . . .
>
> The fakeness of it. Or I just couldn't believe the contrived situations. I just thought it was absolute bullshit, you know. (Terry)

She may have thought it was "bullshit," but this is one of the first shows that comes to her mind when asked which ones she liked and watched. Another woman describes similar criteria for shows she likes and watches:

> I really get a kick out of *I Love Lucy* and *Twilight Zone* and that sort of thing. Not that, like with *I Love Lucy*, not that I want things to be that way at all, that's unrealistic, but I think that it's just interesting to look back at a different time.
>
> Interviewer: Is it because there's anything different about that time, specifically? Take *I Love Lucy*—why do you think you get off on that?
>
> Well, I just think that it's so—it's not realistic at all. I'm not sure why I

like it so much. I don't know—it looks interesting. The cars and the clothes or something. I don't know, because really when I think about it, I don't think I'd want to live in that time. (Lori)

This woman finds a show she specifically labels "unrealistic" to be interesting and enjoyable; in fact, she "gets a kick out of it," in part, it seems, because of its unreality. It will be interesting to compare, in the next chapter, the ways in which working-class women use the term "reality" differently from middle-class women, certainly differently from Lori's use of the term here.

Given middle-class women's greater resistance to answering direct questions about television characters in a literal manner and the fact that working-class women seemed to have less difficulty in answering such questions directly, it is somewhat paradoxical that working-class women often deny that they actually identify with or relate to television characters. At the same time, middle-class protestations of distance from television were often combined with a more self-conscious identification with television characters than was displayed by most working-class women.

Sometimes even the very language involved in my questions—asking women whether they "identify with" or "relate to" specific television characters—seemed confusing to members of both groups, which caused me to wonder whether the meaning of these terms was actually different for different groups of women. Often I would be asked for clarification regarding the meaning of these questions: "Women that I related to?" "What do you mean, identify with?" Working-class women often interpreted this question to mean did they "like" or "dislike" specific characters, or even, as discussed above, to use the question to make the moral judgment as to whether someone was a "good" or "bad" person. Middle-class women often found this sense of the question somewhat difficult to answer ("Did I *like* her?" "Was she *good?*"), as illustrated in some of the passages above.

It is possible, of course, that there are simply more characters on television, which is dominated by middle-class images, with which middle-class women can reasonably identify, than there are potential objects for working-class identification, and so they are perhaps more accustomed to think of television characters in this sense.[19] To an extent, I believe this to be true. Middle-class women are more likely to expect television to offer them objects for identification. Working-class women are less oriented toward the female personalities they watch and notice more the general way of life depicted, as I argue in the next chapter. Should the bias of television content change, both offering more working-class characters and depicting more often working-class lifestyles, perhaps this difference in viewer orientation would change as well.

Conclusion

Middle-class women are more apt than working-class women to identify overtly with television characters on a personal level and to use these personal identifications to work out problems concerning interpersonal relationships in their lives. This use of television particularly emerges when choices and conflicts between work and family are depicted. Middle-class women seem more plagued by such choices than do working-class women, who do not as often perceive themselves to be free to make these choices. Women of both classes enjoy newer, postfeminist television characters, such as Clair Huxtable.

Earlier, less composite "feminist" television characters, however, are praised by middle-class women and criticized, belittled, or ignored by working-class informants. Middle-class women find some television characters to be feminist ideals whom working-class women perceive very differently: women of each class seem to have different ideas of what constitutes female or "feminist" strength. Working-class women are more uncomfortable with television's depictions of female sexuality than middle-class women seem to be, and may therefore be less susceptible to the oppressive ideals that television offers.

It is paradoxical that middle-class women both speak more distantly of television than do working-class women and, at the same time, seem to identify more closely than working-class women with many of television's images of women. Scratching the surface of their speech, one suspects that middle-class women are vulnerable in a deplorably direct way to the set of representations that constitutes the feminine in our culture. Television's ideal women are one substantial part of these representations, and this body of images engages middle-class women in a way that bespeaks their close, personal involvement with the issues they have been created to represent and belies their stated distance from such representations and cynicism about them. On the other hand, middle-class women at times view television as a cultural source of images of female strength, perceiving certain characters to be extremely feminist and admirable. For middle-class women, therefore, television is both a source of feminist resistance to the status quo and, at the same time, a source for the reinforcement of many of the status quo's patriarchal values.

Chapter 4
Working-Class Women Discuss Television

I turn in this chapter to an examination of the dominant themes that emerge when working-class women discuss television, emphasizing in my discussion the differences in my interviews between working-class and middle-class women. While there are some similarities, the differences between the two groups help to highlight the ways cultural experience is distinct for women of different classes. I argue that, in many cases, middle-class women's experience with television is dominated by gender-specific concerns. By this I mean that the terms of their responses are more related to their position as female individuals in a patriarchal society characterized by a gender-based division of labor and power differentiating men from women, than are the responses of working-class women. In a sense, middle-class women's discussions of television are more "psychologistic" than are those of working-class women; more often, they concern the relational problems that theorists have argued take a more primary form for female individuals in our society than for males as a result of our patriarchal social organization (Benjamin 1977, 1978; Chodorow 1978; Balbus 1980; Flax 1983). In contrast, working-class women often express this reception of television using terms that are first related to their experience as members of the working class and secondarily related to their experience as women per se in our society. I find, therefore, that in many cases working-class women respond to television in a more class-specific way, and that television's hegemonic properties are therefore more class-specific in their case. For middle-class women, however, television's hegemony is more gender-specific.

There is a well-established tradition of sociologists attempting to study and articulate the particularities of working-class culture(s) in capitalist societies.[1] Bernstein (1973), in a now much disputed theory, initiated the discussion of class cultures by theorizing that, in Britain at least, class experiences are so distinct that they translate into different overall uses of language for members of the working class vis-à-vis the middle class. More recently, British communication researchers associated with the Centre for Contemporary Cultural Studies at the University of Birmingham have described, at times quite convincingly, what they term "subcultures of resistance" to the dominant culture among the British working classes (Hebdige 1979; McRobbie 1978b), as well as documenting the often insidious operation at an everyday level of ideological hegemony (Willis 1977, 1978). Often the resistant subcultures Birmingham researchers describe have involved the appropriation of mass-produced commodities or mass media products, and the paradoxically transformative use of these products in the expression of resistance to the dominant hegemony.

American researchers have followed the British in searching for evidence of resistance to ideological hegemony at the cultural level among the American working classes. Fiske (1987), formerly associated with the Birmingham group, has been in the forefront of this approach.[2] But important differences between the historical situations of the British and American working classes might lead us to expect major differences between them. Katznelson (1981) and others have documented the relative political passivity of the American working class compared with the working classes in other Western societies. They argue that, owing to immigration patterns, residence patterns, schooling, cultural ideas about assimilation in the United States, and the peculiarities of the American political system, there is a less specific and distinct working-class culture in this country than elsewhere. An important tradition of American media research (Gitlin 1978, 1979, 1980, 1983) has borrowed from the Italian Marxist Gramsci's (1971) concept of hegemony to argue that the mass media in this country, rather than promoting resistance to the capitalist forms of domination that exist, actually encourage ideological passivity to and accommodation of domination.

The case of working-class women raises even more complicated contradictions for students of ideology, culture, and the mass media. In the case of women, do patriarchal and capitalist forms of domination, and related forms of resistance, reinforce one another? Does one promote or hinder resistance to the other? How might the responses of working-class women to hegemonic products such as the mass media differ from those of middle-class women? Can we say that the categories of class or gender or neither are primary in women's cultural experience? How might such a determination be made?

Working-class women resist television but often rely for their critiques on standards drawn from television and from our popular culture more generally. Many respond to what I have termed television's "hegemony of middle-class realism," labeling the pictures of middle-class life presented on television, pictures from which working-class women themselves are often far removed, to be "realistic" (i.e., accurate depictions of reality). In contrast, working-class women are much more critical of television images of working-class life. These images, they feel, are intended to represent their own experience but rarely meet this goal satisfactorily.

In this chapter, I first discuss the different ways in which working-class women use the term "reality" in talking about television; here, I flesh out the idea that television presents women with a "hegemony of middle-class realism." In this section, I note women's distanced acceptance of middle-class television: even television judged to be "real" offers women few character images with which they can personally identify or become emotionally involved. I further develop the theme of television's hegemonic relationship to reality by juxtaposing how women talk about their own experience, and their own experience with others, in relation to their discussions of television and television characters. I contrast women's discussions of middle-class television in the next section, detailing working-class women's often critical reception of working-class and upper-class images on television (although women criticize and distance themselves from these two types of images in different ways). Finally, I analyze the issues of comedy and glamour in conjunction with women's rejection or critique of specific television characters drawn from a spectrum of shows. My goal is to present as complete a picture as possible of the range and issues involved when working-class women discuss television.

What Is Reality? Working-Class Women's Discussions of Realism

When I watch that show [*Cosby*], I think I'm really looking, I forget I'm watching TV. It's so real. (Janice)

Reality is a scarce resource. (Carey 1989)

In my discussions with them, working-class women treat television's relationship to "reality" differently from middle-class women. Whereas middle-class women are often able to identify with television characters and the situations they find themselves in, even while judging these characters to be unrealistic, misinformed, irritating, or outrageous in their behavior, working-class women overall are much more apt than middle-class women to overtly seek realism in the television they watch. Often, working-class women state that they prefer television shows that they perceive to be realistic (although the meaning of this term as used here is far from clear), as in the following quotes:

> I don't like something that I don't think can really happen. I guess I like real-life stuff. (Nancy)

> I like more realistic shows on TV, I guess because they make more sense to me. (Kim)

> It's more realistic stuff, you know? It's not a lot of garbage and it's like that show is what can happen—really happen, whereas a lot of these shows, they make everything seem like peaches and cream, you know? I like realistic stuff. (Marie)

> It's a very good story. I thought it was cute. It was real-life. (Marilyn)

> Now I like things that . . . I mean, things that are plausible is what I really like. Things that can happen. They show all kinds of things now. That's the kind of thing I like. The thing that they show you that is going on that is true. Why? Well, because it's happening around me. That I find very interesting. I like to be informed, I like informative shows. I think we should all face reality. If we're living in this world, we better know what's going on around us, and what might be in store for us whether we like it or not. (Seline)

> You can sometimes learn little things [from television], that maybe that would be a good way of handling that. . . . You know how different people deal with different situations, you might learn something from them. (Janice)

Other studies of middle-class women's media reception have found that they prefer realism in the mass media, particularly in women's reception of books. Yet, often the precise meaning of this term in women's own language, and in the language of the critic, has been difficult to articulate. Radway (1984b) talks of the sense in which middle-class romance readers distinguish between geographical and historical backgrounds, which they believe to be accurate, and characters and plots, which they believe are unrealistic—even though more often than not romance readers identify with the main character. Long finds that middle-class book club members have "a deep allegiance to the conventions of realism" with regard to their discussions of geographical and historical background, plot, and especially character

(1986:604–606). Women expect books to be realistic and like books they find to be so. This expectation is particularly evident in women's responses to characters in books; often they discuss characters as if they were talking about real people rather than constructed realities.

Studies of television reception have similarly yielded realism as a criterion people use for deciding whether they like or dislike particular television shows. Ang (1985), in studying reception of the prime-time soap opera *Dallas,* found that there was a close correlation between a viewer's judgment of a character or setting from *Dallas* as "realistic," and her judgment that this character or the show itself was "good." Overall, those who liked *Dallas* appeared more involved with the characters themselves; like Long's informants, they talked about them as we would talk about people in daily life, in terms of their particular character traits and evaluating "how they are" as individuals. On the other hand, many of those who hated *Dallas* expressed their dislike by reference to the show's "unrealistic" content. Liebes (1984:49), in an interesting study which will eventually yield critical insight into ethnic differences in viewers' discussions of *Dallas,* also finds that at least some viewers (in this case, Israelis of Moroccan descent) talk about the show itself as if it were real.[3]

In the studies of Radway, Long, Ang, and Liebes, informants seem to mean several different things when judging mass media products to be realistic. Primary in this judgment is the belief that individual characters are realistic; in each study, readers and/or viewers liked characters they could identify with and become involved with at a fairly personal level. But when class is added as a variable, in the context of television at least, these categories of "realism" and "identification" take on distinct and different meanings. Middle-class women assert that television is *not* realistic; one feels as though they are culturally expected to make that judgment. Following Bourdieu's (1984) categorization of middle-class culture in the West, we might say that middle-class women are more "cultured": they "know" they are not supposed to take television seriously. Yet they enjoy it and identify with and become involved with its characters nevertheless. While they find television's overall portrayal of the world to be contrived and unrealistic, this does not prevent middle-class women from enjoying the individuals the medium produces, much as Long's readers enjoyed the characters in the novels they read.

Working-class women, on the other hand, talk much of television's "realism"; yet this term, as it pertains to television, derives more from the overall world television portrays than the individual character portraits it paints. Their expectations of the medium, and the basis upon which they decide whether they like or dislike particular shows, are different overall from those of middle-class women, less focused on character and more on ambiance. In general, working-class women seek realistic television shows; in fact, when asked whether they like television shows, many working-class women, as the above quotes indicate, without any prompting at all respond with an evaluation of the show's relationship to reality, while denigrating shows that seemed to lack a realistic quality. When pressed about what constitutes realism, answers more often pertain to plot, physical setting, and moral issues treated, or lessons learned on the show, than they resemble the middle-class focus on individual character portrayal and related qualities.

When pushed even further to describe which particular plots and settings constitute realism in their view, some working-class women paradoxically describe a picture, both material and moral, of middle-class life. In this sense, television exerts an hegemony of middle-class images over working-class women. The particular sorts of pictures of middle-class life that dominate the medium are consistently and strongly preferred by working-class women to television's attempts to portray working-class or upper-class life. These pictures come to constitute a normative vision of reality that may influence viewers' interpretations of their own experience, and certainly influences viewers' ideas about what typical American life is and ought to be like.

Several working-class women, for example, in discussing the middle-class situation comedy show *Bewitched*, mention that in addition to the magical powers of leading character Samantha Stephens and fantasies they had surrounding those powers, what they like about the show is the realistic nature of its portrayal of suburban, middle-class family life. One working-class woman—a housewife who stays at home with her small children—remembers her mother remarking on the authenticity of the housewife aspect of Samantha's role:

> I liked *Bewitched* a lot. I remember my mother always saying how well she portrayed a housewife. I guess just the way she looked and the way she acted and I—I guess the situations that she was presented with were real domestic. I always wanted that sort of domestic life. (Betty)

Here we find that it is the promise of middle-class "normality," embedded within the realistic conventions of the show, that stands out for this woman and is remembered long after the appeal of a truly magical, fantastic existence has faded from memory.

Some working-class women remark on the physical accoutrements of middle-class life in *Bewitched*, expressing their envy of the house and trappings of the Stephens' family lifestyle:

She had a beautiful house, I remember that, but I don't remember really thinking about the neighborhood. I did like her house, though, I thought it would be nice. Same with the *Brady Bunch*. I thought, wow, a big, fancy house.

Interviewer: That was a lot different than what you thought about your house?

Yeah. I always wanted a two-story house.

Interviewer: Do you still want a two-story house?

Yeah, probably. If I—that's right, I've never thought about that. I want a big house someday. (Pamela)

Fully as much if not more than she attends to the fantastic dreams of entering the supernatural world of witches, this woman notices the more "realistic" middle-class dream that *Bewitched* presents, that of the happy family with the large, beautiful house in the suburbs. The pull of middle-class realism is as powerful for this working-class woman as is the pull of the completely fantastic, magical existence of the witches *Bewitched* portrays.

Another working-class woman comments on Darrin's propensity to drink when returning home from work.

I remember they used to drink a lot on that show too. Every time he came home she handed him a drink. And I used to think, why does he have to have a drink when he comes home? It's strange, he must have a terrible time at work. (Janice)

Again, this illustrates that working-class women are more likely to comment on the aspects of *Bewitched*—the accoutrements of everyday life—that contribute to its effect of middle-class realism rather than those central to its more fantasy-oriented aspects.

Working-class women's comments contrast rather markedly with middle-class women's remarks about this show, which tend to focus more on the fantasy of magic and Samantha's strength than they do on the fantasy of middle-class suburban life. Some middle-class women speak in critical terms of her relationship with her husband, the man ostensibly responsible for Samantha's decision to stay home and live a "normal" life:

I wanted to be like *Bewitched*. Well, because she was a witch. I thought she was really stupid for being married to Darrin, because he was such an asshole. He was so dominant, and she wanted to be a housewife, and that was so—unbelievable, that this woman with so much talent and creative powers would want to just be a housewife, and raise her kids. (Nadine)

Another woman reiterates this criticism:

I liked her, and she was pretty shrewd sometimes. But she was too married to Darrin. And Darrin was kind of a jerk. I would not want to have been married with him. Because he never really treated her very well. He never appreciated her as much as I think she deserved. (Sarah)

In contrast to the working-class women cited above who expressed some envy of Samantha's domestic situation, these middle-class women are very critical of Samantha's domestic choices and her allegedly "ideal" domestic situation, and are more focused, if critically, on her relationship with her husband and family.

Regarding Samantha's sacrifice of her magic powers in order to live "normally," a working-class woman comments, "I thought that was really a good thing to do but I don't think I could have done it if I was in the same position" (Linda). Another mentions, "She was really a good wife and mother" (Pamela). These women accept the normative aspect of the show, that Samantha's giving up her magic powers is actually a good and noble thing to do, responding to the show's narrative-level message that the "realistic" life of the typical suburban middle-class housewife is preferable to the unreal, immortal life of a witch.

A working-class woman who shares the disgust the middle-class women quoted above express at Samantha's renouncing her powers nevertheless chooses a different aspect of Samantha's sacrifice for comment. Rather than criticizing the power relationship between Samantha and her husband or her general commitment to being a housewife and raising her kids, Janice finds it entirely unbelievable, almost offensive, that "anybody in their right mind if they could twitch their nose and clean their house [would not do so]. I hate housework. To think that anybody would actually want to do it" (Janice). The middle-class women quoted above praise Samantha, and admire her strength, blaming external factors such as her husband and marriage for her limited use of her powers. Rather than admiring Samantha and envying her strength, Janice finds her somewhat contemptible for not using it. As I point out in my discussion of the Lucy character below, working-class women tend not to judge television women to be as strong when their characters are embedded within situations and given to actions that viewers find either silly or incomprehensible.

Bewitched is interesting in that it paints two different ways of life simultaneously. The fantasy of the typical suburban middle-class housewife and mother corresponds closely to the typical pictures of middle-class life that dominate so much television programming. In the show, this way of life is explicitly contrasted with magical fantasies, of people having magical powers and living a fantasy life. According to the overt text of the show, a woman would be glad to give up the latter for the chance the former offers to achieve perfect happiness. While both sets of respondents thought Samantha's magic powers "neat" and desirable, middle-class respondents seem less affected by the suburban fantasy, working-class respondents more so. Middle-class women, on the other hand, respond more to the particular characteristics of the Samantha character herself, her power and unusual strength as a woman, finding it jarring that so powerful a woman voluntarily subordinates herself to her husband. Even in a show marked by extreme pictures of outrageous, unrealistic fantasy, working-class women pick up the middle-class realism portrayed alongside the magic.

Cosby is another show that garners praise from working-class women for its overall portrayal of American family life. Several working-class women, when initially describing the show, immediately bring up their belief that *Cosby* is a show that portrays a "typical" family. One woman told me of her concern that a family like the Huxtables, rather than the families portrayed on prime-time soaps such as *Dallas* or *Dynasty,* should be taken by foreigners to American culture as representative of our culture; she had heard of *Dallas*'s international reputation and was alarmed by it:

I watch the Bill Cosby show. It's an average family, working parents, nice house, not wealthy but . . . and that to me is more an American family, you know. Like people from other countries see *Dallas* and *Dynasty,* they think that's how we all live. Watch *Cosby,* I think that's more of a typical American family.

Interviewer: So, Cosby strikes you as a typical individual?

Right, with exaggeration but that's for television.

Interviewer: And so you say you like to watch some of these shows that you feel portray a typical American family.

Yeah, that I can relate to. (Janet)

Here we have a woman who turns from the abnormality of the fabulously wealthy to the comparative "normality" of the Huxtables. By comparison with the images presented on *Dallas,* the Huxtables may appear relatively representative of American families; in fact, however, they are far from representative, far more affluent than most white families, certainly more well-off than typical black families.[4] What is identified as typical by this informant is an image of affluent, upper-middle-class life.

Working-class women often relate personally to situations portrayed in shows they feel are realistic. For example, some mention that they enjoy *Cosby* because the show treats situations similar to those they encounter in their own lives and teaches valuable lessons concerning those situations. Some lessons mentioned involve discussions of money problems, and of children's responsibilities relating to property and money. Sometimes it is clear that women who encounter more than their share of these issues in their daily lives particularly value the *Cosby* treatment of them.

Janice's husband is unemployed, and she is supporting him and their two children with her job as a secretary. She watches the *Cosby Show* often, and mentions that she particularly liked the episode where Theo takes the family car without permission and ends up wrecking it. She enjoyed the way the family dealt with him after this incident.

Interviewer: How did they deal with it?

Well, they sat down and talked to him, of course, he got grounded, needless to say. But they got him to admit where he was wrong rather than accusing him or screaming at him. It was, "You tell me what you did." (Janice)

One has a difficult time imagining Janice's family calmly handling a situation where one of her sons wrecked the family car, given her description of the financial pressure she is constantly under. In this context, it is interesting that she saw such similarity between the *Cosby* situation and her own. It is also interesting that, unlike the words of middle-class women discussed in the last chapter, Janice's description focuses more on the situation portrayed, and lessons learned, than it does on her identification, or lack of it, with specific characters on the show.

For some working-class women, learning information about real life is a strong motivation governing their television choices. But more escapist motivations are mentioned as well.[5] At times, these motivations apparently conflict. What Janice mentions that she enjoys most about the Huxtables, in addition to the child-rearing lessons she gleans from the show, is that she gets a good feeling from watching the show. She enjoys watching the family portrayed and their interactions. But

Janice's desire for a good feeling from television at times conflicts with her desire, also strong, for realism in television—television that can teach her something about the world. She herself mentions the contradiction between these desires and notes her own attempt to reconcile the two with the strategy of watching *Cosby*, which she sees as a show that can satisfy both:

> If it's something that really happened, you know, that I feel like I'm learning something about either history or somebody else in a different world, I mean a different part of the country that I wasn't aware of. Something we watch every week would be, if we're home, that new show the *Crime Stoppers* because that's something that usually makes me depressed, but . . . so you know when I watch TV I like to come away with a good feeling. There are some shows maybe that I really want to see that are depressing but I watch them because I want to find out how these things have ended up, but then I also think that when I'm watching something like the Cosbys you can catch something that can be used in real life. (Janice)

In Janice's case, she feels that watching *Cosby* accomplishes both desires, by teaching her about the real world and leaving her feeling good when it's over.

Part of the good feeling Janice reaps from *Cosby*, however, is traceable to her desire that her family be a bit more like the Huxtables and her belief that one day this will be true. She notices that her family does not live like the Huxtables (her husband is unemployed and uneducated and her own earnings low; they have severe money problems). Part of what Janice may hope to learn from *Cosby* is how to change her current reality to bring her family's standard of living closer to that of the Huxtables. Janice recognizes that, both financially and relationally, the Huxtables live quite differently from how she does but explains that she enjoys watching them in part because, "Maybe I think there's hope that my [financial and family situation] will get that way."

With her high school education, however, and her husband's lack of one, a standard of living approaching that of the Huxtables seems unlikely. When Janice has tried to register for night courses to further her education, she has found that the only time she has for studying is "between 11:00 P.M. and 5 A.M.," and she felt "like I was losing my identity" with this grueling schedule, making it very difficult to continue with her studies. In this case, television may temporarily open for Janice an imaginative space where problems which in her life have no easy solution are repeatedly solved calmly, fully, and in the space of a half-hour weekly timeslot. Viewing this sort of problem-solving on television may relieve, temporarily at least, some of the enormous financial and family pressures under which Janice constantly lives.

Nancy invokes characters from another show featuring professional women, *L.A. Law,* in a way similar to Janice's use of the Huxtables as providing ideal images. Despite working as a low-paid secretary, Nancy has visions of having a career. She mentions that she admires the character of Abby on *L.A. Law* because of her career and her success within it. She tries to emulate her, but her ability to do this is limited to externals like clothing, both because of her situation and her understanding of Abby's career:

> I guess I like [Abby], you know, she's successful and she's got a career. I've always wanted to have a career and I think that's what I like most about it, and when I watched it the first few times, I watched what she wore and I thought gee, you know, I've got to dress like that, more professionally. (Nancy)

Like Janet, Nancy enjoys watching television that offers her images of the kind of life she would like to lead. What is obscured is the stark degree of difference between her life and the lives of those she chooses to admire on the screen, and the difficult (in some cases, virtually impossible) steps each woman would have to take to attain the achievements of those they would emulate. For example, with a high school education, Nancy probably would need further education before achieving her ambitions. Her television watching makes the externals, the clothes and glamour that constitute careers on television, seem vital and relatively attainable, yet the steps that would necessarily be involved in getting on the career track remain obscure.

Other working-class women discuss lessons they have learned concerning money management, particularly in relation to children, from watching *Cosby.* One working-class woman, Janet, mentions that she closely relates to the following situation portrayed on the *Cosby Show,* which she describes in detail. The situation involves the Huxtable children buying a car. The college-age daughter in the Huxtable family wants to buy a car, and her father gave her advice regarding which car to buy. This reminds Janet of the time her two teenage boys, wanting a car badly, decided to buy one together. At that time, she had advised them that it would never work. The fact that at the time she worked in a factory and was divorced from her husband, whereas Cliff Huxtable was a medical doctor and his wife a lawyer, does not seem to interfere with her identification with the situation. Or perhaps it aids her apparent identification, since she may have perceived the Huxtables' fictional situation to be more desirable than her own. Wish-fulfillment, rather than "closeness of fit" between experience and image, may be the actual basis of her definition of realism and her identification with this television situation.

Another working-class woman mentions similarly liking the way compromises about money are made in the Huxtable household. As an example of the sort of compromises they have to make, she mentions an episode in which Cliff's wife, Clair, wanted to buy an extremely valuable painting which Cliff allowed her to purchase despite its expense:

> Like the episode where she [Clair] wanted the painting which was a lot of money, but it was from her family. He thought it was a lot but it was something she really wanted. You know, so he made allowances for that although I guess she paid for it with her own money. I'm not sure, but that's how you have to have a compromise. (Marcie)

Marcie was first married at fifteen and was divorced by twenty-two, supporting two children with factory work and later with a series of other working-class jobs. Money had clearly been an important issue for her, given the details of her life. It is not surprising that she mentions incidents such as this one when discussing television, incidents which involve decisions concerning the use of limited resources. What is a bit surprising is that Marcie, who enjoys the *Cosby Show* and watches it regularly, finds it so easy to relate to or identify with a family whose greatest financial issue is whether or not to purchase an expensive piece of art.

In these examples, television seems important in serving women's wishes that reality might bear a closer resemblance to its television image. Or perhaps the particular content of the incidents women watch on television is not as important as the general nature of their content. In several of these cases, the fact that budgeting issues are dealt with at all, rather than the actual size of the budget or the content of what is purchased, seems to be what is most important for the women watching these shows. They are able to extract from a show like *Cosby* those aspects of its situations most relevant to them and to use these television images to help them learn about and reflect upon their own situation, while ignoring those aspects of television that are painfully different from their own world.

Beyond their ability to extract relevant parts of middle-class television, however, what is particularly striking about these examples is that the working-class women interviewed, often beset with financial woes, find it comforting to turn to, for example, money management in the Huxtable household for "realistic" hints as to how to better manage their own financial lives. These working-class women find such decidedly middle-class shows, with their middle-class problems, to be realistic, unlike their reception of working-class shows on television, which I discuss in the section below. Although on one level, the wish-fulfillment such judgments involve may be satisfying, on another level it is alarming to see working-class women accept television's presentation of the middle-class experience as the normal one for our society. What, then, do these women make of their own experience and the experience of their peers? How can women develop a critical consciousness of their own experience and put this consciousness to active political use when awash in a sea of middle-class images? In these cases, television's hegemonic function assumes a double-edged character in this doubly oppressed group.

Class, Television, and Experience

The issue of the relationship between women's experience and their perception of televisual representation takes an interesting turn in the speech of some working-class women. At times, women's expectations that television will be realistic translate into an acceptance of television images as de facto images of reality. Marcie, for example, mentions her belief that Clair Huxtable is a good attorney and that she is a typical wife and mother. I continued this line of questioning by asking Marcie whether she knew any female attorneys and, if so, to describe them.

> Interviewer: You know one woman attorney. Did she remind you of Clair?
>
> No. Not even closely. Because she wasn't as feminine as Clair Huxtable.
>
> Interviewer: Who do you think is more typical of women attorneys?
>
> Clair Huxtable.
>
> Interviewer: Why?
>
> Well, because I've seen other ones on television like on the news and other things like that, and they are all more feminine than the one that I knew. (Marcie)

Even though Marcie invokes images she has seen on television news that have strengthened her perception of the *Cosby Show*'s realism, her remarks serve as a particularly striking example of an instance in which a woman accepts television images to be more representative of reality than even her own experience and points to the possibility that some women rely on television as an authoritative source of information about many areas of life that are removed from experience.[6]

Another working-class woman, Janice, takes a similar position on the relationship between the *Cosby Show* and middle-class reality. Janice works as a secretary for a group of middle-class executives. She states that she enjoys the Huxtable family and finds it representative of middle-class couples who have "a career and a good home life and [do] not bring their work home." She then goes on to say that none of the middle-class men for whom she works (she has become friendly with several) has a life that even approaches that of the Huxtables for its calmness and lack of conflict between the demands of work and family. When asked for an example of a family she knows that does live similarly to the Huxtables, she mentions Harold but immediately contradicts this by saying, "I think Harold's life sounds totally opposite, hectic and kids running to sports and stuff, but I don't know, maybe it's just . . . wouldn't it be wonderful if things *could* be that way [as they are in the Huxtable household]." Janice continues to maintain that "well, I think there *could* be a family out there similar to the [Huxtables]," and to refer to the realism of the show, despite the fact that her experience contradicts this.

Although of course both Janice's and Marcie's remarks are plausible, and there could be women like Clair and families like the Huxtables in reality (and who knows? perhaps there are), what strikes me from their comments is that they do not trust their experience of the middle-class world and the individuals within it, seeming more inclined instead to accept television's representations of that world. This is particularly noteworthy when compared with the confidence they and several other working-class women show in their own experience when television attempts to represent a more working-class scenario, as I will argue in some detail in the section below. It is perhaps not surprising that when television hits more closely to home, which either fortunately or unfortunately it does only sometimes for working-class women, women are much more confident in their own experience, and disdainful of television images that fall far short of their realistic ideals.

One sees evidence of women's tendency to accept televised portrayals as real even in the case of the somewhat more fantastic television program *Dynasty,* which portrays the lives of the fabulously wealthy. One working-class woman, for example, comments on the character of Alexis (Joan Collins), "She's supposedly a career woman, but she was not a career woman like I associate career women to be" (Marilyn). Marilyn goes on to compare Alexis with other career women she knows in her life. It is particularly interesting to note how easily she discounts her own experience, which is that she has never met or known of a woman like Alexis, for the view that "there must be women like Alexis," which she seems to believe only because this image does appear on prime-time television:

> Well, the career women that I know socially and see about, I mean, they are women who are very average women. You can't figure *her* out; she's really far above the average in many ways—in her love approach, in her money spending, her clothes, her dress, I mean, that's a very different standard from the average person. But there must be women like Alexis in *Dynasty*. (Marilyn)

Another woman comments:

> Interviewer: Do you think there are women like Alexis?
>
> Yes, I'm sure there are. (Seline)

Contrast the views that "there must be women like Alexis" with these statements by middle-class women, which betray a totally different approach to the character, "No one could be like an Alexis" (Estelle). Another woman remarks:

> I think Alexis's story is absolutely far-fetched and ridiculous. Nobody can be that rotten. That's my honest opinion. That is absolutely unreal. Absolutely unreal. (Evelyn)

Quite a contrast in the interpretation of images! The far-fetched Joan Collins character, Alexis Carrington Colby, is a character who would stretch anyone's imagination. She is brilliantly and consistently successful in business, and her sexual allure is so powerful that no man can resist her. Yet what is interesting about the women's different responses is that working-class women are more accustomed to expecting reality on television and to describing it with these expectations in mind; this makes *Dynasty*, with what must be to most a startling lack of realism, less interesting to working-class women overall, at least according to the conversations many working-class women had with me. They do not quite know what to make of the character of Alexis herself, an individual whose character traits must strike women as very unreal, challenging their faith in the realism of television images. The middle-class women with whom I spoke seemed freer to be critical of the character of Alexis herself and, at the same time, to enjoy this character while judging her to be extremely unreal.

From a hegemonic point of view, it is interesting that both the middle-class and working-class women I have quoted criticize *Dynasty*'s lack of realism or accept its images as realistic on the basis of the belief that, essentially, rich and poor people are the same. Both overlook differences between the two, but they do so in different ways. One middle-class woman, Evelyn, has noticed, and subverted, *Dynasty*'s ploy: to make us think that rich people have many more, and more serious, personal problems than do those poorer.

I don't think the things on *Dynasty* are plausible. They make you feel that because people are rich they have nothing but problems. And then they're always jumping into bed with someone else, and I really don't believe that. I don't believe that at all. Just because a person is rich, doesn't put them in a different category and make them different from other people. (Evelyn)

Rich people, she claims, are emotionally the same as poor; they are not fundamentally different, nor do they act so. They simply have more money. While this woman may be similar to the working-class women quoted above in her lack of experience with rich people, she is more apt than they are to criticize the televised images with which she is presented.

In contrast, the working-class woman quoted simply does not mention that the fundamental difference between people she has met and those pictured on the television screen is the economic class in which each travels. There must be, she claims, women like Alexis Carrington Colby out there somewhere. Perhaps accidentally, she has not met them. The level of material wealth which *Dynasty* portrays is perhaps so threatening to women of both classes that they cannot consciously think about the material discrepancies between their way of life and what is shown on the screen.

In addition to the denial of their own experience of reality in favor of the televised version, one can sense in working-class women's statements a search for words that would be adequate to conceptualize class differences, armed as are most of us only with concepts and a vocabulary that steadfastly ignore the importance of class in our social system. By promoting a level of identification that, in effect, urges viewers that we are all the same, a show like *Dynasty*, whose principals sport lifestyles that in fact differ radically from those of the vast majority if not all of its viewers, contributes heavily to the class-blind quality of our society's language and our vision of ourselves. Most perniciously, this blinding seems, in some cases, particularly effective for working-class women. More middle-class women with whom I spoke are able to maintain more distance from this particular we-are-all-the-same message, seeing sameness on an emotional, rather than a material, level ("no one could be as rotten as Alexis"). Or, as one middle-class woman puts it,

> If you view it as a goal and become frustrated because you're not like that and you don't have furs and you don't have chauffeurs and you don't go on jets—on your private Lear jet here and there . . . I think it's okay—I don't look at what they have as much as the way they react to other people.

Few working-class women, in contrast, refer to the *Dynasty* way of life explicitly, or comment on the level of material difference between the *Dynasty* lifestyle and their own. Perhaps it is even more threatening for working-class women to examine this issue in detail, given that their prospects for upward mobility are even more limited than those of middle-class women. The unattainable quality of *Dynasty*'s lifestyle is the same for both classes, but the magnitude of this problem differs, ranging from issues of relative comfort on one end to actual survival issues at the other end of the spectrum. The real meaning of being unable to "keep up" with the *Dynasty* crew differs, therefore, for members of different classes and is potentially more painful for working-class women.

Even those working-class women who find shows like *Dynasty* and *Dallas* to be unrealistic and who criticize them for this refer more to plot details than either to character or to the lavish materialism involved. One working-class woman, for example, mentions that the *Dallas* plot-line wherein the entire previous season's events were shown to be a dream sequence really bothered her because, "This could never in a million years happen, and I couldn't stand it so I stopped watching it" (Nancy). The implausibility of this particular plot offended her. Another woman mentions that Pam's story on *Dallas* just seems too implausible to her, because

> Everyone seems to fall in love with her. If it isn't one rich guy, it's another rich man. I just don't think it's possible. When I don't think a story is possible, or an everyday happening, I don't enjoy it. (Seline)

In contrast to the way many middle-class women react to these shows, these working-class women find them unrealistic and tend not to like them for this reason. Some middle-class women also found shows like *Dynasty* and *Dallas* to be unrealistic but, for the most part, were not prevented by this perception from enjoying them and from using them in a personal way, nonetheless, by becoming affectively involved with the characters, their families, and their relationships with one another.

Race, Class, and Hegemony: Are the Huxtables a Typical American Family?

Television's hegemonic potential is not confined only to its representation of class and gender. Television portrays racial differences as well, and at times, its depictions of race intersect with those of class and/or gender. Returning to the *Cosby Show*, it is particularly striking to witness television's hegemonic qualities, in this instance, vis-à-vis class and race. The issue of race itself is rarely dealt with explicitly on the *Cosby Show*. Some analysts interpret the show itself as Bill Cosby's personal attempt to culturally retrieve the black family after its image had been destroyed by decades of sociological reports about its demise.[7] Yet rarely do women of either class mention the fact that the Huxtables are a black family. When this does come up, many hasten to assure me, as one woman put it, that the Huxtables are "just family," race-free, in a sense (this woman goes on to mention that the Huxtables "didn't seem like a black family").

Consider the way in which the race of the Huxtables does come up for some in their experience of the show. One working-class woman, Nancy, had an argument with a friend at work who attempted to argue that the Huxtables were not a representative black family. Nancy loves the sort of family relationships portrayed on the show and resents the suggestion that the Huxtables are not a typical black family.

> I like the family relationship [on the *Cosby Show*]. I had a big discussion with a friend of mine because he claimed that was fantasy and that there is no black family in reality that lives that way, and I got very angry with him.

> Interviewer: Why?

> Because I don't agree with him. There are black families out there, I knew some personally and I know that they do, yeah, they're just like . . . he was under the impression that black people are poor and uneducated and they have no class [laughs]. It really bothered me that he felt that.

> Interviewer: You don't think it's true?

> No. I mean a lot of them, yes, are in poverty or are lazy, but then I see a lot of Puerto Ricans and a lot of white people living in the same way. It evens out, but I've known a lot of people who were very nice and

lived very well and had good jobs and had a nice house. . . . We had some next to us and they used to take care of us and they were wonderful, very clean people. . . . He was saying it was a very unrealistic TV show, that there was no such thing.

Interviewer: And then based on your own experience with this family you think it's not unrealistic?

Yeah, yeah, that's how I feel. (Nancy)

The vigor with which Nancy argues that the *Cosby Show* is realistic is indeed a tribute to the ability of television images to establish, for some, an alternate vision of the real world. Yet, even if Nancy did know one successful, middle-class black family, surely there is enough evidence in the world around her to confirm the high incidence of poverty and unemployment among blacks; in fact, she lives in a city area that borders an extremely poor, largely black section of town. There should have been ample evidence in her experience to support the position alternative to the one she argued.

Nancy's attitude attests to the real triumph of that aspect of the hegemonic ideology that states those who work hard will succeed. It is as though she believes it would be racist to admit that some blacks, or that blacks as a group, have not succeeded; that to believe this would be tantamount to labeling blacks as lazy and incompetent individuals. Otherwise, how to explain their failure? Her statement indicates the possibility that shows like *Cosby* could have an extremely conservative effect on perceptions of the true position and needs of minority group members in our society. If shows like *Cosby* are perceived as an advance for minorities, as capable of correcting racist misconceptions that blacks are poor, they undoubtedly strengthen an individualistic interpretation of poverty's causes and its remedies. Paradoxically, then, the increasing appearance of minority images on popular television, packaged as they are within the terms of the white middle-class hegemony, may progressively discourage accurate perceptions of minority groups, poverty, and prejudice in our society.

The Hegemony Fractured: Working-Class Women Respond to Working-Class and Upper-Class Television

In contrast to their reaction to these middle-class shows, several of the working-class women with whom I spoke were much more critical of television shows featuring proletarian settings. It is not entirely surprising that working-class women criticize television's all-too-few working-class shows for their lack of realism on many different dimensions. Hitting closer to home than television's middle-class norm, these shows are perhaps easier to fault for those whose experience comes close to them, as they seek a more perfect fit between life and the screen and fail to find it.

Alice, for example, garnered criticisms from women who denigrated the show and its characters for their lack of realism. For example:

> I used to watch, sometimes, *Alice.* With Flo. I used to watch it when Flo was on.
>
> Interviewer: What did you think of that show?
>
> Forget it. You know, it was realistic in the sense that, you know, mother—single mother raising a child, working in a restaurant. But then she was dating attorneys, doctors—doesn't that seem a little. . . ?
>
> Interviewer: So that brought it out of the realm of being realistic?
>
> Right, because how many women that are working in diners date attorneys? I mean, they date truck drivers or whatever. Flo was more of a realistic character because she did date truck drivers.
>
> Interviewer: Was the character of Alice realistic?
>
> Well, she was realistic in a sense, but a person with that kind of strength would care—well, she was a strong person—wouldn't stay a waitress. You wouldn't stay working in a diner out of loyalty to the other waitresses and the boss. She would start her own restaurant, she would go out and do something different, go to night school. (Gladys)

According to Gladys's perception of reality, one can always improve one's situation through hard work and determination. *Alice,* which depicts a strong woman working in a dead-end job and apparently making little attempt to improve her situation, contradicts Gladys's conception of the way a real woman with Alice's qualities would behave in this situation. The show certainly contradicts her apparent judgment of how a real woman *should* behave in this situation. Both normatively and descriptively, Gladys judges *Alice* to be an unrealistic show. Perhaps *Alice* is most disturbing in that the show confronts her with images that contradict what she would like to believe is true: that no strong, intelligent woman need remain a waitress for very long. Such a view accords with Gladys's perspective on her own situation. She herself was currently attempting to improve her life by taking courses at a local college. Poor and abused as a child, after years of struggle as a single parent, she had finally made a successful second marriage; with the help this afforded her, Gladys could finally see the light at the end of the tunnel. Perhaps the last thing Gladys was interested in viewing on television was a bright woman apparently stuck in a dead-end job as a waitress.

Marcie, another working-class woman, criticizes the work situation as portrayed in *Alice* for its lack of adherence to her ideas about what the boss-worker relationship should be like. She believes workers should show more respect to their bosses than do Alice and Flo:

Interviewer: Do you think that show is very true to life?

As far as the working place, no. Because I've done that type of work, and for one thing, when I say I like the way they handle [Mel's] chauvinistic attitudes, he's still their boss and they're working for him and they owe him a certain amount of respect. That's my opinion.

Interviewer: And so you think on the show they don't really show him that respect that they would actually owe him in real life?

No. Because even though like they say about his chili, you know, I know it's just to get laughs, but in real life, even if I worked for this man and I hated his chili, I wouldn't [tell him]. Yeah, I might, if they said do you have any suggestions I might suggest not trying the chili, I wouldn't be dishonest with my customers, but I still wouldn't belittle the man. (Marcie)

The light-hearted attitude toward work presented on *Alice* offends Marcie, or at least provokes a response close to home. She holds strong opinions about the sort of interaction which is correct between a boss and his or her workers. The comic treatment this set of relationships receives in the situations and characters shown on *Alice* subverts some of the—to her mind—sacred rules that ought to govern here, and she is not amused. Again, Marcie has some difficulty in allowing comedy to wreak havoc with reality, and in this situation she is well-grounded experientially in the reality upon which this comedy is based, having had a long history in the paid labor force during which she worked for a variety of bosses. Marcie prides herself on being a good worker; we see this pride reflected in the decided and critical judgments she makes of the workers on *Alice*.

Significantly, and in apparent contradiction to her above remarks, Marcie begins her discussion of *Alice* by giving some evidence that she enjoys the show precisely because it depicts workers conspiring to subvert their boss's authority. She mentions that she enjoys watching the three waitresses work together to manipulate the chauvinistic Mel:

I liked the way the three waitresses manipulate Mel, because he is so chauvinistic. And they have their own ways of getting around him. That's mostly why I like that show. Or the character of Alice. (Marcie)

So in fact, despite her disapproval of it, the manipulative behavior the working women display toward their boss does seem to touch Marcie in an important way. It is, she claims, the main reason she derives pleasure from the show. She may harbor unconscious fantasies of rebellion against the bosses to whom she has shown so much respect throughout her life, and it is to this that the show speaks. Her conscious judgments of the show do not reflect the power of this fantasy, however. Consciously, she finds the work situations depicted on *Alice* to be grossly unrealistic, and this seems to interfere with her overall enjoyment of the show. In her reception of *Alice*, Marcie shows evidence, therefore, both of accepting hegemonic values (workers should respect their bosses) and resisting them (by liking the way the waitresses manipulate the chauvinistic Mel).

Undoubtedly, Marcie has experienced both these emotions in her own life. She has lived through familial as well as work experiences that bear some similarity to Alice's situation. Divorced at an early age, Marcie brought up two sons single-handedly, with little help from her ex-husband or family. She struggled through her life working at a series of relatively low-paying, unskilled jobs. Yet when asked whether the working single-mother Alice's situation reminds her of her own, she denies any particular identification or close feeling for this character:

Interviewer: Do you think you like shows, a show like *Alice*, because it reminds you of your situation, of what it was?

No, no. I think I probably . . . like I say, I enjoy the three of them together. If you take Alice alone, I don't know that I would enjoy her as much. I like the interaction between the three. You know, I think they complement each other. I just view it as entertainment because, like I say, there's not much about her son and their relationship or about how she struggles financially.

In these comments, Marcie zeroes in on what are in her opinion the main ways in which the show *Alice* is inadequate in its representation of the life of a single working mother. What the show does offer her is an entertaining trio trading comic wisecracks, probably unrealistic but enjoyable nevertheless.[8] *Alice* does not, however, offer a realistic representation of some of the most deeply important issues in Marcie's life;

and the implication in my discussion with Marcie was that she looked for, and missed, precisely these qualities as she watched, and judged, the show.

Sometimes women's judgments that television shows bearing no resemblance to their real-life experience are more real than those that apparently do are quite striking. This was particularly true in Marcie's case. During her interview, Marcie had compared another popular show, *Who's the Boss*, favorably to her judgment of *Alice*. *Who's the Boss* stars Judith Light playing Angela Bower, a high-powered advertising executive who hires Tony (Tony Danza) to run her household and help in raising her child. Of course, like Alice, Angela is a single mother. Yet unlike Alice, she is an upper-middle-class, highly paid professional. In one episode, Angela is fired from her job because of mishaps at home and, failing to locate another position easily, decides to go into business for herself as an advertising consultant. The whole family helps out, her mother acting as her secretary, Tony redecorating, until she gets started.

Marcie prefers *Who's the Boss* to *Alice* because to her, the former is more realistic. She particularly enjoys the way family finances are portrayed on *Who's the Boss:*

> Interviewer: What about comparing a show like *Alice* to a show like *Who's the Boss*? If you had a choice of watching one of those two shows, which one would it be?

> *Who's the Boss.* Because it's more realistic a lot of times. Like with her starting a new business, you know, they all pitched in and helped to get this place ready. Now that's something people would do, and they did without a lot of things to help her get started, and when she was finally, ah, in the black there was a little celebration. You know, it was like a group effort. It's like they're saying you have to sacrifice certain things to get ahead, to gain, and it's a gamble. (Marcie)

Who's the Boss appeals to Marcie, in this instance, with its classic portrayal of American achievement ideology. In the episode Marcie describes, hard work truly does lead to success, in this classic illustration of the Horatio Alger myth. It is interesting that this episode as she describes it also includes an example of family (or a pseudofamily group) cooperating in a business effort—more of a working-class than a middle-class scenario, which perhaps makes the middle-class nature of the way of life depicted on the show, and the ideology it carries, more palatable. In addition, the effort is successful (in our society, however, small businesses rarely succeed, as the somewhat grim statistics indicate).

Whereas the scarcity of economic detail on *Alice* displeases her (or perhaps it was, as Gladys identified them, Alice's bleak prospects that Marcie really finds repellant), Marcie is drawn to this upbeat presentation of a middle-class family cooperating economically and doing so more successfully than most. Marcie seeks economic detail from the entertainment television she watches, but it must be detail of a particular sort: upbeat, certainly, and involving interclass movement of various kinds, rather than depicting people as fixed in their position within the class structure. In some respects, she identifies more closely with the middle-class people on *Who's the Boss* and with their economic situation—perhaps because it is more upbeat—than she does with the working-class characters on *Alice,* whose situation is more vulnerable to her knowledgeable critique of its unreality.

Marcie's ability to identify easily with middle-class television is further illustrated by her comparison of the "realistic" *Who's the Boss* to the "unreal" *Dallas.* Referring to another episode of *Who's the Boss* on which Angela had to delay putting a pool in her backyard until the business got off the ground, Marcie praises the greater realism of *Who's the Boss* over images of the wealthy on the nighttime soap opera *Dallas:*

> There was a thing [on *Who's the Boss*] like one time where it's either a pool or this. They don't have that much money that they can do what they want to do when they want to do it like *Dallas.*

> Interviewer: And so you feel that's why you would rather watch a show like that than *Dallas*?

> Because it's more realistic. They're not wealthy people, but they're, they're like working-class people. She was paid very well where she worked, but now she's on her own and she dresses very nicely, but it's still a homey atmosphere. And like the place isn't furnished elegantly, it's furnished very nice, it's a nice house. (Marcie)

Marcie finds *Who's the Boss* "homey" compared with the stark, forbidding luxury portrayed on *Dallas.* She states that she enjoyed imagining the personal sacrifices the family members make on this show.

When compared with the lavish wealth of *Dallas,* almost any middle-class family would look more realistic. But television's skewed imagery leads Marcie to judge a successful advertising executive to be working-class, and leads the relatively middle-class setting of *Who's the Boss* to be incontrovertibly more realistic than television's supposedly proletarian *Alice.* In this instance, again, we see the power of television's middle-class images to claim for themselves an aura of reality lacked by the representation of other ways of life. Yet distance is maintained from

Dallas, which is dismissed for its lack of realism. Is the judgment of realism, in this instance, a means to maintaining distances too painful to imagine bridging?

Janice, another working-class woman, differentiates between the depiction of Angela's career on *Who's the Boss,* which she finds "realistic, she has to work a lot of overtime or bring a lot of work home" and which she therefore enjoys, and the depiction of the work-boss relationship between Angela and Tony, which strikes her as unrealistic:

> I can't imagine a situation [like that] not because I can't imagine a man doing that job, it's just that, them arguing all the time, I can't imagine any employer that has you living with them, taking care of their children, disagreeing with you that much and keeping you there.

The split in her response to the different work situations depicted on *Who's the Boss* is revealing. Janice finds the representation of Angela's professional life to be realistic and enjoys it. But she criticizes the more working-class representation of Tony's job situation and his relationship to his boss (Angela), a situation that perhaps strikes closer to home. Janice's responses illustrate well the split characterizing working-class women's responses to the depiction of different sorts of work situations on television.

Perhaps television's role as wish-fulfillment goes only so far. Possibly, it is too disturbing for working-class women to watch and to accept as real the lavish wealth of a show like *Dallas,* given that they seek reality from television and compare television images to reality more often than middle-class women. Middle-class prosperity as depicted on *Who's the Boss* and on so many other shows, however, provides a potentially more acceptably "realistic" set of wishes for working-class viewers, who might consider it plausible that they could achieve the level of affluence shown. My sense, in talking with working-class women, especially those thirty-five and under, was that overall there was an optimistic belief in their own ultimate upward mobility. In some instances, I found this striking given obstacles women would have to overcome to achieve this.

My interviews also provide some indications that, when the subject is too close to unpleasant aspects of a home life familiar to them, some women become uncomfortable with the televisual image. One working-class woman, Cathy, remembers herself laughing hysterically when watching *The Honeymooners,* a show about a working-class couple. This woman had been a battered wife for many years but had never related her experiences to the many arguments or threats of violence depicted between husband and wife in that show. Again, here it may be that comedy interfered with the identification process, that women avoid identifying with images that evoke too realistically real-life pain.

Gladys states quite clearly what she desires from television. She had just described in great detail a soap opera to which she was addicted, criticizing many of the characters and situations for their lack of realism. However, when asked if she would prefer more realistic characters or situations on television, poor women, for example, or women who worked for a living, she denies it. While she likes television to be fairly realistic, she wants a rather whitewashed (perhaps more middle-class?) picture; she does not wish to see too problematic a reality:

> It takes the fantasy away. When it's something that's totally unreal you expect it to stay that way. Who wants to see welfare mothers or working women who go home to a bunch of screaming kids? You don't want to see that on TV. (Gladys)

Gladys goes on to illustrate her point in the context of describing the show *Kate and Allie* and her reaction to it. Kate (Susan Saint James) and Allie (Jane Curtin) were two divorced women, old friends, who decided to move in together with their children to form a household following their divorces. Allie, the old-fashioned one, kept house for Kate, the glamorous career woman. The show is interesting in that it plays the roles of the two women—traditional and modern—off each other. Plots revolve around various problems one or both of the women experience in the course of their lives. *Kate and Allie* has been widely praised among television critics for its realism and for the sensitivity with which the relationship between the two women in particular is portrayed (Horowitz 1984; Lague 1984; Leonard 1984; MacKenzie 1984).

My informant describes the show in these unflattering terms:

> Well, it was these two women with their problems. I don't know what it was like 'cause I just didn't like it too much. I just watched it because it was supposed to be so good. (Gladys)

She ends up, not surprisingly, criticizing the show, somewhat ironically, for its lack of realism:

> Well, I guess the repartee, and the way they discuss and handle them [their problems] seems still unreal. I mean, life is really slow. It's not always an incident or entertaining, funny issue. Real life is just—can be quite a drudge. You know, the same old problems. You have to make your challenges. (Gladys)

On the one hand, we are told that the drudgery of real life is an unfitting subject for television—"it takes the fantasy away." On the other, *Kate and Allie*, a show about problems, is unreal, failing to capture the dull drudgery of real life. Gladys seems caught between the desire for more realistic television and the desire that the content of this realistic television not be too depressing. There is an implicit message here that television should, therefore, depict relatively affluent groups, the middle-class rather than struggling workers, certainly not the underclass, welfare mothers or even working wives with the difficult task of balancing work and family responsibilities: that television realism should, in fact, be middle-class realism.

In sum, then, many working-class women maintain a critical distance from both familiar (while often inaccurate) working-class images on television and more forbidding, upper-class television images. Working-class women are often extremely critical of working-class television, focusing on empirical inaccuracies in the portrayal of working-class work and social lives. Some women criticize upper-class television similarly, finding it empirically "unrealistic." Some working-class women also criticize working-class television on normative grounds, finding flaws with the values attributed to the working-class characters it portrays.

The critical edge of many women's responses to both working-class and upper-class television is blunted, however, by women's adherence to a normative idea of "reality" that derives from cultural representations of middle-class life, including middle-class television. While many of the working-class women's comments on working-class television display truly critical insight into the situation of the working class in our society, their attention is immediately captured (perhaps metaphorically) by television's "flow" to more mainstream, hegemonic, images that portray middle-class life in all its accoutrements. Women therefore end up asserting hegemonic rather than critical values when moving from criticizing working-class (or upper-class) television to describing the television they prefer.

Character, Comedy, and Realism

It makes sense that women are only figures of comedy. . . . When you think of traditional figures of comedy—the short guy, the ugly one, the man with the big nose, the Negro or Jew or member of any minority group—comedy is a way of turning their misfortune into a joke. It's a way of being accepted—"Look at me, I'm funny" and "Don't anybody laugh at me, I'll laugh first." (Madelyn Martin, writer of the *I Love Lucy* show; quoted by Friedan [1964:274])

Comic characters, particularly those inhabiting zanily comic shows, provoke distinctly class-differentiated responses from the women. I interviewed. Women's comments on the *I Love Lucy* show provide an interesting example of these differences. Although the show is popular with women of both classes, middle-class women more often find much to admire in the Lucy character, while working-class women tend to find much to criticize. Members of both classes think Lucy a funny character, but for middle-class women she has more of a positive identity, often as a comedienne in distinction from her character's comic personae. As discussed earlier, they notice the liberatory aspects of the Lucy character more often than do working-class informants, identifying her as a strong, independent role model for women. While some working-class women notice her strength, they tend to label it in less positive ways. They term her "manipulative" and "sneaky," a woman dependent on "feminine wiles" to get what she wants from men. In addition, working-class women respond negatively to the absence of what they would define as "realism" on the show and to the comic qualities of the Lucy character.

Working-class women, while often perceiving the same qualities that middle-class women see in Lucy's character, frame them somewhat differently. For example, this working-class woman notices and remarks on Lucy's strong will, but qualifies her statement with an awareness of the character's "finagling" and manipulative use of her "feminine wiles":

Lucy should definitely be remembered as a very strong woman. There are all these aspects of her where she's finagling, you know, she's always kind of getting her way. She has all these feminine wiles that, you know, you'd never see 'em act the fool the way she did. But I think that more important is how strong she was. She was a real strong-willed person. She was very courageous. She was not concerned with what people thought. She did what she wanted, she had a great spirit. I thought she was great. (Cathy)

While Cathy describes Lucy's dominance on the show, she tempers her description by recognizing the "finagling nature" of the Lucy character. Other working-class women echo her sentiments.

Working-class women find it difficult to identify with the character of Lucy in part because the extreme level of slapstick comedy that characterized the show interferes with their search for, and expectation of, realism on television. Many working-class women with whom I spoke find that the perception of realism is necessary for them to identify consciously with a fictional character. In fact, several women specifically mention that the absence of realism on the *I Love Lucy* show and in the Lucy character herself interferes with their ability to identify with this character. Indeed, instead of her strength, many working-class women stressed the dumb, dingy, and crazy aspects of Lucy's character, at the same time that they admitted having watched her regularly because she was so funny:

> I watched, you know, the dumb shows like *I Love Lucy*. It was just funny. It was stupid. It was—you know, it was like Lucy and this family and these neighbors and—that's sort of—silly.
>
> Interviewer: Did you like Lucy?
>
> She was very, you know, dumb, or she did a lot of silly things and stuff like that. But the way she came across on television shows was kind of silly. (Kim)

Other women remarked in a similar vein:

> *I Love Lucy*? She was a dingbat. You know? (Marie)
>
> I enjoyed Lucy very much. The dingy—it seems like the show, I mean that there's people who are just . . . don't even think about anything they do and they get themselves all into these stupid messed up things. And at least she was funny. (Carol)
>
> Lucy [was] always getting into trouble because she wasn't thinking or . . . you know, being more brave than making—and always somehow—getting into mischief or something like that. That's how it always . . . having some crazy idea and then going to all these lengths—yeah, and getting herself into a mess. (Linda)

These women all stress the dumb, dingy qualities of the Lucy character. While maintaining that she was certainly funny, and that this in large part accounts for her popularity with them, they do not mention this funniness in the context of Lucille Ball's strength as a comic, as do the middle-class women quoted in chapter 3. The working-class women quoted here find Lucy funny, but funny as her character is funny, in a way that is zany and lacks dignity. Rather than attributing to Lucy the actress the dignity and recognition that her talent might command, these women focus instead on the attributes of Lucy the character, a character from whom they feel quite distanced.

The perception of Lucy's identity as a comic character differs between social classes as well. Many middle-class women admire her skill as a comic *actress*, seeing the show as a fine piece of comic work, something good for children and the whole family to watch. Working-class women, however, tend to view even the Lucy character's comic qualities less favorably. Their descriptions tend to focus rather critically on her dinginess or how dumb she seems in disparaging ways matched by none of my middle-class informants. Some even complain that Ball's skill as an actress detracts from the reality of her character.

While noting that the *I Love Lucy* show is extremely funny, and that they enjoy it as such, working-class women show few signs of identifying with the Lucy character, nor for the most part do they appear to like her very much, and certainly most do not admire her as a character. Even when one woman mentions the actress's skill in portraying her, she mentions that the strong acting only supports her criticism of the unrealistic nature of the show. Instead, they like the show in a very escapist way, appreciating its zany humor for this reason. One woman, brought up in poverty by her divorced mother and violently abused by both her mother and stepfather, nevertheless has fond memories of watching *I Love Lucy* with her mother:

> I laughed hysterically at *I Love Lucy*. In fact, I have real fond memories of my mother because she can laugh—she's a great laugher. And *I Love Lucy*, she would just laugh until she cried. (Carol)

Watching *I Love Lucy* provided a valued escape for herself and her mother while she was growing up. When asked whether she identified with Lucy, however, Carol focuses on Lucy's life as a wife and mother in maintaining that she, like the woman disavowing the label "dingy" above, also viewed the character's situation quite negatively and in no way wanted to be like her:

> No. I never had a desire to be the little homemaker, the wife, the mother. Didn't feel anything maternal. It wasn't—I didn't get anything in return. (Carol)

Of course, given the home life in which Carol grew up, it is no wonder that domesticity holds few attractions for her. In her own experience, family life had been made repellant by violence and sexual abuse; in no way could Carol resonate emotionally to the nuclear family ideal underlying even television's zaniest situation comedies. While she values the escape that the comedy itself secures, Carol, as do other working-class women with whom I spoke, fully rejects or interprets in a negative light the images, ideals, and meanings underlying the comedy.

Many middle-class women with whom I spoke, however, both em-

brace *I Love Lucy*'s comedy and find more to admire about its underlying meanings as well. While admitting the *I Love Lucy* show's comic
lack of realism, and while admitting the stark unreality of the Lucy
character herself, many middle-class women nevertheless have more
praise for Lucy than do working-class women. While admiring the
actress's skill in portraying Lucy, middle-class women comment upon
and praise at some length the strength of the Lucy character herself. As
discussed in chapter 3, some even see her as a feminist figure, a strong
woman to be admired. Neither Lucy's position within the family nor
her comically rebellious desires to escape this position seem to interfere
with their identification with and, at times, admiration for this very
comic character. In fact, it is specifically Lucy's domestic struggles that
cause her character to resonate with a fair number of the middle-class
viewers I interviewed. Lucy seemed to ignite their imagination regarding the possibilities of rebellion against domesticity. The entrapment
middle-class women experience is, perhaps, overall less painful than
that experienced by working-class women, more amenable to a comic
televisual heroine than if their experiences were more deeply trau-
matic, even life-threatening, as was the case for some of my other
informants, who preferred television to be either *more* escapist than the
domestic situation comedy or less unreal in depicting women's lives.

Another character several working-class women criticize for being
unrealistic is Alice on the show *Alice*. Three women mention their
feeling that Alice was simply too intelligent to be working as a waitress
and that her situation as a waitress is portrayed unrealistically. It is
interesting that two of these women mention that they enjoy the character of Flo, Alice's sidekick, much more than Alice. They seem to find
Flo, portrayed to be a less intelligent woman, more believable, feeling
that Alice is too smart to be working at such a dead-end job:

> I would say, like, Flo was more of a comic type of character. That was
> real, but a strong person wouldn't [stay in that situation]. (Gladys)

> [Flo] just did her part better. I mean, the character, you could believe
> her. She lived in a trailer, I think, she always had these people in and
> you could just believe that that's really what a waitress would do.
> With her hair up like that, her uniform unbuttoned to the first. You
> weren't offended by her, that was just her part. There was one time,
> now I didn't care for this show particularly, I think when she and Mel
> actually made it together. It ended up bad because it put too much of
> a relationship between them, and it didn't work. But it was very
> believable. You know, she was always talking about who she was
> dating, who she was going out with, that just sounded right to me.
> (Cathy)

The distinction made here between these viewers' expectations of a character whom they perceive to be "strong" or dramatic (Alice) as opposed to a character whom they perceive to be comic (Flo) support the analysis of women's responses to television's comic women in the discussion of *I Love Lucy* above. These women specifically mention their affection for and enjoyment of the character Flo, Gladys noting that she stopped watching the show when Flo left it. Similar to the judgments working-class women made of the Lucy character in the *I Love Lucy* show, these women rarely express truly positive or praiseworthy sentiments about a comic character (Was Flo strong also? If she was, why would she remain working in Mel's diner? Was Alice the only strong figure in the diner? Why was Flo a more realistic character than Alice?).

Other shows depicting working-class women on television inspired similarly ambivalent reactions from some working-class viewers. For example, several told me that they enjoyed the show *Laverne and Shirley,* which pictures the adventures of two young working-class women, but they phrased their comments in terms of noticing and praising the show's humor rather than in their ability to identify with or relate to the main characters. Again, women may have found the zany comedy of this show and its lead characters prohibitive, preventing the perception of realism in these images and preventing any real identification on their part, despite their enjoyment of its humor.

Leading characters on middle-class shows at times inspire similar reactions. Some working-class women mention liking the comic show *That Girl,* yet distance their praise with belittling comments concerning main character Ann Marie:

> I liked *That Girl* because she was independent and lived by herself and was trying to make something of herself. 'Cause I always wanted to move to the city and live in an apartment. Though I think she was very stupid. She does a lot of really stupid things. (Kim)

> I liked shows like that. You know, good girl makes good. Who is real silly and plays dumb and yet she comes out. . . . I enjoyed the light humor. I never took it seriously or believed, you know, that was the way things should be. (Betty)

The former comments come from a woman, Kim, who seems slightly embarrassed to admit that she had watched any television and knows any television characters at all. It was therefore almost humiliating to her to admit any real identification with or affection for this comic television figure. The latter comment came from a traditionally oriented working-class woman, Betty, who left junior college to get married and later quit her part-time job to stay home with her three children. Marlo Thomas's character on *That Girl*, Ann Marie, ostensibly lived an independent life that indeed differed from Betty's notions of "the way things should be." While Betty seems quite content with her decision to stay home with her children, she does discuss with some apprehension the fact that she will indeed be forced to work when her children are a bit older, although she prefers not to think about this reality at the moment. Taking this television show too seriously might force her to think too seriously about an issue she would prefer to relegate to the back of her consciousness: her ambiguous prospects in the paid labor force. Upon the birth of her second child, Betty had quit a part-time job she particularly enjoyed. She missed working and knew that at some point she would want to, and have to, return to work.

Betty's consciousness of herself is of a woman who has maintained traditional family values in the face of many worldly challenges. She prides herself on not feeling the pressure to combine family and work or career as do many of her friends, and as is depicted in so much of our culture. When Betty says she felt *That Girl* never showed "the way things should be," she says this with some pride in her critical assessment of the show, a pride that seems to me to relate to the pride Betty shows more generally in her ability to maintain traditional values in the face of a rapidly changing world.

Betty's story is particularly interesting because her mother's traditional life and marriage had broken down in the sixties, when she read *The Feminine Mystique* and became interested in having an independent career of her own. Most of Betty's childhood had been spent in a female-headed household made especially poor by her mother's return to school. Betty's own desire for a more traditional family life is understandable, yet her own rejection of her mother's response to homemaking does seem to require some active suppression of issues pertaining to her own work life and future. This became quite clear in my interview with her as well as in her response to middle-class television. In fact, Betty's mother often brings up this issue with her, forcing her to respond in some manner, either by thinking about her relationship to work or by actively *not* thinking about it (the latter seemed her predominant strategy, although she herself was aware that it was probably a temporary one).

For these working-class women, the aspects of unreality they perceive in the show, perhaps related to its comedy (as I discuss below), seem to interfere with their full identification. Kim, for example, seems unwilling to admit fully any real admiration for a character as silly as Ann Marie. Also, because the two shows picture essentially middle-class images, working-class viewers may for good reasons find the shows more unrealistic and understandably more difficult to identify with. Yet again, there are ways the ideal of feminine independence, even when presented in so comic and tempered a form as in Ann Marie's character on *That Girl*, may touch on issues that are troubling or threatening to women, as in Betty's case, causing women to repudiate any identification with or even much appreciation for such shows and their characters. Middle-class women with whom I spoke, in contrast, had much less trouble identifying with these particular images, which apparently struck a responsive, more positively embraced chord with their all-too-rare images of middle-class female autonomy.[9]

These findings lead me to suspect that overall, women of different classes respond differently to comic female figures. In the context of the Martin quote which begins this sub-section, perhaps women's sense of their own misfortunes or exclusion varies in quality between the classes and is reflected in their differing responses to prototypically comic women. Or perhaps comedy's lack of realism, when literally interpreted, accounts for the paucity of working-class women's identification with comic characters on television, as when the Lucy character and the show itself are criticized for being unrealistic, not true-to-life, or when Ann Marie and her life are described as not depicting the way they "should be."

Entertainment television in general offers few images of women who are working class. The female working-class characters that do appear on television occur almost exclusively in comic formats which, because working-class women generally seek realistic television images, may prohibit their identifying closely with working-class characters at all. Many working-class women's responses to middle-class characters, however, while more positive overall than is their response to those working-class in origin, shows little real identification with these characters, but rather displays overall a more distanced appreciation of them. Women may like middle-class characters or admire them but do not seem to identify with them, do not discuss them enthusiastically in ways that emphasize the connection between their circumstances and those of the television character, or do not exhibit the kind of real interest or involvement in a character's personal situation sparked by the experience of personal recognition. While middle-class women seem more directly touched by more of the television characters they watch, working-class women, who may enjoy the same programs, often remain at a critical distance from, or unengaged on a personal level by, their characters.

Class-Based Responses to Real-Life Intrusions on Comic Television

Scholars have theorized that television programming is in general a site for a continuous merger between the world of the narrative and the world outside. The indistinct boundaries between fiction and reality lead to the illusion that television is an interactive medium (e.g., that real-world events have some impact upon the fictional images with which we are presented). Television's property of flow, wherein fiction follows nonfiction, middle-class shows follow working-class follow upper-class shows, gives these distinctions an aura of unreality:

> Television's foremost illusion is that it is an *interactive medium*, not that we are peering into a self-enclosed diegetic space. This generalized stance of the apparatus as a whole, due in part to the property of "flow," tends to carry over to the more cinematic narrative modes of the episodic series and the continuing serial, if only because these "diegetic" fictions are continually interrupted (especially on American television) by more discursive structures in the form of voice-over announcements, commercials, and promotional "spots." . . . The very concept "diegesis" is unthinkable on television. (Feuer 1986:104)

Feuer illustrates this thesis with an interesting example of television's constant shifting onto and away from the diegetic level of analysis. She cites the way in which nine o'clock and ten o'clock dramas are often interrupted with promotional spots for the eleven o'clock news in a manner that calls attention to apparent parallels between the fiction and a "real-world" event the news will cover:

> For example, a "news report" on college students' ritualistic viewing of *Dynasty* was announced during the commercial break preceding the last segment of *Dynasty* and then broadcast during the news report directly following *Dynasty*. . . . Such disregard for the diegetic is a *conventional* television practice, not an exceptional one. Television as an ideological apparatus strives to break down any barriers between the fictional diegesis, the advertising diegesis, and the diegesis of the viewing family, finding it advantageous to assume all three are one and the same. (Feuer 1986:105)

On early television one can see examples of this flow between diegetic levels in the use by sponsors of fictional television families and domestic scenes for commercially promoting their products. For example, the family in the early situation comedy *Mama* is pictured at the end of the show sitting around their kitchen table drinking Maxwell House coffee, their sponsor's product; this practice broke down after television sponsors became separated from the production of specific shows (Barnouw 1975).

Feuer's theory is provocative, but focuses on textual analysis rather than the study of reception by actual audience members. What differences between audience groups might emerge as audience members receive, process, and ultimately interpret this flow of images? The class differences I found in women's attitudes toward television and the "real-life" portrayed on it are particularly interesting in light of Feuer's thesis, in that they offer some qualification of the meaning of this scholarly debate for actual groups of television viewers.

In the case of the *I Love Lucy* show, for example, the social class of female viewers makes a difference in the way the character of Lucy is perceived. While middle-class women move out of the diegetic space in describing Lucy as a character, working-class women with whom I spoke rarely do this. One middle-class woman, for example, when asked about Lucy the character, responds with a remark concerning Lucy's skill as an actress:

> Interviewer: What did you think of Lucy as a character?
>
> I think she's a great comedienne. I don't think the things she got into were plausible, but they were funny. I mean, you took them because it was human, not because it was human, like natural, but it was adorable because it was funny. (Evelyn)

As with other middle-class informants, this woman notes the discrepancy between television shows she would describe as realistic and those that make pleasurable viewing for her. There is for her, as for many other middle-class women, no necessary correspondence between the two.

The ways in which these working-class women commend Ball's comic skill differ subtly, reflecting their different expectations of television and their desire for realism in its images. The following woman quoted is torn between her desire for a more realistic television image and her almost begrudging desire to recognize the work of a very skilled comic actress:

> What did I think of Lucy as a character? To me she was always an actress. It's very hard to really believe all the things she was able to accomplish, but she did. But she was always an actress as far as I can see. It was acting, but she was always a very successful actress, that's true. She was a big hit with most everybody. So, *I Love Lucy* was a popular show I'm sure. Most everybody enjoyed it. (Seline)

With her choice of words, Seline seems somewhat hesitant in her praise: "*but* she was always an actress" implies that, if she'd been a really successful television character, this would not be the case. Of course, as she goes on to note, it's true she was a very successful actress, but she remained an *actress* rather than a *character* nonetheless. In the same vein, consider Janice's remarks:

> I thought she [Lucy] was funny. I can't imagine anybody living like that. But I mean, if I watched that show, it was just to get a laugh out

of her, not even thinking about anything that would be true watching her.

Interviewer: What did you think of her? How would you describe her?

I was looking at her as Lucy, Lucille Ball, when I watched it, I guess. More like she was telling jokes or whatever, you know. It's just the crazy things that she did. I just never thought of it as a true, as a real family situation, of anybody living that way or acting that way. I just thought of her as a comedienne, just a very unrealistic redhead, you know. (Janice)

Like Seline, Janice somewhat pejoratively describes Lucy as a comedienne, as unrealistic. The show depicts a sort of family life that "no one lives." Judging from her responses, the unreality of the depiction seems again to interfere with Janice's enjoyment of the show, or at least, she feels it necessary to separate the "unreal" Lucy character and her show from what presumably are more genuine, real characters and shows. She watched "just" to get a laugh out of her, Lucy was "just" a comedienne, "just" very unrealistic. Janice's tone implies that these qualities make Lucy a character of less value than a truly realistic, serious character (versus comedienne) would be.[10]

Middle-class responses to *I Love Lucy* indicate generally more comfort with the fact that the Lucy character is somewhat unrealistic and that one notices not only the character's qualities but also Ball's skill as an actress. Working-class women are less comfortable with the shift between diegesis and reality that watching the *I Love Lucy* show, with its popular and widely-known star, seems to entail. While middle-class women move out of the diegetic space in describing Lucy as a character, feeling at ease in discussing Lucy's qualities as a character in conjunction with Lucille Ball's skill as an actress, working-class women with whom I spoke rarely do this. When they do, as in the case of the woman quoted above, they do so reluctantly, as though this lessens the pleasure they derive from watching and interpreting television fiction. In fact, even when describing the Lucy character in some of the same terms middle-class women used (e.g., her strength, dominance, and ingenuity), working-class women remain firmly within the fictional world created by the show.

Brooke, another middle-class woman, subtly illustrates the way the consciousness of television's unreality adds to, rather than intrudes upon, some middle-class viewers' enjoyment in television watching. She describes how interesting she thought it was when the actress playing Clair on the *Cosby Show,* Phylicia Rischaad, had been pregnant in real life, that her "real" pregnancy had been hidden on the show:

When she was pregnant in real life, I kept trying to see that, never could catch that. She did the show. They had her in bed a lot. She did a lot of bed scenes that year. Same thing with Diane on *Cheers*. In fact she and Carla were pregnant at the same time, they didn't figure that they could have the two of them on the show pregnant at the same time. That wouldn't work. They just camouflaged it on *Cosby* and on *Cheers,* too. It's easier to do that than it is to make the plot with them like that. If Diane had gotten pregnant by Sam, I don't think that would have worked. And Clair Huxtable didn't need another child. That would have been too much, too much, they are too smart for that. I think that would have just about done it if she had gotten pregnant. They put Lucy on there pregnant way back when. (Brooke)

This digression shows Brooke's delight in discussing the actual relationship between these television shows and real life, her consciousness that they are *not* real life, and most notably her thoughts about the actual construction of the world of the television shows she watches. She "kept trying to catch" evidence of Phylicia Rischaad's real-life pregnancy in her television character to subvert the intentions of the producers as they attempted to hide it, and she seemed disappointed that this evidence of Clair's fictiveness was denied her by the clever manipulation of her character. What was Brooke looking for when she kept trying to catch a glimpse of Clair's real-life pregnancy in her television character? What is the source of the pleasure that might have occurred had the show's illusion of a nonpregnant Clair been pierced by a glimpse of the actress's true state? It seems Brooke would have enjoyed the kind of play between fiction and reality that would have occurred had *Cosby*'s writers and producers managed to work in a pregnancy for Clair during Rischaad's actual pregnancy, as happened with the *I Love Lucy* show years back. She would have enjoyed the ability to get that much closer to the real person responsible for Clair's fictional portrayal. Yet for many working-class women, as my discussion of the *I Love Lucy* show illustrates, evidence of the actress's role in creating the Lucy character seems to disturb rather than to delight them, intruding as it does into the reality of the television portrayal and abruptly highlighting the fact that television is often not a very realistic medium as they define it.

Comic Glamour, Character, and Realism

Overt, obvious glamour itself seems to interfere with working-class women's enjoyment of and identification with television's female characters, as it is yet another quality that detracts from the realism of characters. This becomes evident when working-class women's responses to the Ginger and Mary Ann characters on *Gilligan's Island* are compared with those of middle-class women. As discussed in the previous chapter, middle-class women respond rather favorably to the "glamorous" qualities embodied in the character of Ginger, a former Hollywood movie star. She inspires some hostility, however, in working-class women. When asked to discuss or describe Ginger and Mary Ann, there is almost a defensive quality to some of their responses, as though the more modest, quieter Mary Ann image must be defended against Ginger's flagrant sexuality:

> Ginger, in the middle of the shipwrecked island, had the eyeliner and the makeup and the walk and the high heels on the desert, that was important to her. (Kim—the tone here is somewhat hostile)

Another remark:

> Ginger seems like the type of person who was very possessed with herself. You know, how she looked and how she—what other people thought of her and that she—with all those dresses and those high heels in the sand, that struck me as kind of strange. Maybe that was the only thing she had, but I sure wouldn't be wearing that on the beach!

> Interviewer: Did Ginger represent some kind of ideal that women should look like?

> No. She always seemed like she was just a washed-up Hollywood movie star that thought of herself as more than she is. She just seems like she just kept playing at what she used to be, and maybe she wasn't really that big, but she thought she was. (Carol—the tone is rather derisive)

Some go on to describe Mary Ann in an almost defensive manner:

> [Ginger was more glamorous.] But still, Mary Ann was portrayed in a way that, you know, she had a nice little figure, and they put her maybe not in a negligee, but she had a little bikini top on and a little skirt, but she was still—you know, she wasn't unattractive. (Betty)

> Mary Ann was the cute but sensible one, you know, I think that she had a little smarts about her. Actually, both of them did. But Mary Ann I think was sensible. More so than the movie actress. (Kim)

Some overtly identify with Mary Ann, at least to some extent:

Interviewer: Would you rather be like Ginger or Mary Ann?

Mary Ann . . . she was perky, she seemed smarter, she was treated fairly or equally or whatever by the others in that situation. (Barbara)

More directly, Linda commented, "Ginger, I think Ginger's a typical nowadays movie star and Mary Ann was more me. You know, the sweet, warm Mary Ann." Carol more hesitantly remarked, "I didn't really feel that I was too much like her. I don't think I was too much like Mary Ann—well, maybe more."

Linda, a working-class woman, goes on to explain her identification with Mary Ann; she is a more "real" image, as opposed to Ginger's unreality:

Interviewer: Did you identify more with Mary Ann? Or did you want to be more like Ginger?

No. I mean . . . sure there's been times where I'd like to be more, like, glamorous. But myself, as far as being a movie star and living on Gilligan's Island . . . I enjoyed very much dressing up and being like that. And so I do like the glamour there, but to be a movie star I think is unreal. (Linda)

It is interesting to note here that Linda is a young woman who is rather preoccupied with her image as a "sweet, warm" woman. Having been through several unhappy romances, she waits for Mr. Right to make her very traditional dreams of marriage and family come true. Her criticism of the way Ginger's character flaunts her charms and her praise of Mary Ann's sweetness and warmth accords well with Linda's description of her own personality and the ideals relevant to her own character. Linda and other working-class women seem to have some discomfort or hostility when confronted with the overtly glamorous, movie-star image of womanhood. Middle-class women react a bit more positively to this image; some even admit to admiring it and aspiring toward it. While working-class women label such images unreal and find them impossible to identify with or relate to, these qualities seem less of a problem for middle-class women.

Conclusion

Together with the previous chapter, this chapter lays the groundwork for a more general theory regarding the relationship between the way women talk about television and their social class membership. Class differences coalesce around two main points: the search for realism on television and identification with television characters. Working-class women tend to value realism on television more highly than do middle-class women, who have fewer expectations that television will be realistic. Often, working-class women judge televised depictions of middle-class life to be realistic, particularly as compared with their assessments of some of the few working-class shows on television, which women generally find quite unrealistic. Middle-class women, on the other hand, sometimes speak about television as unrealistic but, more often, employ other criteria in assessing television shows, sometimes pertaining to the strength of their attachments to specific television characters.

On these bases I conclude that working-class women are more susceptible to what I term television's "class-specific" hegemony; that is, working-class women are particularly vulnerable to television's presentation of the material accoutrements of middle-class life as the definition of what is normal in our society. Their television watching may contribute, therefore, to a degree of alienation from the reality of their own material experience and potential or, at least, may contribute to a sense of personal failure women experience for not achieving this media-defined norm and may thereby confound working-class women's oppression in our society.[11]

Middle-class women are more likely to become engaged on a personal level with television characters and to identify with them, in the general sense of the term, than are working-class women—to experience, in short, what I term to be a "gender-specific" hegemony vis-à-vis television. More specifically, these differences are highlighted by class differences in women's responses to different sorts of images of women on television. Both television's portrayals of independent women and television's stereotypically sexy females are more heavily criticized by working-class women than by middle-class women, who emphasize positive attributes of these images in discussing them. Middle-class women, therefore, seem more susceptible to television's portrayals of either physical or behavioral ideals for women, whereas working-class women are shielded somewhat from this aspect of television's portrayals of women by their greater distancing from these images. The former may find that their experience with television contributes to their oppression *as women* in our society by reinforcing stereotypical interpersonal and role behaviors as desirable for women and by displaying as normal and attainable physical ideals that only distantly resemble the appearance of most women.

Of course, this is not to argue that working-class women are not oppressed by images of women on television or that middle-class women are not affected by images of the upper-middle-class and the wealthy that abound on our screens. Surely each group is affected in similar ways by the types of images predominantly discussed by the other in my study. Also, these differences in response may simply be the result of the relative absence of working-class television characters overall and their presentation in comic form when they are present.

There is some evidence, however, that the class differences I have described run deeper, touching the character of women's experience of television itself. My consideration of class differences in women's discussions of the relationships between television and reality and between television and experience point toward these deeper differences. I can only conjecture at this point, however. My main goal here is to call attention to the fact that these differences in discourse do emerge in my interviews. Whether they in fact indicate an overall, broadly determined class difference in the way women experience our culture must be confirmed or denied by more extensive future studies.

Chapter 5
Women Remembering Television: Pre- and Postfeminist Generations

My discussion thus far has been centered upon differences in the ways working-class and middle-class women talk about television. In this section I compare discussions of television by women who were in their sixties or older at the time of my interviews with those by women age twenty-nine or under.[1] The meaning of television as an institution has itself changed over the generations, and we know very little about these changes. Different generations of women have come of age at different ideological moments in our culture and at times when television itself has occupied different places and held different cultural meanings. Given these variations, do the generations themselves receive television differently? There is almost no attention to the forms these differences might take in the literature about television.

Generational differences are of particular interest to feminists. In the wake of the women's liberation movement, many are concerned with measuring women's acceptance of its ideas in our culture at large. Women's discussions of television, their acceptance or critical rejection of television's conventions for portraying women in the wake of this movement, may serve as a barometer for women's response to more general feminist ideas in our culture.

Breaking down women's discussion of television's female images by generational groups forces a difficult, complex confrontation with the ideas women of different generations might hold.[2] These differences may be the result of, first, the women's movement and women's differential exposure to it and, second, differential exposure to television as an institution. In fact, generational variations in women's discussions of television both strengthen and add a new dimension to my arguments about class, realism, and identification in relation to women's readings of television.

Work, Family, and Television Viewing

Women in their sixties at the time of this study have lived through many changes in our society.[3] Over the past several decades, they have witnessed widespread social criticism of some of our most basic beliefs about women's nature, mothering, and the proper relationship between women's identity in the private, familial sphere and their activity in the public, paid labor force. Many ideas that were accepted in the social environment of this group's youth are now looked upon with scorn by their daughters and members of their daughters' generation. Coming of age for the most part before the second wave of feminism in the late 1960s, these women made many of their seminal decisions concerning family and career training before feminist ideas became prominent in our culture.

Women under the age of twenty-nine, in contrast, have for the most part come of age in a time of cultural confusion and change regarding women's proper roles. Those in the older portion of this group often feel themselves torn between two traditions, the ultradomestic fifties with its powerful cult of motherhood and the feminism of the seventies, which ushered in the seemingly irresolvable conflict many younger women experience between their desire to pursue a career and their desire to become mothers (Hewlett 1986:32). Other studies of the way women in this age group make decisions about work, careers, and motherhood support these conclusions. Speaking of younger women, Kathleen Gerson describes the forces that have contributed to their confusion:

Younger female cohorts are most responsible for the rise in the percentage of women workers, decline in the birthrate, and the increasing proportion of childless women in the later stages of their reproductive lives. The personal decisions of young adult women, most of whom came of age in the 1970s, underlie these rapid social changes. . . . This generation reached adulthood during a period of accelerated social change. Born in the aftermath of World War II, most of its members grew up in so-called traditional households. Ironically, the mothers of this generation are the women who vacated the workplace in large numbers to devote themselves to home and family. Yet the world this generation has inherited, and helped as adults to create, differs greatly from the world it knew as children. As members of a generation on the cutting edge of social change, they have collided with social institutions in flux. They have become both the recipients and the agents of far-reaching changes in work and family life. (1985:10)

This group of women is particularly interesting to those wishing to study processes of social change because they are poised between two strong yet contradictory social currents.

Women at the younger end of the spectrum of my second age group have not yet made their career and family choices, yet they too face a contradictory world for women. In addition, many feel the influences of their older sisters and friends, who have advised them of the diffi- culties of attempting to combine work or careers with family and motherhood. Gerson's work reveals that among many women of the 1980s, the superwoman myth—the idea that women can do it all, and do it all well—is beginning to crack, ushering in what some have called the era of postfeminism.[4] One might assume that for younger women the myth will come more and more under attack, resulting either in the reappropriation and strengthening of older myths of female strength or in the creation of new ideas and ideals for women, or both.

The term "postfeminist" is often used to describe the mindset of this generation of women, women who have come of age after the heyday of the women's liberation movement and reaped the benefits of the social reforms and changed attitudes that the movement gained— often at the cost of upset and humiliation to the women who fought for them—but who categorically refuse to call themselves feminists. Post- feminist thought is seen as rejecting feminist ideas that stress too public or masculine a role for women in favor of combining women's public role with more traditional ideas placing women in the family. On television, postfeminist images of women show women performing a variety of roles in both work and family without experiencing much of the juggling act many women have felt in recent times (Hewlitt 1986; Hochschild 1989). In contrast to prefeminist television, which por- trayed women primarily in the family and showed only single women to be active in the workplace, and feminist television, which empha- sized women's workplace experiences and de-emphasized family life, postfeminist television presents women in both spheres, living without conflicts between them.[5]

We might expect that women of different generations, having lived through changing social ideals for women and having faced very dif- ferent opportunity structures,[6] might respond quite differently to each stage of television's representations of women. In my study, I do find important generational differences in reception. Older women are freer to simply take note of television's evolving images of women in the workplace. Often, they enjoy these new images, admiring the free- dom of the women pictured, their professional competence, and their opportunity to enter traditionally male careers or fields of work. Having come of age in an era when expectations about women's proper roles in the family and at work were in many respects different from what they are today, older women are more able than younger women to view postfeminist ideas, and feminist ideas themselves, as wonderfully freeing for women, a vantage point they can hold without really having to live these ideas or experience their contradictions. Since mass media so often minimizes the contradictions of postfeminism for women, postfeminist images can retain their idealized form for some older women whose experience with them may be personally limited.

In contrast, current television, in its attempt to portray both feminist and postfeminist women and to depict them as occupying a reasonable variety of jobs and family positions, touches young women's experiences, and for some, their conflicts, in a timely fashion. For older women, current television offers a glimpse of a new way of life most have never attempted. Yet younger women are themselves coming of age in our postfeminist culture, a culture that accepts certain feminist ideas but places them alongside very traditional notions of family and women's role within it. Some have already experienced, or have seen others experience, some of the frustrations inherent in attempting to combine work with career in a society still essentially structured around a more traditional division of labor between the sexes.[7] Younger women overall are more skeptical of feminist television images than are older women. A few younger women in my sample used a strategy of "splitting" feminist images by talking only of the more feminine, relational, family side of women who were actually shown primarily at work. More temperate in their portrayals of the family, postfeminist images fare a bit better.

Many young women in my sample receive early, prefeminist family television, much of which is still widely viewed on syndicated reruns and cable stations, in a markedly nostalgic way. This results perhaps from younger women's early experience with television watching as an activity of family togetherness. Particularly for women from broken homes, young women's viewing of family television is remarkably emotion-laden. A few young working-class women from broken homes, on the other hand, criticize family shows for portraying a reality they do not experience. While most young women do not consciously aspire to the lifestyle pictured within these shows, they are touched by their idealized pictures of what seems to them a bygone era, and in some ways a nicer, less impersonal, and less materialistic era in our culture. In some of the working-class women in my sample, this early viewing of television's idyllic middle-class families lays the basis for their later judgments of television according to the standards of middle-class realism.

Older women, in contrast, do not respond, for the most part, as strongly or emotionally as do young women to disjunctures between their own family reality and the situations they view on television. This is in part due to the fact that older women did not grow up viewing families on television throughout their youth, as did the vast majority of the younger women with whom I spoke. Older women, not having grown up with television, and not having experienced it during their earliest years in their own families of origin, are not as emotionally inclined as young women to take television's representations of the family as prescriptive. Also, the fact that young women have come of age in a time of increasing divorce rates and rapidly changing family norms gives media images of the family more power for them.

In a more general way as well, women's differences in experience with television are tied to their overall interpretations of it. Interesting differences emerge in the manners used by younger and older women to discuss television. In conjunction with their reception of it as a technological wonder, older women generally are more predisposed to view television positively and to give representations of women on television the benefit of the doubt in their analysis of them, despite their sometimes rueful recollection of the pretelevision world we have lost. On the other hand, younger women, in line with their experience of television as the common culture of their generation, are more likely than older women to identify television with the forces of conformity. Their experiences with television have given rise to an overall tendency to be critical of television images of women. In this chapter I illustrate these generational differences further with examples from my data. I first discuss women's responses to newer television images of women and work. A discussion of women's responses to television images of the family follows. Class differences in response, which were salient in my younger group, are also discussed.

Women at Work: Responses to Working Women on Television

Feminist images on television portray women primarily in the public sphere as members of the paid labor force. In a striking break with prefeminist conventions within which television portrayed women primarily in the private, family sphere, feminist television de-emphasizes women's familial relationships and centers its representations instead on their public lives. Such representations emerged gradually during the late 1960s to early 1970s on the heels of the women's liberation movement.

As there is no absolute break between prefeminist and feminist television, there is also no easily identifiable break between television's feminist and postfeminist periods. Instead, feminist representations have been transformed gradually in the 1980s with the advent of post-feminism on television. While women are still shown at work, more and more work representations are combined with depictions of women in the family. Images of single professional women are, as in the case of *Murphy Brown,* often tempered by taunting remarks about these char-acters' forbidding and eccentric personalities. The unstated but nev-ertheless ever-present normative implication of postfeminist television is that women should combine work with family, and that normal women prioritize the latter.

Television as a Liberating Force: Generational Responses to Women in Nontraditional Jobs

Several older women in my study are great fans of television's working women, praising them in a variety of contexts. When these images are not confounded by too much explicit sexuality, these women seem to enjoy newer images of working women. Such images offer them a glimpse of a way of life—a feminist life, in many respects—that offers a variety of experiences many older women have never experienced in their lifetimes. Many seem aware that they will never have similar experiences but are comfortable in their vicarious enjoyment.

Consider, for example, women's comments on the following images. One woman mentions that she finds the combination of work and careers depicted on the female cop series *Cagney and Lacey* surprising, although she takes television's word for it that the images are realistic:

> *Cagney and Lacey,* I like that . . . I like those two gals. Maybe because *they're so different from anything I could possibly think that I could have been in those days,* maybe because it's such a great difference, I mean, to see these two gals in such activity. That I find interesting. I also find it interesting that she [Lacey] can still be a mother of two children and do this type of work. In fact, in my mind sometimes I'm even a little surprised that it can happen. Or again, could this really be the truth, but I won't argue the point since I imagine there must be women who are in the field who can do anything and everything. (Estelle) [Emphasis added]

Another older woman also found *Cagney and Lacey* fascinating, for similar reasons:

> I watch *Cagney and Lacey.* I like it because they are two women cops, working, you know—what they go through. They have to work with

mostly men, and they really are getting somewhere. It's an interesting . . . uh, to me a soap opera is one day this one is in bed with the
other one, then the next day she's with somebody else. It's just plain
sex. Where these shows, it's very interesting. (Marilyn)

Marilyn expresses a clear preference for shows that portray women
in adventurous situations, where "they work with mostly men" and
"really are getting somewhere." She distinguishes this from the much
more conventional domestic placing of women that soap operas offer
and of which she apparently disapproves because of the amount of
sexuality shown. In both cases, it is interesting that the particular
combination of work and family depicted in these newer television
shows is remarkable to these women, serving in slightly different ways
as an example to each of roles that they now believe are real and
possible for women.

Some younger women enjoy *Cagney and Lacey* also, but they comment on their lack of identification with the characters, calling them
too "tough," not actually realistic, in line perhaps with most women's
disinclination to pursue a career in police work. One woman describes
her reaction to the show as follows:

It was exciting, they were really tough. I liked the action. I never
really thought of that [police] work as something I'd like to do.
(Nancy)

Another young woman, Lori, comments similarly, "I like watching it, I
think the characters are really interesting, but I can't see it for myself."
Both Nancy and Lori focus their comments more on their admiration
of the show, and their personal distance from its main characters, than
do the older women quoted above, who feel much freer to fantasize
about Cagney's and Lacey's actual lives, for example the contradictions
they might experience (it's "interesting that she [Lacey] can still be a
mother of two children") and their accomplishments ("they really are
getting somewhere"). Younger women speak very differently of the
show in a general sense, commenting more than older women do on
whether they can actually imagine themselves in many of the positions
the characters occupy. Older women fantasize more in relation to these
images, make remarks in the form of "what if," while younger women
are more concrete in their remarks, more specific in their fantasies,
actually attempting to put themselves in the place of the characters
they perceive. Of course, in this instance life cycle rather than generational differences may explain the bulk of this variation in response.
Younger women are understandably preoccupied with the career

choices they are imminently facing, while older women are more apt to look back over their lives and fantasize in a what-if manner.

The spread in generational response widens when I analyzed discussions of *Charlie's Angels,* an earlier show depicting three very glamorous female detectives. Marilyn, the older woman quoted above, goes on to praise *Charlie's Angels* in a manner similar to her description of *Cagney and Lacey,* claiming that she likes the stories it has and, interestingly enough, mentioning that she especially enjoys the absence of sex on this show relative to the amount of sex shown on soap operas:

> I'm not a soap opera watcher. I don't care for them. I like *Charlie's Angels,* I used to watch it, you know, stories. They didn't have no sex or anything like that. Well, you got to have some of it! I'm not saying none of it, but, you know. . . . (Marilyn)

Her comparison of *Charlie's Angels* with the allegedly sexier soaps is particularly remarkable given the abundance of sexual imagery on this show. In fact, *Charlie's Angels* has received much attention in the critical literature largely because of its "tits-and-ass" emphasis (Schwichtenberg 1981; Gitlin 1983). Yet Marilyn emphasizes the action and adventure on the show, which provoke very pleasing fantasies for her.

Another older woman echoes Marilyn's sentiments, focusing her description on the pleasure she derives from watching the girls work together, rather than on any reference to its sexual content or imagery: "*Charlie's Angels* was very enjoyable. Those girls work beautifully" (Nora). What interferes with her pleasure in this show is the unreality of the team's continual successes:

> To myself I kept saying, "Anyway, it's only a television show," because of the things that were accomplished all the time, the successes they had with everything they had to do. We know for a fact that doesn't happen all the time, anywhere. . . . But, it doesn't bother me. I continue watching them because I enjoy watching it.
>
> Interviewer: That wasn't a show you watched just to see what they were wearing?
>
> No, not necessarily. No. It was fast-moving. It was a fast-moving show. (Nora)

It seems clear from these comments that at least some older women are able to enjoy a show like *Charlie's Angels* for its liberatory spirit, which lies in the fact that it depicts competent women successfully working in a male-dominated profession. The women I have quoted are not overly bothered by the contradiction between this facet of the show and the fact that the women starring on it appear, are taped, and have functioned culturally as prototypical sex objects. They seem not to notice the degrading qualities of the Angels' sex-object image in these cases. The Angels' sexual images, unsullied by explicit sexual relations, do not come in for criticisms from them, and older women enjoy the Angels fully as much as the probably less objectified images of *Cagney and Lacey.*

Younger women's responses to these figures are often couched in different terms. Rather than responding to the work the women do on the show, younger women focus on the personal appearance and sexuality of the women themselves, which in the wake of the women's liberation movement they find demeaning.

> I hated *Charlie's Angels.* I thought it was terrible. I just figured it was one of those based-for-men shows. Three women wearing tight clothes [laughs]. I felt it was more geared for men than women. A lot of the stuff they did, I just couldn't take realistically. (Nancy)

Another woman remarked:

> *Charlie's Angels*, no, I never liked that show. I just didn't like watching those women. And the plots were so stupid. It really offended my intelligence. (Alisa)

The three other younger women who commented on this show made negative comments as well. The sense was that younger women feel themselves not taken seriously by a show premised on three young, super-glamorous detectives.

These passages illustrate, in the case of some older women, a fascination with television women in unconventional, traditionally male-dominated fields (law and police work). They are surprised at the form that the combination of work and family roles takes in these characterizations, and they find it explicitly noteworthy that on *Cagney and Lacey* it is possible for a woman (the character of Mary Beth Lacey, played by Tyne Daly), in postfeminist style, both to successfully hold a traditionally male job and to bring up two children. Older women also find it exciting that three women can perform dangerous work together with the enviable grace of Charlie's three Angels. Television, in depicting situations that are in these instances far from their own experience, here introduces new images and ideas regarding women's roles to the consciousness of women who might otherwise be unaware of such possibilities or, alternately, might be convinced of their impossibility.

For many of the older women I interviewed, seeing such images on television makes them real, although they might be critical of them in some ways as well.

The younger women I have quoted notice and choose to comment upon their own lack of identification with the *Cagney and Lacey* policewomen. While not entirely negative in commenting on the show, young women are uneasy about these images, mentioning that they find it difficult to relate to them and implying that this personal relating, or at least some sense of recognizing themselves or their own possibilities or desires in these television images, *should* come more easily. Young women seem to expect role models or figures of identification from feminist and postfeminist television and may be uneasy when newer television images thwart their expectations. Thus, their hostility to the *Charlie's Angels* images, feminist-era women supposedly liberated yet quite governed by commercial notions of glamour. The young women feel that they see through the facade of liberation and are offended by the sexual stereotyping that underlies the image.

Some of television's professional women are received more favorably by younger women and more critically by older respondents. One example of such an image is the character of Joyce Davenport (Veronica Hamel) on the television cop series *Hill Street Blues*. Joyce is a very tough public defender. In addition, she is the lover of the captain, Frank Furillo (Daniel J. Travanti). Gitlin discusses her character in some detail, calling her "the first woman television regular at once professional, tough, elegant, intelligent, and sexy" (1983:275), a "New Woman" who, "in proper feminist fashion, fends off Furillo's desire to get married—or at least to go public with their 'relationship'—with barbed reminders about the importance of her career" (1983:312).

Rather than responding overtly to her competence or to the adventurous nature of her job, as was the case in responses to *Cagney and Lacey* or *Charlie's Angels,* older women respond more to Joyce's sexuality, which strikes them as rather hard-edged and which, put together as it is with her work identity, offends them. One older woman has this to say about Joyce:

> The woman lawyer [Joyce] is a very contradictory character as far as I'm concerned. From her law approach, I would say she's good as far as a lawyer. I'm sure when she quotes, she quotes the law properly, . . . she's very good as a lawyer, and her approach to him is a very different kind of an approach, her lovemaking. That doesn't necessarily mean that one can't be an emotional person, but she comes across as a hard woman, and of course, she really isn't all the time as far as he is concerned. So what does my reaction to that mean, I

wonder now? I don't really think I believe that, but I don't enjoy it, let's put it that way, maybe that's the reason, I don't believe it and I don't want to watch it, that's all. (Estelle)

Estelle, a middle-class woman, finds the particular combination of qualities Joyce's character entails unrealistic. Yet beyond this judgment, Estelle finds that she does not enjoy Joyce's character for other, and deeper, reasons. Joyce represents a "hard" yet sexual image, sort of a television version of the super-feminist in both work and play, which Estelle finds to be foreign or offensive. Apparently Joyce's activities on *Hill Street Blues* do not offer Estelle enough pleasurable material with which to conjure the same sort of adventure fantasies inspired by the more popular *Charlie's Angels*. The same is true for Evelyn, from my older group, who remarked, "I used to watch *Hill Street Blues* but then they also always wound up in bed at the end of the story, which had nothing to do with police work." While not specifically mentioning the character of Joyce, Evelyn also is bothered by the particular combination of public and private, particularly sexual, life depicted in *Hill Street Blues*.

Several young working-class women respond to Joyce quite differently. They emphasize her intelligence and her career competence, rather than the sexuality of her image. Coming of age in the wake of the sexual revolution, young working-class women seem untroubled by the particular combination of tough competence and sexuality that Joyce represents. This young working-class woman, for example, speaks about the character of Joyce:

The lawyer's very intelligent. I like her very much.

Interviewer: Do you identify with her?

Oh, some, yeah. I think she is perhaps . . . a lot like me because she did want to have children and stuff. And I can relate to that, to her relationship. 'Cause she can be very caring and helpful. She's a lot tougher than I am, but that's something she has to be for her job. (Linda)

While this woman claims that she does identify with the character of Joyce, when asked why, she gives as explanation the fact that Joyce "wants to have children," and is "very caring and helpful" in her relationship, while on the show Joyce is depicted for the most part in her "tough" role as public defender, the aspect of her character with which this woman does not identify.

Linda responds favorably to what she sees as the incipient postfeminist aspects of Joyce's image,[8] her ability to combine more traditionally feminine personality traits with a masculinized, tough role at work. It is Joyce's family plans to which she most closely relates. Older women don't see the same qualities in Joyce's character which she perceives, judging Joyce's personal side as they do to be as hard-edged or masculinized as her professional personality. Women seem to focus on that aspect of the work-and-family dichotomy that most preoccupies them in their own lives. A character like Joyce gives fodder to thoughts of either.

We might almost talk here of a postfeminist realism for younger working-class women like Linda, who is quick to assign radically feminine qualities even to television's most hard-nosed women professionals. Just as middle-class women do not have the same motivation as working-class women for seeing television's middle-class images to be real, so older women do not have the same motivation as younger working-class women to assign stereotypically feminine home lives to television's feminist females.

This tendency toward postfeminist realism in description is further illustrated by Betty's reaction to the character of Laura Holt (Stephanie Zimbalist) on the private-eye show, *Remington Steele*. Like Joyce, Laura Holt is in fact quite a feminist figure in many respects, having begun the investigation agency called Remington Steele entirely on her own (she had hired Steele, played by Pierce Brosnan, when clients repeatedly requested a meeting with the real Remington Steele, a male name she had invented to inspire confidence and improve her business). Yet Betty, a young working-class woman, emphasizes other aspects of Laura's character, describing Laura as follows:

> She's a good person. She's determined. Independent, intelligent, and witty. Attractive. And she's resourceful. Kind of a down-home girl. And they [Laura and Brosnan] often talk about their relationship in the show. It's strictly business but they'd like to make it something more. Sometimes they've approached the subject of children and family. And that's part of the program—they spend a lot of time sort of teasing one another. (Betty)

Betty centers her description on the teasing and banter about family that occurs in the context of the work relationship upon which the show focuses. It is interesting that Betty is a housewife who had three children by her mid-twenties and who very traditionally stays at home and takes care of them. *Remington Steele* is her favorite television show, the only one she watches regularly, and she implies that this is due in large part to the tension between work and family she enjoys seeing treated somewhat comically (the couple banter and joke with one another on the show constantly, in her account).

Another young woman, Nancy, illustrates this ambiguity in young working-class women's response to television's professionals with the split between her admiration for, and lack of identification with, the character of Ann Kelsey, the law-firm partner played by Jill Eichenberry on *L.A. Law:*

> I like the one lawyer on *L.A. Law,* the one with the layered hair. They've just made her a partner. She's got the layered hair.
>
> Interviewer: Why do you like her?
>
> Because she's one of those go-getters. She won't let anything stand in her way. That's what I like about her. (Nancy)

However, when asked whether her affection for this character is combined with identification with her, Nancy does mention that her own work identity is quite different:

> Interviewer: Do you think of yourself as a go-getter?
>
> I can be [laughs]. It depends on, you know, like for myself or at my job, I usually don't, you know, jump out and do it right away. But I can be for someone else, like my mother or my family. I can move fast for them [laughs]. (Nancy)

It is interesting, in this description of herself, to note the split in Nancy's answer between her sense of her work identity and her sense of family identity. In her family role, she conforms more closely to the commonly accepted postfeminist notion of the "new woman"; regarding her family, she is a go-getter, fast-moving and aggressive. At work (first as a photo-lab clerk and now as an office receptionist), she is not usually like this, for reasons not entirely apparent from my interview with her. While admiring Jill Eichenberry's go-getter qualities on her job, Nancy is still unable—or unwilling—to put similar qualities into operation in her own work life, although she finds this much less problematic to accomplish when working on behalf of family members. Perhaps these splits between attitudes toward work and family are too troubling for her to actually notice them or to confront the contradictions they entail.

Along these lines, Nancy also comments on the character of Abby Ewing (Donna Mills) in the prime-time soap opera *Knot's Landing.* Nancy mentions that, actually, she used to dislike Abby intensely because she was so ambitious, revealing an overt hostility to the work aspects of the media's conventions of a feminist woman. Now that Abby is being portrayed so often in the context of helping her drug-addicted daughter, however, Nancy finds that another, more acceptable side of her personality is emerging which, in her eyes, makes the character much more likeable:

> I like Abby Ewing. They just did a thing where her daughter was a drug addict and you see a whole different side of her character, and I thought, it made me like her, I didn't like her before.
>
> Interviewer: Why?
>
> She's very strong-willed. Very go-for-it, and nothing stands in her way. I'm not that ambitious. (Nancy)

Here we see an example of a woman almost "splitting" the character of Abby into two parts and choosing Abby's family-relational aspects rather than her explicitly feminist, work-related qualities upon which to base her evaluation of, and connection to, this character. This is one functional way a viewer might choose to deal with television women's conflicted images, images that may produce correspondingly conflicting emotions.[9]

Postfeminist realism, then, operates similarly to middle-class realism for young working-class women. As was the case with middle-class realism, some working-class young women admire television's very "feminist-oriented" women, the go-getters, even while it is clear that they do not quite identify with their images. These women like to view television women who are striking in their confidence and competence at work. Yet they couch their admiring remarks more in terms of women's familial roles rather than elaborating on their competence at work. Young working-class women have been blitzed by a media feminism that presents the liberated woman as generically middle-class and professional, and essentially ignores working-class women's concerns.[10] Perhaps their response to this complex of feminist representations is to embrace "liberation" itself, but to focus on realms of its representation that are more familiar to them, and more possible for them to attain. Thus, professional women are admired, but when discussed in detail, it is their family lives that are scrutinized. In its postfeminist tendency to show career women almost always in conjunction with their family roles, television itself increasingly encourages this emphasis.

In general, then, the generations respond to television differently, as it touches upon their respective experience as working women differently. Older women are inspired by newer representations of working women, images that are far from representing their past or present experience but that fire their imagination. Certain combinations of tough sexuality in extremely competent professional women can be offensive to them, however. For older women, feminist and postfeminist television can serve to enlarge their horizons, to help them imagine possibilities for women they never actually witnessed or experienced in their own lives.

Younger women, in contrast, are more apt to be bothered by discrepancies between possibilities they imagine for themselves and those they see illustrated on the screen. Some younger women apparently enjoy watching women in nontraditional jobs less than do older women, conscious as they are that such roles are unlikely (though possible?) for them. Working-class young women view postfeminist images through what I term a lens of "postfeminist realism." Again, seeking to relate to these images, working-class women find parallels to television women's family lives, but find their disproportionately professionalized work lives more unfamiliar. In consequence, several young working-class women speak strikingly of the family lives of many of television's newer images of women, even when these women are portrayed according to feminist conventions and shown much more often at work than at home. Postfeminist representation, in their case, reinforces television's hegemony of middle-class realism rather than actually serving to open up new possibilities for them. As I illustrate in the following section, young middle-class women comment more positively on postfeminist images, feeling no similar need to "split" their responses to them into either work or family comments. I discuss this and other contrasts between their responses and those of older women, as well as of young working-class women, below.

Generation and Class in Women's Responses to Family Television

Televised depictions of the American family have changed, obviously, along with changes in television's images of women's relationship to work and family. As discussed earlier, prefeminist television was dominated by the traditional, mythical nuclear family, wherein the father (usually middle-class) went off to some unexplained managerial position, the mother stayed at home tending her suburban one-family home, and the children led apparently idyllic lives, experiencing little to shatter their faith that the peace, prosperity, and happiness of their lives would continue indefinitely (what Herbert Gold called "happy people with happy problems" [Gitlin 1983:93]).

Televised families have undergone some major refigurations since those early days. Single-father families have come and gone; single mothers have made an appearance; conglomerate families are common. Wives and mothers now work, for the most part, outside the home as well as in it. Children have taken over much of the authority once ascribed to the omniscient father in, for example, shows such as *Diff'rent Strokes* and *Family Ties*; this change has made for some interesting developments in the foci of situation comedy, the form within which most of these family shows appear.[11]

Older women offer comments about family television that indicate relatively little involvement with it. They are not particularly attentive to women's changing roles within the family, certainly not as attentive to it as they are to women's changing roles within the work force, which seems to be more interesting to them or at least is more often a topic of their discussion. Their comments on older family television shows display little, almost no nostalgia for the families of days gone by.

Yet some early family shows inspire in older informants a more positive remembrance. The working-class matriarch, still a theme in family television today, is a favorite with my older informants. The working-class show *Mama,* for example, an early situation comedy, starred Peggy Wood as "Mama" Marta Hansen, the matriarch of a Norwegian-American family living in turn-of-the-century San Francisco.

Mama's starring character shares the qualities of strength and determination that separate Alice Kramden from her middle-class contemporaries. Mama is the rock of her family, and although she does not have a rebellious husband on the order of Alice's Ralph to manage, her large family (husband Lars [Judson Laire], a carpenter, daughters Katrin [Rosemary Rice] and Dagmar [Robin Morgan],[12] and son Nels [Dick van Patten]) present management problems of their own.

One repeated problem on *Mama,* as in *The Honeymooners,* is the family's limited budget. In one episode we are told that Mama takes care of the family budget, every week paying the bills and dividing whatever is left over among the family members, according to her determination of their need. This is illustrated as she attempts to determine in the course of a budgeting session whether there is enough money for Nels to go to college, as he would like. At first there is not, but as the family members offer one sacrifice after another, Mama's "Is not enough" finally becomes "Is enough!" With Mama at the helm, there is no limit as to what even this poor, hardworking family can accomplish.

The character of Mama inspires a considerably strong and affectionate remembrance in one older woman with whom I spoke, who remembers Mama as a pillar of strength:

I watched *I Remember Mama*. That was a very popular show, 'cause she was a very strong character. We didn't think so, but she was the strongest character of all, . . . I remember something about, thinking about her that she was always referring to something in security; like a bank book, that people always really thought she had money, but she never did. But she gave them that feeling of security, that there was always something there so that there should never be any fear. But actually, when you realize that she really didn't have anything—they just, were very poor . . . not a poor working family, but a very moderate working family that you saw, . . . It was a very outstanding show though, I know; everybody would always say yeah, that's like *I Remember Mama*—an *I Remember Mama* type of thing.

Interviewer: When you say it's outstanding, what do you mean?

That it brought in a great deal of family life that evidently everybody related to, in some way or other, I would say.

Interviewer: Some people you knew made comparisons actually?

Yes. That's right. People would always point out "Yes, that's a situation that we've been through." Something like that. I think association with the characters in that particular part was very good. (Evelyn)

This interchange illustrates a great deal of affection for at least this one early television mother, who seems to constitute, for Evelyn, a powerful image of great female strength, although Mama, like other early family women on television, was in some senses a traditional wife and mother. Older women, who may have trouble identifying with so much of today's family television, seem to have found the Mama character easier to identify with. Another older woman supports her assertion that *Mama* inspired easy identification.

I watched *Mama*. That was cute! She was a tall blonde woman. I enjoyed watching her. I really felt that I could understand *Mama*, you know, because you're a mother. (Amy)

Again, *Mama* resonates with the experience of older women who watched her. Unlike so many other early family shows, recollection of *Mama* calls forth recollection of the experience of identifying with family characters on television.

Other older women also praise early family shows from their vantage points as mothers within nuclear families. These women found such shows to be hearty fare for children and the entire family; they felt that the strong paternal authority many of them portrayed illustrated the right way for a family to operate, or at least realistically depicted the dominant family experience of the time:

> Yes, *Father Knows Best,* we used to watch that all the time. Yes, I loved all the family shows . . . even *Ozzie and Harriet,* with their boys growing up; that's the kind of show I would like my children to see.
>
> Interviewer: Why did you like *Father Knows Best*?
>
> Why? Because his advice was generally right, and he was a typical father. He cared about his children, and it was uppermost in his mind to make the right decision for his children and with his children. (Evelyn)

She goes on to compare *Father Knows Best* to a more recent, feminist-era show, *The Waltons,* claiming that although the newer show portrays a more egalitarian marriage, the older show was appropriate to its time and did not offend her:

> Interviewer: So you really liked to see a father who gave the right kind of advice for his family.
>
> Or the mother . . . or the mother. Now *The Waltons,* I think the mother had as much to say as the father. I mean it was always a family and a unit. And that's what I liked on TV. To me that was very important, and I believed in letting my children watch those kind of things.
>
> Interviewer: So it doesn't bother you if, say, in a show like *Father Knows Best,* the mother doesn't say much?
>
> No, no . . . because of the meaning of the father image? No, I don't think so. Well, but you see, you have to understand that years ago, the father did rule the house. The mother really had less to say than the father in most families. The father made the decisions. (Evelyn)

Another woman describes a similar affection for and identification with *Father Knows Best:*

> That was a good show. Lots of people must have watched it the same as I did. Because, it was something that was close to home, you know. There was always a situation. They were situation shows, that if you had children, you could associate with them. (Nora)

Again, we find an older woman identifying with the situation depicted in this very traditional family show.

Nostalgia and Resistance in Younger Working-Class Women's Responses to Family Television

Older women, then, take a particular attitude toward family television. Some talk of using early family television shows instrumentally to help in bringing up their families; others describe with satisfaction and approval how a wholesome portrayal of family life involved them. While some characters—Mama, for example—inspire enthusiastic identification among older respondents, older women generally view family television in a more limited, sometimes instrumental, fashion as a tool they used to help teach their children proper social and family values.

Ironically, their strategy worked. For young women approximately the ages of many of the daughters of my older group, family television is received with much more seriousness than it was by their mothers. For younger women, family television in many respects has defined their notions of what the family is. Prefeminist family television in particular strikes a plaintive chord of response in young working-class women, many of whose family experiences in reality have borne no resemblance to that depicted. In our society's collective memory, aided strongly by its representation on television, the traditional nuclear family is holding its own as a poignant point of reference for many, even for those who have never personally experienced it.

Thus, there is a striking nostalgic streak in responses to family television particularly among the young working-class women I interviewed, a strain of thought absent from older women's discussions of television. Young working-class women from intact nuclear families speak of admiring the idyllic pictures of family life they have viewed on television, sometimes comparing these to aspects of their own family lives that do not quite measure up. But plaintive, nostalgic reactions to early family television are particularly strong among women who grew up in homes with divorced parents or in families unconventional in some other manner, an experience that is increasingly common in our society.[13] Apparently, watching early family television taps into deep-seated feelings of deprivation that young working-class women feel when their families have deviated from the mythic nuclear model.

One young working-class woman, from an intact nuclear family herself, conjures up the image of the good old days, which to her mind family television represents:

Interviewer: What about families on television today versus the older shows you were saying you enjoyed?

I think a lot of them [families on television today] are divorced or . . .

they go along with the society of today: divorced, having problems. . . . I think they reflect what a lot of families of today are like.

Interviewer: Are the images of today an advance in any way?

No. I think I like the good times back when the majority of families
stayed together. (Linda)

Apparently, the myth of the good old days is still alive and kicking in
today's young women, some of whom, like Linda, desire to return to a
time when families were more traditional. Linda's comments are especially interesting considering the fact that she herself comes from a
traditional, still-intact nuclear family with a working father and a stay-
at-home mother. She strongly desires to recreate this family life in her
own future.

Another young working-class woman, Pamela, also from an intact
nuclear family, mentions that it was fun to watch certain family shows
on television because they were so happy: "I don't know, they [the
Partridge Family and the *Brady Bunch*] were just fun to watch. They were
always happy and everything." Pamela goes on to criticize the mother
on the *Brady Bunch* in an almost angry manner because, as she put it,

She used to bother me 'cause she was just too perfect, you know, she
just gave her undivided attention to all her children. I didn't like the
way she had to have a maid to help her clean the house when she
didn't work. She was just a housewife and she had a maid. I don't
think I ever thought she was very realistic. (Pamela)

These critical comments clash somewhat with her response to my
next question:

Interviewer: Do you remember ever wishing your mother was more
like those mothers?

Yeah, I used to wish that my mom would, when I got home from
school, would have snacks for me. I remember that, 'cause they
always did on television. She would always be happy to see them and
have something for them to eat.

Interviewer: And your mother never was happy to see you?

Oh, she was! That was a big thing, when I used to come home from
school, if my mom wasn't there for some reason I would really hate
that. I wouldn't like to come home and have no one there. So it was
important for me, but she wasn't real eager to find out, "Oh, how was
your whole day?" and give you something to eat, she wasn't quite as
enthusiastic as the one on television. (Pamela)

Even working-class women from intact, traditional nuclear families, like Pamela and Linda, can react quite emotionally to the feeling that their own family experience deviated from that portrayed as the norm in family television or to the fear that their own present and future family lives may not measure up. Some women even express these reactions on the heels of criticizing these television families for being ridiculously unrealistic.

Given that working-class women from intact families seem driven to feelings of inadequacy by family television about their own less-than-perfect families, certainly we would expect women who recall growing up in divorced families to have some similar responses. In fact, women from divorced families have strong feelings about early family television and even about some of the later shows depicting happy families in a somewhat more modern family form. For example, Cindy, the product of an unhappy broken home who grew up the victim of an abusive stepfather, has this to say about the meaning of *Father Knows Best* for her:

> *Father Knows Best* was my favorite, always was. I was always in love with him.
>
> Interviewer: The father?
>
> Oh definitely yes. My father left right after we moved. My parents got divorced.
>
> Interviewer: When you were eight?
>
> Right. So Robert Young became my ideal man.
>
> Interviewer: Was he a lot different than what your father was like?
>
> I suppose. I don't know if I even knew my father. He was just sort of a vague memory. And so, I idealized him and didn't know ever what he was. I still don't know who my father is, he doesn't want any contact. I've tried to write him but he won't respond.
>
> Interviewer: So you had a strong reaction to *Father Knows Best*?
>
> Mm-hmmm. I always thought he was kind. I had a stepfather who was very cruel—well, not very, but we didn't get along at all, we just . . . so I always sort of fantasized about a father like Robert Young. (Cindy)

This poignant passage illustrates how closely these family shows can move viewers when exposure to them is timed with the experience of family difficulties. Cindy goes on to describe the way elder daughter

Betty Anderson (Elinor Donahue) on the show became somewhat of a role model for her:

> I always sort of looked up to Betty. She seemed more aloof, brighter, more put together than the younger one [the younger daughter]. You know, the looks, the dates, the lots of respect she had that I would have liked. (Cindy)

Perhaps because the family situation itself hit so close to home for this viewer, one of the show's female figures began to function as a role model for her.

Other young working-class women from broken homes describe their responses to intact television families somewhat similarly:

> Interviewer: Did you watch any old family shows, such as *Leave It to Beaver,* during your heavy television-watching period?
>
> I did, but that was sort of—that was a little bit—just sort of envy, you know. . . . I watched it a few times, but it wasn't regular. (Kim)

That Kim expresses a preference for early family television over that which is more recent may also relate to a yearning for the simple nuclear family that dominated the early images.

Kim goes on to speak in a defensive, almost hostile tone when denying her identification with certain more recent (mid-1970s) family shows. This tone is most evident when Kim describes her response to the *Brady Bunch,* a show popular during her childhood which depicts a large happy family resulting from the remarriage of a widow and widower. She criticizes the unreality of the undisrupted, untroubled family bliss the show depicts:

> It's more the family situation, you know, and I was never really part of that, so . . . well, I'm saying that maybe I wasn't—I didn't identify with those [family] shows, you know, maybe that's why I didn't identify with them.
>
> Interviewer: How about a show like the *Brady Bunch?* Did you watch that a lot?
>
> I watched that, yeah, I remember that, the *Brady Bunch,* the *Partridge Family* . . . it wasn't real, you know, it wasn't—you know, they were in situations where . . . the *Brady Bunch* was, yeah, that family, they came together and they got together really well, and they were little, little men and little ladies, the kids were. But that's, you know, that

wasn't really real to me. There were no hardships or no real arguments, there was no—nobody getting into trouble or having real-life
problems.

Interviewer: When you were younger, what was your family like?

I didn't have that happy—not that it wasn't happy, supportive, and
very nurturing, it was, you know, but my mom was busy, my brother
was in school, and my dad wasn't really there, and so that's why I
didn't relate to those sort of shows where it was very fun and they
were all—you know, I mean I had fun with my family, but it wasn't in
that way. You know, my brother and I were never like the kids in the
family. It was more—I had to seek things out, either through friends
or, you know, I guess other people. I didn't have a lot of family, you
know, like I don't have cousins or aunts and uncles around that I
could, you know, be like an extended family. (Kim)

Kim's exposure to this show causes her to make some apparently
painful comparisons between her own family and what she saw on the
screen. Watching family television has made Kim yearn for a big family; her own fell far short of this ideal. Even before her parents' divorce,
like many modern families Kim's was small and rather fragmented,
each member busy with his or her own jobs and activities. Also like
many modern family members, Kim had relatively little contact with
her extended kin group. In these respects, she finds the *Brady Bunch*
unrealistic. In the style of many working-class women, Kim criticizes
television rather harshly for what she takes to be its lack of realism in
this respect.

In the same vein Barbara, another product of a broken working-class
home, mentions *Little House on the Prairie*[14] as her favorite television
show: "I just liked them 'cause they were so, you know, homey and
down-to-earth. Always doing things for each other." When pressed as
to whether she sees herself living in this manner in her own future,
however, Barbara denies it. "I just don't see it, really. I don't know. I
don't think I'd want to stay home and be a . . . I don't think I would
even be a good mother to stay home, 'cause I don't have much pa-
tience."

The ideal of the intact, closely interacting, mutually sacrificing family is appealing, yet young working-class women do not envision this
sort of family life in their own futures. No wonder young women
experience feelings of nostalgia and conflict where the family is concerned! Barbara also mentions how "neat" and "fun" the large family
pictured on *Eight Is Enough*[15] seemed to her. Both *Little House on the
Prairie* and *Eight Is Enough* picture lives that are painfully different

from Barbara's own experience as the only child of a divorced, single mother.

The following serves as another example of the sort of painful comparison which this show evokes in young women from families unorthodox in some way. Monica's family, though intact, was culturally unusual. As Mexican-Americans, her family members had relationships and customary interactions that differed in important ways from those she saw in family television:

> I remember seeing the *Brady Bunch* and wondering why my family wasn't like the *Brady Bunch*. I remember that very clearly. I must have been eight. I was young. And I remember sitting there and saying, "Why can't my father be like Mr. Brady," you know?
>
> Interviewer: Go out to work, and come back . . . ?
>
> Right, and kiss my mother when he comes in and all that. And I remember I started the tradition in my family of kissing my father when he came home, because that's what I saw Marcia [Brady] do.
>
> Interviewer: You mean nobody did that before?
>
> No, we didn't. You know, and we'd go out and get his thermos from the truck and the gate, but . . . my father was very stern. It's not like I would go and sit on his lap. You know what I mean? He had his place, and that was to keep us under control. When you have eight of 'em, that's a hell of a lot of people to feed and keep under control at the same time. So I started that in my family. I saw Marcia go and kiss her daddy. I hate to say it, but I was sort of white-oriented, culturally, you know, and in my ways, I wanted to be like them. You know? And so I came home one Sunday and I said, "Mom, you know . . ." and she said, "Well, why don't you do that?" So from then on my sister Irene and I would go and run to my dad when he came home and kiss him. And he'd just have this gruff face. (Monica)

Monica goes on to describe a childhood and adolescence fraught with conflicts about her Mexican heritage, and the way it rendered her different from others she knew. While in many ways she feels the pull of her traditional roots, in others she aspires to become a fully assimilated, culturally indistinct American. Monica's remarkable anecdote illustrates the way in which family television often seems to make younger working-class viewers conscious of how their families differ from the norm, or how they do not fit in with supposedly correct and desirable ways of life in our society.

Middle-Class Responses

Young middle-class women take a different approach in commenting on family television. As is characteristic of their responses generally, when commenting on this genre rather than responding to particular characters within it middle-class women are more distanced than working-class women, almost cynical in their speech. One young woman mentions preferring the earlier family television because it now appears "contrived" to her, and she enjoys this overt lack of realism:

> The older it is, I mean, the fifties stuff I like better because it's even more contrived and ridiculous . . . and the expressions they use and stuff. And I enjoy *Leave It to Beaver* more than, say, the *Brady Bunch* now because it's further away from culture now, society now. And the situations are more ridiculous. (Terry)

Of course, this quote may be read on its surface to indicate simply a preference for more unrealistic television. On the other hand, if we push this interpretation a bit further, asking *why* the nostalgia for early television, what is it about early shows that makes them attractive to some viewers, we come up with some clear differences between the family situations and relationships in shows from each period that might explain the nostalgia for early television both middle-class and working-class women share.[16]

Middle-class women from divorced families tend to respond to family television with a degree of nostalgia similar to that expressed by working-class women from similar family backgrounds. Sarah, for example, is from a family in which her parents divorced when she was very young. But rather than projecting anger at family television for depicting the unified family she had lost, Sarah instead found refuge in television, becoming a heavy watcher and often watching with her brother and other remaining family members. In fact, Sarah, who after the divorce lived with her mother, tells of difficult visits to her father's house during which she felt so bored and ignored that she would spend her time reading *TV Guide* to escape her loneliness. For her, television occupies a cherished place, at times filling in for the lack of family contact in her repertoire of early memories.

Also, in accordance with middle-class responses generally, young middle-class women show more positive identification with television families than do working-class women. This is particularly true of middle-class women from intact families. Consider the case of Holli, who comments on how similar her family is to the one depicted in the *Brady Bunch* and how widely noticed this is among their friends and acquaintances. How different is this experience of our common culture from that of most women with less normative family backgrounds!

Young middle-class women overall have a more positive response to television's postfeminist women than do young working-class women. They do not feel the need to "split" these characters in their discussions about them, seeming to appreciate it when characters represent the successful integration of professional work with family concerns. Several young middle-class women mention the character of Emily Hartley (Suzanne Pleshette) on the *Bob Newhart Show* as someone they particularly admire. Emily, Bob's wife, was also a schoolteacher. The perceived egalitarian relationship between the two strikes several young middle-class women particularly well:

> I liked that show. Because it was more of an equal relationship. She seemed more professional and he was agreeing, he was more, allowing her to be equal . . . it was more of a balance, maybe that's why I identified with this show. (Sarah)

> I liked Emily. I thought Emily and Bob really had a nice marriage. She had a sense of humor. She would tell Bob to cut it out when he was bugging her. And he accommodated to her and she accommodated to him. (Nadine)

The Emily Hartley character inspires this admiration from young middle-class women, but little comment from older women or from young working-class women, who do not seem particularly intrigued with the show. Perhaps this somewhat rare image of a relatively egalitarian family strikes a chord for young middle-class women absent from the responses of the other groups.

No young working-class women comment on the *Newhart* show explicitly, although several working-class and middle-class young women do praise the character of Clair on the *Cosby Show* in a similar manner. There is some evidence that the newer *Cosby* appeals to young women of both classes (and attempts to appeal to women of all ages) in that it offers a view of a postfeminist woman (Clair), which de-emphasizes her individual personality and conflicts while emphasizing traditional family values. One young working-class woman explains her affection for the show by noting that it depicts a way of life in which people are governed by motives other than materialism:

> These days I find like a lot of people I'm very materialistic. I am.

> Interviewer: And you're saying on this show [*Cosby*] people are less materialistic?

Well, not so much that they're [not] materialistic, but the fact that they have good relationships, you know, they talk to each other. From the show you can tell that one sister doesn't get along too well with the other, or the father and mother don't agree sometimes, but they don't stand there and argue in front of their kids. My parents, they were terrible . . . and they [the Huxtables] communicate. (Nancy)

In discussing *Cosby*, Nancy shifts from describing the idealized way of life pictured on the show, a hypothetical "those days" so different from "these days" when a lot of people are materialistic, to a brief moment of recognition of the lack of communication she witnesses in her own family, a sequence of comments that implies a yearning for the sort of life she sees portrayed in this, one of her favorite television shows. The *Cosby Show* is somewhat unique in that it elicits comments from young women more similar to their nostalgic responses to early family television than to other current shows.[17] Older women, while noting the good feeling the *Cosby Show* gives off, seem more inclined to identify with the parental point of view on *Cosby* and to mention the lessons they learn from the show, or its realistic portrayal of parent-child interactions, as they do in comments on older family television as well.

Family television touches both generations and, among younger women, both classes in almost an opposite manner. Older women, more experienced in adult family life, are somewhat less interested in current and past family representations on television. Those they do discuss are summarily described; family television does not seem to inspire strong emotions in my older group. They have used early family television to teach their children proper values and dismiss it at that.

Younger women, in contrast, respond quite emotionally to portrayals of the family on television. One almost has the sense that they are seeking some clue, some cultural direction from television to advise them in this difficult and increasingly nebulous area of their lives. This is not surprising since for most younger women family television is responsible for much of their normative picture of the family; it tells them what family life should be like. Overall, family television is a source of acute pain for many young women from broken homes, who tend to compare their lives to its pictures.

In accord with my argument in the preceding chapters, middle-class and working-class young women have different expectations of television. When women apply these differing expectations to family television, the resulting emotional reactions differ in both intensity and tenor. Young working-class women tend to be more incensed at family television's lack of realism than are young middle-class women, who also identify more often with television families. Middle-class young women find some postfeminist families and the women in them, Emily Hartley for example, a source of inspiration without the "splitting" mechanism, offering them positive images that give them some hope for their own futures. Some young working-class women also respond to the character of Clair on the *Cosby Show* in a similar manner.

Conclusion

In addition to witnessing many changes in social norms concerning women's roles in work and family, older women have lived through many changes both generally in the position of television in our society, and more specifically in women's television images. Older women enjoy newer television images of women in the workplace, sometimes responding to those images as though the pictures themselves broaden their own horizons, which for many have been limited particularly with respect to opportunities in the labor force. They like seeing women in nontraditional roles and are excited by the range of possibilities now open to women at work. Older women are bothered, however, by some of television's newer norms for portraying women's sexuality more explicitly, in concurrence with their independence.

At the same time, older women seem less involved with family television, displaying less emotion about it than do younger women and offering fewer reactions to it. Unlike younger women, older women's experience with family precedes in time and importance their viewing of television's images of the family. Perhaps, as was true for working-class women's response to images of the working-class on television, older women respond more positively to images of women at work because their own experience in nontraditional careers for women is limited, while they are less impressed with images of the family on television because their own experience as adults in the family is so extensive. In this respect, newer television images of working women serve as a liberating force for older women, freeing them to envision new possibilities for women, possibilities they have never experienced and have rarely seen in their own lives. Family television, on the other hand, is more often summarily dismissed, a tool older women used to teach family values to their children.

Younger women, in contrast, have less experience in the family than older women and have come to understand the family in conjunction with viewing the idealized forms on television which their mothers allowed and sometimes encouraged them to see. Having grown up with television and often watching television together with their families when they themselves were very young, younger women exhibit a sharply emotional and somewhat contradictory response to family television in particular. The idealized nuclear family of much older and some newer television touches young women deeply at an emotional level, due in part to this early experience with it and perhaps also to their relative lack of experience in the family as an adult. This is true despite the fact that few young women see such a family, at least in its older, more traditional versions, in their own future, though some expressly wished to be able to create this kind of family life someday. Women who are the products of unhappy or disrupted families in real life respond especially strongly to television's very idealized family forms, images many recall from childhood viewing days.

In contrast to their comparative lack of family experience, many younger women have somewhat more experience in the work force than women over sixty, or at least have had more freedom to prepare themselves for a wide range of positions. While older women are more involved with television shows that portray women in work more often than family settings, young women are more critical of these shows and more involved with family television, which frequently addresses experiences they have not yet had as well as some of the most intense experiences of their lives. Younger women, therefore, do not encounter television as a source of liberating notions about women and work but are more aware of women's constraints vis-à-vis the workplace from their own experience and those of their friends and sisters.

In a somewhat different manner from my older group, young women of both classes are experiencing fully the newer social pressures of our postfeminist society, pressures to live up to both older ideals of women's service to their families and newer ideals of women's capacity for work or career performance and achievement equal to that of men. But perhaps it is working-class women who are feeling most pressured by these ideals, in conjunction with their often troubled backgrounds and limited opportunities. Young working-class women sometimes respond to television's professional women by "splitting" their image between its work and family sides and by choosing the family side with which to identify. This response is not surprising since television's working women, like so many other television images, are overwhelmingly middle-class and occupy jobs that are relatively out-of-reach for many working-class viewers.

At the same time, several young women of both classes do show some appreciation when television attempts to portray women involved in both family and career activities (Emily of *Newhart* or Clair on the *Cosby*

Show, for example), particularly when they perceive some acknowledgment of women's need to prioritize one of these roles (almost always, the family). It is almost as if such well-adjusted postfeminist women, shown primarily in their family roles, help to relieve younger women of their anxiety and confusion regarding the need to juggle and manage alternative roles perceived as desirable, necessary parts of their future lives.

Conclusion: Television Reception as a Window on Culture

IN THIS BOOK, I have compared the ways in which women of different social classes and generations talk about popular television entertainment. My discussion is offered as a starting point, a way for us to begin to define the shape and dynamic of cultural processes at the individual and social group level in complex societies. Qualitative methodology, as I have employed it, presupposes that events at this individual level, though not the only level we should investigate, are nevertheless meaningful and contribute to our greater understanding of culture.

In interpreting my study, I start from two convictions which are often construed to be contradictory in the literature on mass media reception: first, that the mass media in general and television in particular serve as important mechanisms for disseminating and reinforcing ideology in liberal capitalist societies and, second, that individuals and groups of individuals receive media actively, that to receive television involves the active interpretation of its images and their meaning. Viewers bring their own perspectives, often critical ones, to the viewing experience.

More often than not, these two sets of assumptions are held to be incompatible in our field. It is often assumed that, if one accepts the terms of hegemony theory, then one holds that the mass media audience is passive and that one's attention will focus on media form, content, and control rather than on problems of reception. This assumption unfairly oversimplifies the premises of the notion of hegemony, however, and misrepresents the intentions of those who have adapted this theory to mass media study. The theory of hegemony is, at heart, a theory of human action. Unlike many social theories, hegemony theory highlights the role of the thoughts, beliefs, and practices of human actors in the process of social change.

Marx's dictum that "men [in this case, women] make history, but they do not do so under conditions of their own choosing" may be applied to media scholars' use of hegemony theory as well. While consciousness of—and conscious resistance to—a society's dominant ideas are important motors for the process of social change, we do not always control the conditions which form our consciousness. While it may be human nature to continually seek further knowledge of those conditions, we can never become fully enlightened about the determinants of our consciousness; this point has been made abundantly clear by the works of Marx and Freud and the commentators on them.[1]

The study of media reception, therefore, like the study of all complex processes of thought and action, to be complete must involve considerations of both conscious and unconscious thought processes, of creative and resistant impulses as well as determined and controlled responses. It is a large task. Not surprisingly, most attempts to study media reception emphasize only one small part of the total picture. Hegemonic discussions, unfortunately, have de-emphasized the critical response of audience members; studies of the active audience have de-emphasized media's hegemonic nature. Like most others, my study is also a limited investigation of television reception, but it is one I hope will fill some gaps currently in our literature.

Overall, I take the position that television reception is a complicated process, one that cannot be adequately summarized either by the term "resistance" or by the terms "passivity" and "accommodation." With the open-ended interviewing method I employ in the study, women are able to express elements of both, and often do, in their responses to my questions and in their discussions overall. Theories that cannot account for both are bound to understate the complexity of the problem. It is much too simplistic to argue that women resist domination when they watch and talk about television.[2] Although in many respects television texts are open to competing interpretations, in other respects they bear the unmistakable marks of the hegemonic culture that creates them. It is wishful thinking, I fear, to believe that viewers are unaffected by these ideas as they are present in both mass media texts and concomitantly in our culture at large.

It is also simplistic, however, to argue that television viewers are simply passive recipients of the medium's hegemonic messages, or that members of a culture simply imbibe, passively, the ideological messages of that culture. Individuals and groups show themselves capable of creativity and independence both in thought and in strategies of action in many ways in our culture.[3] People often express, verbally and actively, resistance to dominant ideas and realize the contradictions among competing aspects of our cultural ideologies. Women watching television are no different. Often they find themselves frustrated with their family and/or work situations, and are dissatisfied with the ideas our culture makes available for expression of this frustration. The process of receiving television may include strategies for expressing, as well as for coping with, this frustration. Evidence of this abounds in women's responses to my interviews. In my discussion, however, rather than making an overarching claim as to the ends television watching serves in our society, I emphasize the different forms in which these responses to questions about television occur between class- and age-differentiated groups.

In the course of my study, marked class differences emerged when I compared discussions of television offered by working-class and middle-class women. Working-class women's search for realism on television seems in large part responsible for these differences. Often, working-class women begin their discussion of television characters by assessing their realism. In fact, their search for realism leads working-class women, in the end, to a more distanced, perhaps resistant, stance toward television they like, and to identify with relatively few television characters.[4] More often, they are extremely critical of television characters, and there seems to be little propensity on my informants' part toward identification with these characters, even with characters on shows women told me that they enjoy and watch often. For middle-class women, on the other hand, the realism of situations and even characters is seldom an overtly discussed issue. They often harbor favorable, somewhat personal feelings toward television characters inhabiting shows they describe to be silly or unrealistic.

A convenient way to sum up these differences might be to observe that while middle-class women focus their criticism on television shows in a very general way, they more often respond positively to individual characters on these shows, even characters they may find comic or unrealistic. In fact, middle-class women more often identify with television characters, in particular with their situations and dilemmas vis-à-vis family and other relationships, than do working-class women. Paradoxically, then, middle-class women generally seem to like television less overall but to identify with its characters and situations more than working-class women.

Working-class women, on the other hand, while overall claiming to value television more highly, are often critical both of television shows themselves and of the characters on them, primarily for their lack of realism.[5] Working-class women's lack of identification with television characters is perhaps not surprising when one considers the middle- or upper-class bias of most television content. What is more surprising and disturbing is their judgment that many of television's middle-class shows offer accurate pictures of reality; this suggests that some women learn from television to see middle-class life as "real," and raises alarming possibilities for television's impact on women's consequent interpretation of their own experience.

Working-class women resist television but, paradoxically, the standards of critique they use are not their own. In large part, working-class women criticize television content for its lack of reality; yet the concept of reality used here corresponds to television's portrayal of middle-class life. The potential resistant thrust of their critique of television, therefore, is blunted by television's hegemonic impact itself.

Comparing older with younger women's responses, I find that, at the older extreme of the life cycle, gender-related considerations govern women's responses to television more than class, for both historical and developmental reasons. In younger women's responses, class differences are more prominent. At both ends of the age spectrum, women respond most to what many feel they are missing in their lives. Older women, while critical of television's working women in certain respects, speak longingly of the interesting and different sorts of jobs women are pictured holding on current television. One has the sense that for older women television is an important cultural reminder of many of the experiences not widely available to women in the prefeminist era of their youths; in this respect, television is almost a liberating, or enlarging, force for them.

Younger women focus more on family than on work. Aware of new ideals for women in the workplace that conflict with older prescriptions for women in the family, younger working-class women often view family television with an interesting mixture of criticism and sadness. Children of broken homes are sometimes painfully nostalgic for the intact nuclear families early television depicts. Middle-class women are somewhat less critical of family television, some gratefully acknowledging it as a refuge from unhappy childhoods.

A comparison among women of different ages reveals that, at different points in its history and for different groups of women, television can serve either as a fairly conservative or as a relatively radical repository of cultural ideas. Older women feel that their horizons are broadened by what they see on television, especially by the roles television women play at work. Many younger women find that television encourages their longings for and exacerbates their feelings of loss about traditional family forms. Paradoxically, from a feminist perspective, television can be construed as feminist or progressive for older women, inspiring criticism of sexual mores but drawing their eager attention to depictions of women at work. In younger women, postfeminist television in particular inspires criticism, admiration, and nostalgia, a mix in which resistance blends with an often backward-looking sentiment. Younger women are happy to see images of women successfully combining work and family, but they are skeptical as well. Few see such realities in their own futures. Younger working-class women often split feminist or postfeminist female characters and talk only about their family lives, either not relating to their generally middle-class work situations or not believing that they combine this work happily with their family roles.

In sum, my findings lead me to conclude that the hegemonic aspects of the way television operates are more gender-specific for middle-class women (e.g., in ways related to the operation and perpetuation of patriarchy) and that television's hegemonic function works in more class-specific ways for working-class women (e.g., in ways related to the organization of the class system in our society). I certainly do not mean to suggest that working-class women are not oppressed by their gender. Rather, I argue that how they interact with television culturally is more a function of their social class membership than their membership in a particular gender group. At either end of the age spectrum, women of both classes tend to respond more to gender-related variables than to those related to social class, with younger women more critically suspicious of television's images picturing women's changing social positions, and older women more hopeful and accepting of the stories these images tell; both trends are tempered, however, by strongly opposite, and contradictory, responses.

In conclusion, women's reception of television is affected by both their position as women in our society and their membership in social class and age groups. In comparing the remarks of women of different social classes, I find that television contributes to their oppression in the family and in the workplace both *as* women and, for working-class women, as members of the working class. While women criticize television and resist much of its impact, it is clear that television contributes to these two dimensions of women's oppression. In addition, women of different age groups experience television's political impact differently; both older and younger women are at once critical of, and compelled by, pictures of television women in the family and at work.

My findings stand in contradiction to those theorists who would argue that viewers use the mass media to resist cultural hegemony all the time, or to hegemony theorists who might argue that the mass media operate as a cultural monolith, presenting the audience with politically determined content that is received uniformly across all groups.[6] Instead, television is both a source of resistance to the status quo for different groups of women and a reinforcer for the patriarchal and capitalist values that characterize the status quo. Mass media in general and television in particular function complexly and paradoxically in our society, simultaneously fostering conformity and encouraging resistance to it among dominated groups.

My research leads me to suggest that, until more conclusive evidence accrues that either capitalist or patriarchal cultural hegemony prevails in our culture, or that resistance to it is widespread, we must look beyond the institution of television for a clearer picture as to how its participation in either trend articulates with our cultural practices as a whole. If women's tendency to resist hegemony through creative interpretations of television truly stops in the kitchen, then this evidence of resistance must be counted as something else. Theorists of resistance must develop some means for assessing the political effectiveness of the resistance they chronicle.

Overall, this book maps the terrain of class and generational differences in women's interpretations of television entertainment programming in the United States. My work will serve, I hope, to raise issues involved in investigating women's media reception; further work, of course, will be necessary to refine and deepen our understanding of these issues. Scholars in Europe and the United States have lately attempted ethnographic audience study. As I have discussed in the introductory chapters, most of these studies have focused on audiences and groups within audiences outside the United States. In some ways, the vast diversity one encounters within American culture makes it a natural laboratory for ethnographic study, yet in other ways, the constant interchange between subcultures in this country makes it difficult, and forbidding, to identify specific subcultures upon which to concentrate. Introducing the variable of gender makes such groupings even more difficult to attain.

The reception of television and the other popular media gives us an important window into the cultural lives of groups within our society. Such studies can help us begin to talk meaningfully about cultural life within a society as vast and complex as our own. I hope that others will build on the work I offer here, and that ultimately we will develop a clearer picture of how cultural processes operate and reproduce themselves for women in our society.

Appendix: Methodology

The Study

For this project, I located two groups of women: twenty working-class women and twenty-one middle-class women. I chose a spectrum of ages ranging from seventeen to seventy-eight to facilitate the generational comparison between women sixty and older and those twenty-nine and under which I make in chapter 5.

Sampling Techniques

I used snowball sampling as a means of finding my informants.[1] In snowball sampling, one starts with a member of the desired group and asks that person for a friend, neighbor, or relative in order to continue interviewing within the same class group. In this way, one obtains an informal sampling of a social group. Snowball sampling makes no claim to yield a representative sample of a group; in any case, my numbers here are too small for me to make such a claim. This is preliminary research, meant to raise questions and issues that must be investigated further with future larger studies.

In order to avoid the bias sometimes inherent in this sampling method, in which all of the individuals in the snowball are somehow connected with one another, I used several snowballs to start off each group. Similar to the informants in Rubin (1976:11), the women I interviewed at the start of each snowball came to me in a variety of ways—through waitresses I met, friends who taught working-class students, a working-class church, hairdressers. Like Rubin, I conducted my interviews in different communities surrounding the San Francisco Bay area, although I attempted to exclude the city of Berkeley itself, since its population is so unrepresentative of the country at large. Most interviews were conducted during the years 1985–86. Several supplementary interviews were conducted in southern Florida and in the Lexington, Kentucky, area during the years 1986–88.

Methodological Techniques

My interviews lasted for at least two hours, sometimes more, and often included follow-up interviews and visits. While I used the interview schedule below as a general guide, rather than sitting my informants down to ask them questions, I wanted them to talk to me about television and about their lives in a freer manner. I therefore left my questions open-ended and let the interviews travel in directions that seemed most consonant with women's particular interests and views on the subject.[2] However, I did start to ask about particular shows when after about half my interviews it became clear that many women were bringing them up.

Some interviews yielded little information of value for the study, unfortunately, in part because of the open-ended format I used. However, I am convinced that I would not have gathered the information I did had I created a more closed, structured interview situation. In the end, out of a total of forty-six interviews conducted, I used twenty interviews with working-class women and twenty-one with middle-class women, for a total sample of forty-one interview subjects. Interviews were taped and later transcribed. In addition, I wrote notes directly following each interview regarding the general tenor of the interview, my impressions of my informant, and other miscellaneous details. It is from this data that the information discussed in this study was culled.

I began interviews with a discussion of women's basic life circumstances. I asked them for a great deal of background information concerning their parents' occupations and education, their own occupation and education, past job experiences and future job plans, the quality of their relationships with family and friends, their future family plans, and other related issues. I then moved into the television part of my interviews with the request that women tell me about the television they had watched.

My interviews were in this stage very open-ended, although as my interview schedule indicates I had a general plan in mind. I wanted women to talk to me in their own words about the television they had watched and remembered, to tell me what came to their minds when they thought about television. Once I had attempted to start our discussion of television in this vein, I would ask questions about characters women mentioned, asking them whether they liked or disliked them, identified with them or not, and why. I asked similar questions about the television shows women brought up, asking them for some detail as to why they liked (or disliked) specific shows.

Not all women found it easy to respond to this sort of open-ended questioning about television. If a woman I was interviewing found it awkward to begin speaking in this vacuum, or started feeling she did not remember much television she had watched, I would pull out my list of the top-rated television shows for each year of broadcasting,[3] and ask women to look at the list to see if this would refresh their memory. This usually was sufficient to get a discussion going of particular shows. Overall, the tenor of the interviews was chatty and casual. I sought a relaxed atmosphere because I felt it made our rapport easier to establish, and women's responses more genuine. Again, I did not always succeed in putting women at their ease, but for the most part, I feel that women were basically relaxed and enjoyed the opportunity to express their views in their discussions with me.

I desired, as much as possible, that women themselves structure their discussions of television. I wanted to be guided by women's own rhythms when determining whether, and in what ways, television was important to them. Of course, while this was my ideal, it was one I was unable to realize in its fullest sense, since it was inevitable that to some extent my own categories and preconceptions about what I wanted to know influenced both the interviews themselves and my subsequent interpretations of them.

I began the project out of a dual-edged interest in the mass media. I was convinced that consuming media gave women (including me) great pleasure; I was convinced also that consuming the media images that are dominant in our culture makes women's lives in many ways more difficult, and more painful, by reinforcing stereotypes about our appearance and behavior which are unconsciously limiting and often damaging to our self-esteem. Like most of the women I interviewed, my attitude toward television was conflicted, a mixture of both sets of beliefs. Our similarities in attitude contributed, I feel, to making most interviews relaxed, rather pleasant experiences, somewhat chatty and informal.[4] Of course, some of my informants were more tense and nervous than others. Overall, however, I felt most enjoyed the experience, and gave freely and generously of their time and opinions. I am grateful to all the women who found the time and the inclination to share their observations on television with me.

Defining Social Class: A Methodological Note

Deciding upon a working definition of social class to guide my choice of informants was more problematic. The class issue, particularly when applied to women's class membership, is not a simple one. Even when sex is not considered, class divisions in our country are far from clear. Over the past two decades, there has been a tremendous amount of debate in the sociological literature over what the operant class divisions in the United States are at present. From a strictly Marxist point of view, classes are defined in terms of the positions of different occupational groups vis-à-vis the mode of production. If a group produces surplus value, they are defined as working-class; if they do not, they are not working-class. A Weberian approach to class analysis focuses more on other realms of life, apart from the economic. Classes consist of groups that share a common set of circumstances and expectations in life, which is determined by measurement of the distribution of goods rather than their relationship to production.[5]

Typical sociological models of class differences determine class boundaries with reference to one's position within the division of labor (see Dahrendorf [1959] for an example). As Bottomore et al. (1983:74–77) note, Marxists have had problems in relating the social stratification of capitalist society to the basic social classes as defined in their model. However, both Marxist and more traditional sociological models of class have in common their stress on structural position in determining class membership, as opposed to the belief and values of the individual, which the Weberians have traditionally stressed (Parkin 1979:4).

Poulantzas (1973, 1975) offers perhaps the most systematic attempt to apply a Marxist theory of class applicable to modern capitalism (Parkin 1979:17). When one searches for workers who produce surplus value in our current capitalist society, one is struck by the large number of workers who cannot be said to do so. Where can white-collar workers, service-sector workers, and others be put? Wright (1978:31) argues that, when applied to the United States, these criteria yield a small number of workers indeed. He offers a theory of "contradictory locations" within class positions, arguing that the new middle class under monopoly capitalism contains features of both the traditional Marxist proletariat and the bourgeoisie.

The assessment of women's class position adds a new wrinkle to an already complicated picture. Most male theorists of class have assumed that women's class position is to be determined from their association with men, usually their husbands or their fathers. Parkin states the accepted position well:

Now female status certainly carries many disadvantages compared with that of males in various areas of social life including employment opportunities, property ownership, income, and so on. However, these inequalities associated with sex differences are not usefully thought of as components of stratification. This is because for the great majority of women the allocation of social and economic rewards is determined primarily by the position of their families—and, in particular, that of the male head. Although women today share certain status attributes in common, simply by virtue of their sex, their claims over resources are not primarily determined by their own occupation but, more commonly, by that of their fathers or husbands. And if the wives and daughters of unskilled laborers have some things in common with the wives and daughters of wealthy landowners, there can be no doubt that the *differences* in their overall situation are far more striking and significant. Only if the disabilities attaching to female status were felt to be so great as to override differences of a class kind would it be realistic to regard sex as an important dimension of stratification. But in modern society the "vertical" placement of women in the class hierarchy, through membership of a kin group, appears to be much more salient to female self-perception and identity than the status of womanhood *per se.* It is perhaps for this reason that feminist political movements appear to have had relatively little appeal for the majority of women. (1971:14–15)

The popular opinion holds that women have more in common with men in their class than with women outside it. Giddens (1973:288) agrees with Parkin, arguing that, in fact, women's own work is peripheral to the class system. Felson and Knoke (1974) offer evidence that indeed, women themselves evaluate their own class membership in terms of their husband's income and class position.

Feminists have, over the last two decades, disagreed with this position. Acker (1973) argues that one should look at the mother's status as a criterion for class membership of women and that we should consider women's mobility in light of their mother's status (presumably, those elements of the mother's status that are independent of one's father's status). Smith-Blau (1972) offers evidence to support this theory in noting that, for working-class girls, maternal aspiration is critical in determining their subsequent possibilities for class mobility. Epstein (1970) supports Acker's theory by asserting that individual girls, at least in the middle class, need role models showing them that marriage and careers can be combined.

Ryan (1979) attacks the male view of women's class membership on historical grounds, arguing that in nineteenth-century America the structural similarities between working-class and middle-class women outweighed incidental differences between them, and leaving open the question of what legacy this leaves us with in the twentieth century. Oakley (1974:34–49) notes that the roles of working-class women became more differentiated from those of middle-class women as the nineteenth century wore on. With the establishment of a doctrine of female domesticity as an ideal, although the doctrine did permeate downwards from the middle to the working class, economic reality prevented most working-class women from living up to it, as they were forced to work outside the home in the vast majority of cases even into the early twentieth century. It may be true, therefore, that significant differences between the position of women in different classes may be a comparatively recent phenomenon, sensitive to the fluctuations of history.

Radical feminists have been arguing for several decades that women constitute a separate class or even culture in our society. Hacker (1951) argued early on that women actually constitute a separate subculture, with their own language and idioms, distinct from men, although she did not specify to which *class* of women she was referring. Later, theorists of patriarchy argued that the primary division in our society was between men and women, rather than between more strictly defined economic classes. Millett (1971:26) claimed that "our society is still a patriarchy," in that all the power continues to rest in the male domain. Hartmann and Bridges (1974:76) and Middleton (1974:180–181) claimed that patriarchy operates independently of women's class positions. More recently, feminists have begun to question these blanket positions and pay more attention to women of the working class and possible differences, as well as similarities, between these women and women of the middle and upper classes.[6]

My project falls within the latter tradition. What I have done is to select women who would be defined as working-class according to traditional, sociological measures. For the most part, this means that either their fathers, their husbands, or they themselves are engaged in blue-collar or pink-collar work—butchers, printers, factory workers, hairdressers, or clerical workers. In the case of women brought up solely by their divorced or widowed mothers, I have taken the mother's occupation into account. In the case of independent women, I have looked at their own occupation in making my judgment. In some cases, when someone's husband, father, or single mother worked in a job that appeared to be borderline (unskilled clerical work, for example), I have considered education (lack of high school diploma, high school diploma alone, or some experience with community college or night school) in addition to occupation as an indicator of working-class status.[7]

My middle-class informants were professionals, most of whom had attended college and received a B.A. or an advanced degree, or they were married to men, or were the daughters of fathers, with these characteristics. The same combination of qualities used in assessing working-class women's class status was used in determining that of the middle-class women in my sample.

The Women

What follows is a brief—too brief—description of each of my informants. Since quotations in the text are identified by pseudonyms, I thought it would be useful to present a short summary of the basic life situations of each of the women I interviewed.

Working-Class Women

KATHERINE was sixteen at the time of the interview and lived with her older sister and her mother; her parents were separated. Her mother supported them with her work in a factory warehouse, doing heavy work such as carrying papers and bottles in boxes. Katherine had dropped out of high school and was currently enrolled in a special program for high school dropouts. She was pursuing interviews for summer jobs in construction work at the time of the interview. She was very hopeful about the future and seemed to have rather nontraditional attitudes about her own possibilities.

BARBARA was seventeen at the time of the interview. She was a senior in high school. Her mother was divorced and had worked at a series of jobs to support the two of them, including work in greenhouses and flower shops. Barbara had lately become very attracted to a fundamentalist church, although her mother was not involved in it. Many of her friends and activities were centered around the church. She was critical of the other kids in high school who had moral attitudes different from her own.

ROXANNE was eighteen at the time of the interview. She had dropped out of high school but was considering working for a general equivalency degree. Roxanne was living at home with her divorced mother, who supported the family with work as a keypunch operator. She talked of her life and relationships with men as of a soap opera. Roxanne was very involved in the progression of these relationships and much less oriented toward her work plans.

LINDA was twenty at the time of the interview. Her father was in the air force and her mother had cleaned houses but now was a housewife. Her father had taken a high school proficiency exam, and her mother had a high school diploma. Linda was working as a bookkeeper for an automotive repair shop and trying to attend night school, taking some business classes. She had ambitions to work in women's retailing in some capacity.

MARIE, age twenty-one, was married but separated from her husband. She lived with a two-year-old daughter and worked as a waitress at the time of the interview. She was receiving part-time training to become a beautician. She had left high school upon becoming pregnant at age sixteen (the pregnancy was terminated) and began working as a waitress at that time. She had been brought up by a fundamentalist mother but rebelled against the church in many ways and had left home at an early age, in part to get away from its restrictions. She had a very active social life; her steady boyfriend at the moment seemed to be involved in some illegal activities.

PAMELA was twenty-one at the time of the interview. Her father worked as a meat-cutter for Safeway. Her mother did not work. Neither her father nor her mother had a college education. Pamela grew up in a small town where very few people had gone on from her high school to college. Pamela was attending the local community college and had ambitions of becoming a social worker. She felt she was much different from and much more ambitious than most others in her town. This made her feel a bit alienated from them but also from her fellow college students.

CINDY was twenty-two at the time of the interview. She had attended a local community college part-time, but had dropped out and was working in a record store at the time I spoke with her. She was the child of a divorced woman who had supported them with work as a secretary. Cindy had rather countercultural, nontraditional attitudes and was not a great television watcher.

KIM was twenty-five at the time of the interview. She was working in the production department of a local newspaper. Kim was attending community college part-time and hoped to work in design. She was the daughter of a divorced woman who worked in a restaurant. Kim was very interested in pursuing her career and in becoming successful, but she did not seem to be confident about how to proceed.

MONICA was twenty-six at the time of the interview. Her father was a migrant farm laborer, her mother a domestic worker. They are Mexican-American. Neither parent had a high school education. Although Monica herself was college-educated and currently pursuing an advanced degree, thus raising her class status significantly, I nevertheless include her here because of the diversity of her background and the insight she had developed into her own past experience.

BETTY was twenty-nine at the time of the interview. She was married to a fireman. She had worked part-time before the birth of her first son and was currently the mother of three sons, whom she stayed home to raise. Betty had a high school degree, although she had started junior college, as she joked, in order to find a husband. She was home-oriented with admittedly traditional values; while somewhat embarrassed by her traditional ideas about woman's role in the family, she was also proud of this traditional morality and of her family.

NANCY was twenty-nine at the time of the interview. She was currently working for an accountant, doing some secretarial work. Nancy had a high school diploma and had attended community college for one semester but had left school to work. She had married a serviceman at seventeen and was divorced. Her father was a manual worker, and her mother's health had been too poor for her to work. Nancy had traditional family values and was very devoted to caring for her mother.

JANICE was thirty, married, with two children aged three and five. At the time of the interview, she was working as a secretary, and her husband was an unemployed construction worker. Janice had a high school equivalency degree, while her husband was a high school drop-out. She was interested in taking night classes in computer science but found this difficult with her already overcrowded schedule. Janice's father had worked as a laborer, her mother as a clerk. Both had died early. Janice was rather distraught over her husband's unemployment and the pressure on her to provide for her children and to take care of him. Yet she remained hopeful about the future.

CATHY was thirty-five at the time of the interview. She had married at an early age and had three children by a very abusive husband. She left him in her early twenties and had supported her three children herself with her work as a keypunch operator. At the time I interviewed her, Cathy had become interested in getting a college education and had begun taking night courses part-time.

GLADYS was thirty-five at the time of the interview. She had just been married to her second husband, and had two children, aged seventeen and two. She grew up in Appalachia, the child of very poor parents (Gladys never knew her father). Although she attempted to attend college, she was forced to drop out upon the birth of her first child and to support her family with a series of basically minimum-wage jobs. Currently her husband was in the Navy, and she was planning to attend the local community college part-time, hoping to take accounting courses. Gladys felt grateful that, given her very poor background, she had gotten as far away from Appalachia as she had.

CAROL was thirty-six at the time of the interview. She had dropped out of high school after becoming pregnant, and married at seventeen. Currently she was divorced and raising her son on her own with her work as a hairdresser. She had been the child of a single mother who married and divorced several times and labored hard at a series of working-class jobs to support her. She had been sexually abused by one of her stepfathers as a child and had been in and out of reform schools in part due to this difficult relationship and her mother's not altogether sympathetic response to it. Carol was somewhat unhappy in her personal life, having been in several rather destructive relationships with men.

MARCIE was fifty-three at the time of the interview. Currently she worked in a photo lab. Marie had been divorced twice. She first married at fifteen when she became pregnant, and dropped out of school at that time. Her husband became a miner after finishing high school.

She had two sons, was divorced, and later remarried another miner. She herself began doing factory work when she was seventeen. She later worked in the small grocery store she and her second husband bought and, still later, worked in a gift shop after they sold the store. She had struggled hard all during her life. Marcie told me after her interview that she had not enjoyed it at all (I had found it fascinating to listen to her talk about herself and about television).

JANET was fifty-four at the time of the interview. She had been married to a salesman, had three children, and was currently divorced. She had attended less than one year of junior college, when she dropped out to get married. Currently, Janet did clerical work. Janet was very bitter about her experience in her marriage and the way it had ended. She had never been happy as a housewife and mother, and things were hard for her as a single mother after her husband left. She spoke ruefully of opportunities she had never had.

SELINE was sixty at the time of the interview. She worked as a dance instructor, although she had had a series of other working-class jobs in the past. For most of her life Seline had been the divorced, single mother of two children, solely responsible for their support. Her husband had owned a tire company. She was the daughter of a railroad worker and a grocery checker. Seline had recently remarried, a man who owned and worked in a drugstore. She had dropped out of high school to leave home and work. Her life had been relatively difficult; she struck me as alternately feeling very competent and utterly lacking in confidence.

MARILYN was sixty-three at the time of the interview. She had a high school degree and had married during her last year of high school. After twenty-five years of marriage, she was currently divorced. She had raised two children while her husband worked in the textile business. Following her divorce, Marilyn had worked in the textile business also.

AMY was seventy-five at the time of the interview. She was married to a carpenter and had a high school diploma. She had raised four children and had always been active in sports, sometimes doing volunteer work for the YMCA and in other sports-related contexts. Currently she bowled regularly. Amy was an extremely competent, independent woman with a "can do" attitude about life.

Middle-Class Women

KRISTINE was twenty at the time of the interview and a college student majoring in art. Both her parents were medical doctors (her mother was a psychiatrist). Her mother had been born in Israel, and emigrated to this country to attend medical school. Kristine's mother was extremely feminist and was devoted to the idea that women could compete with men in men's professions. Kristine felt her mother expected her to fit this mold and disapproved of her desire to be an artist since this was too feminine a calling. (She had once suggested Kristine go into "computer art," a field which was opening up and which Kristine figured sounded more masculine and therefore acceptable to her!)

LORI was a twenty-year-old college student studying political science and art. Her father was a business executive, her mother an executive secretary who worked part-time. Both her parents had college degrees. She was a somewhat rebellious college student, wearing punk fashions and following closely the music of many punk rock bands.

SARAH was twenty at the time of the interview. She was a student at a fine-arts academy and planned a career in fashion photography. Sarah's parents were divorced. Her father, an architect, owned a construction company; her mother worked as an administrator for a social welfare organization. Both parents had postgraduate degrees. Sarah had lived with her mother following her parents' divorce and always found it difficult to visit her father after that. While he took an active interest in her brother, she feels he fundamentally ignored her. Part of the reason for her parents' divorce had been his traditional expectations about women's proper behavior, his wife's in particular; she felt these carried over into his devaluation of her abilities.

ALISA, age twenty-one at the time of the interview, was pursuing a four-year college degree and was majoring in accounting. Her father was a successful commercial developer, her mother a real-estate agent. Neither parent had completed college. Alisa was very practical and sensible in her career plans and rather conservative in her personal life. She had a steady boyfriend and intended to marry him.

JENNIFER was twenty-one at the time of the interview and had just graduated from college, where she majored in English. She planned a career in stage design. Her father worked in government and was a sculptor on the side; her mother wrote children's books. Her mother was British. Jennifer always felt somewhat an outsider to American mass culture, in part because of her British mother. She had never watched much television and felt more attracted to classic British novels (and classic British actors).

RACHAEL was twenty-one at the time of the interview and married to an engineer. She was currently pursuing a B.A. degree and planned to become a teacher. Rachael's father was a teacher, her mother had a high school diploma and worked for the IRS. Before she was married, she felt pressure to go into business so that she could provide what she considered a decent living for herself. Upon her marriage to an engineer with a good income, however, she switched her major to education figuring that now she had the freedom to pursue what she wanted.

DEBBIE was twenty-two at the time of her interview. She had just graduated from college and was planning to do graduate work in science. Her father was a college professor, her mother a housewife who worked at times as a food service person. Her father had a Ph.D., her mother a high school degree. She was a very independent woman who had grown up with five brothers.

TERRY was twenty-two at the time of the interview. She was completing a four-year college degree in English. Terry's father was an engineer, her mother a school librarian. Both her parents had postgraduate training. She had grown up a rather rebellious child, in a continual tug of war with her mother. Terry often exaggerated her wrongdoings in tales to her mother in order to provoke a response. In fact, although maintaining a rebellious edge, she was an intelligent, rather sensible woman with elegantly expressed opinions about a number of social issues.

VIVIAN was twenty-two at the time of the interview. She had just obtained a college degree in general liberal arts and was currently working in a store. Both her parents had college degrees. Vivian's father was an aerospace engineer, her mother a bookkeeper. Her mother had moved to this country after growing up in Germany under the Nazi regime. Her father had retired following a long period of unemployment, and her mother resented having been forced to work during the time while Vivian was young. Vivian's mother worried that she had no clear career plans.

HOLLI was twenty-three at the time of the interview. She was the daughter of an architect father and a housewife mother. Both her parents had college degrees. Holli was considering a career in law. Her mother was a rather traditional suburban matron who continually expected her to become engaged to a well-to-do boy and was much less interested in Holli's career plans. Holli had just met a man from a prestigious eastern school and was thinking of becoming engaged to him.

NADINE was twenty-five at the time of the interview. She was currently pursuing a graduate degree in economics. Both her parents were college professors and had Ph.D. degrees. Nadine was an independent woman, the child of a very independent and successful mother who had had nine children as well as a successful academic career.

STACEY was twenty-seven at the time of her interview. She had a college degree and had worked as a teacher before the birth of her daughter. Now she remained home to take care of her child. Her husband was an officer in the military. Stacey's father owned a small business and her mother was a lawyer, having gone back to school while her many children were still small (she employed full-time help). Stacey felt that the younger children in her family, who had been brought up more by full-time help than by their mother, had not been as well-adjusted as those receiving their mother's care (she herself had been one of the older children). She did not wish to make the same mistake.

ELLEN was thirty-five at the time of the interview. She was married, the mother of two, and completing her college education. Her husband was an engineer. She had gone through a long period of living an unconventional life during the sixties, and then had been attracted to a religious cult. Now she was very interested in being a wife and mother, as well as in completing college. One of her children was handicapped, and Ellen was becoming interested in the problems of the handicapped.

BROOKE was thirty-eight at the time of the interview. She had a degree in business although she worked as a secretary. She was married to an engineer. Her father had a college degree, while her mother had a high school education. She often thought she should be more ambitious about her own career, but she was not very motivated. She and her family were quite active in their church. She did most of the housework at home in addition to her full-time job.

GRACE was forty-two at the time of the interview. After growing up poor and working hard to better herself, she married a doctor and had one daughter. Currently, she was divorced and supported her daughter by teaching college. During her marriage she had pursued graduate education, and she felt that this was one of the causes of the breakup. Her husband was happily remarried but she had been in and out of several relationships. Grace was somewhat bitter about how her life had turned out.

SANDRA was forty-eight at the time of the interview. Her husband was an attorney. She herself was a housewife with a high school degree. She had raised five children. She was still very home- and family-oriented, always having freshly cooked food at home for her family.

LYNN was fifty-three at the time of the interview. She had been married for twenty-five years to an attorney and was fairly recently divorced. She had raised two daughters. She had a business college degree prior to her marriage and finished her college degree by going to school part-time after she was married. Lynn worked as a secretary before her marriage and after her divorce.

BETH was fifty-six at the time of the interview. She had a college degree and worked as a bookkeeper. She was married to an engineer and had one daughter, who was in college, and whom she worried was not motivated enough about her career. In her experience, a woman could not count on a man to take care of her (she was somewhat dissatisfied with the type of provider her husband had been—apparently, he had been unemployed for some time during the period of widespread layoffs in aerospace engineering).

EVELYN was sixty-five at the time of the interview. She was a widow; her husband had been a teacher and held an M.A. degree. Evelyn had dropped out of college to be married. She then raised two children and worked intermittently during her marriage as a secretary. She was a confident, independent woman.

NORA, age sixty-eight at the time of the interview, had lived overseas for many years working as a secretary in the foreign service. Later she worked for the Department of Labor. Following retirement, Nora returned to school in her sixties to complete her college degree. Nora was twice divorced. Her first husband had worked for the foreign service; her second husband had been an attorney. Nora was really a remarkable woman and had lived an unconventional life in several countries overseas.

ESTELLE was seventy-eight at the time of the interview. She had a two-year degree in health education. She was a widow; her husband had been an accountant. Estelle had raised two children and had not worked during her long marriage. She was struck with wonder at how quickly our world and attitudes toward men's and women's roles were changing.

Sample Interview Schedule

The following set of questions was used in a general way. The schedule served as a guideline to set the parameters within which interviews were conducted.
1. How old are you?
2. Are you in school? Where and what major, year, history, and so on? [or] What is the highest education level you have completed?
3. What is your occupation, if working? Work history? Salary?
4. What is (was) your mother's occupation? Where does she live? What is her age? education? salary?
5. What is (was) your father's occupation? Where does he live? What is his age? education? salary?
6. What is your marital status/marital history?
7. What is your parents' marital status/marital history?
8. How many brothers and sisters do you have, and how old are they?

9. What is your religious background?
10. What is your ethnic background?
11. What is your geographical experience (where have you lived, how many times have you moved)?
12. How important have grandparents been to you?
13. How would you characterize generally your relationship with your mother, father, and children?
14. Have friends been important in your life, and how? What type of women do you choose as friends? Can you relate this type to any media characters?
15. What is the history of your relationship with men?
16. What is your job or career history? Your goals, plans, and ambitions?
17. How have you or will you reconcile these goals with marriage or a relationship?
18. Have you had any specific experiences at work you can trace to your being female?
19. Do you have children or plan to? How will you or have you reconciled this with your working life?
20. Are you a feminist? How do you define this term? Was your mother a feminist? Are your sisters feminists? Are your friends feminists?

Media History

21. What is the history of your experience with television (do you/ did you watch a lot of it, do you/did you like it)?
22. When did you or your family get your first television set (if applicable)?
23. What have your favorite shows been?
24. What influence(s) do you think television has had on you?
25. Has television influenced your idea of how to be a woman?
26. Who are your favorite women on television?
27. Who are your favorite men on television?
28. Have you had crushes on any television characters and/or actors/actresses?
29. What are your three favorite television shows of all time?
30. Did you limit your children's television watching time (if applicable)?
31. Was your own television-watching time limited when you were growing up?
32. Who decided what television shows to watch in your family when you were growing up? Who makes those decisions now? How?

Notes

Introduction

1. See Freud (1925, 1933).

2. See Dubois (1978) for a history of the women's suffrage movement in this country. Morgan (1970, 1984) chronicles the more recent "second wave" of feminism.

3. I will confine myself to looking at American society; sometimes I quote other Western writers, for example, Freud, who have been very influential in American thought, or British or French theoretical writers who have influenced our thinking about images. But in my study I interviewed women of the United States.

4. Some of these changes relate to the gains of the feminist movement mentioned earlier. Others include women's overall entry into the workplace in greater numbers, the rising divorce rate, and changing conceptions about female sexuality and heterosexuality in general.

5. Some feminists argue for the existence of a female "essential" nature (Marks and de Courtivron 1980:90–110), while others follow Hartmann (1980:371) in her dictum, "Biology is always mediated by society." See, for example, the debate within sociology between Rossi (1977, 1984) and Breines, Cerullo, and Stacey (1978).

6. See Stacey (1987) and Rosenfelt and Stacey (1987).

7. Most historians refer to the U.S. feminist movement of the sixties as the "second wave" of feminism to distinguish it from the "first wave" of feminism, which began as the suffragist movement in the nineteenth century. See Dubois (1978) for a discussion of the first wave of feminism, and Ryan (1975) for an overall view of the history of women in the United States.

8. On this concept see Babcox and Belkin (1971) and Morgan (1970).

9. See Mansbridge (1986) for a detailed discussion of the defeat of the ERA.

10. Although, according to Ferguson and Rogers (1986), this shift may have been exaggerated by current commentators.

11. On these points see Ehrenreich (1986), Ferguson and Rogers (1986), Stacey (1983, 1987), Rosenfelt and Stacey (1987), and Rapp (1988).

12. See Gerson (1985) and Hewlett (1986) on women's contradictory roles; see also Sidel (1986), who speaks specifically to the problems of poor women.

13. See the Appendix for a more complete explanation of Marxist theories of class and their relationship to gender.

14. Media are implicated in racial oppression as well (Gray 1986; Gates 1989). Unfortunately, I was not able to give racial oppression the attention it deserves in this study.

15. Rainwater et al. (1959) give us an early study of working-class women, with some interesting information on cultural concerns. Rubin (1976) and Komarovsky (1967) discuss the working-class family and touch provocatively, if briefly, on cultural matters. On working-class men and culture in America, see Coffin (1955), Geiger and Sokol (1959), Hodges (1964), Shostak (1969), Greenberg and Dervin (1970), Simon and Gagnon (1970), and Mendelsohn (1971). Some work more specifically focusing on the "deviant" groups in American society also touches upon working-class men and cultural issues; see especially Becker (1963) and Matza (1964).

16. The "Birmingham School" refers to the work of a group of social scientists studying culture and the media at the Centre for Contemporary Cultural Studies in Birmingham, England. See Hall (1980a) for a good introduction to the problematic of these cultural analysts. I discuss their work in more detail in chapter 1.

17. For studies of British working-class men and their culture, particularly of their formation of subcultures in part through the appropriation of specific elements of mass culture, see Willis (1977 and 1978) and Hall et al. (1976). Studies of women have been confined primarily to working-class girls' youth cultures; see McRobbie (1978b, 1981, 1984) and McRobbie and McCabe (1981).

18. See Hall's excellent deconstruction of the term "popular culture" (1981). For general discussions of the work of the members of the Birmingham School, see Hall et al. (1976), Hall (1980a), and Gurevitch et al. (1982). Johnson in Clarke et al. (1979) summarizes the theoretical origins of the cultural studies paradigm well. This will be discussed in greater detail in chapter 1.

19. The concept of hegemony is widely used in current studies of the mass media and culture in complex societies. It originated in the work of Gramsci (1971), who coined the term to describe "coercion through the consent" of the dominated. See Gitlin (1980) for a good explanation of its application to mass media study.

20. Katznelson (1981) discusses the fact that while there is a strong tradition of working-class resistance through labor unions and labor struggles in the United States, what differentiates the situation for the American working-class from that in Britain and other Western countries is the fact that in the United States there is a split between the labor-related identity of the working-class and their identity at home. As he puts it, in Britain, a worker is a worker both at work and at home, while in the United States, a worker is a worker at work, but something else (his or her ethnic identity, perhaps) when at home (Katznelson 1981:18). This causes problems for the student of American working-class culture, which as a culture is much less united and militant than its counterpart in Britain, for example. In effect, the identity of the American working class is much more fragmented than working-class identity in other capitalist countries.

21. This point is discussed in greater detail in the Appendix's presentation of the methodological issues involved in this study. Also see McRobbie (1980), who summarizes the problems Birmingham School researchers have encoun-

tered in applying their categories to the study of women. On the general problem of the inability of scholars to fit neatly groups of women into Marxist class categories, see Giddens (1973:288), West (1972), Hartmann and Bridges (1974), and Eisenstein (1979).

22. See especially Radway (1984b) and Long (1986).

23. Exceptions are Lull et al. (1983) and Hobson (1982).

Chapter One: Theoretical Framework

1. Some might lump together the hegemonic and the British Cultural Studies traditions into one larger "critical" tradition of media study, which stands in contradistinction to less "critical," more mainstream, work, since both the former traditions owe much to Marxist (particularly Althusserian and Gramscian) theoretical roots. When one focuses on the audience, as I do here, the distinction between "critical" and "mainstream," so basic to most characterizations of communication research in the United States and Great Britain, is rather limiting. As some have pointed out, American critical research has often neglected the question of the audience (Fejes 1984); in Britain, however, "audience" study (although the notion of audience is more broadly conceived than in the United States, almost as a "cultural" audience) has been a primary theme of critical communication researchers.

Cultural studies as developed by the Birmingham School—particularly in their presumption of an active and resistant audience and their use of qualitative methodology in studying that audience—have begun to exert a wide influence on other contemporary studies of the media audience, both in the United States and abroad. For instance, Tamar Liebes and Elihu Katz (the latter one of the originators of the "dominant paradigm" in mainstream research and once identified solely with this paradigm and with uses and gratifications research) have launched a series of intercultural studies of reception of the television series *Dallas* (Katz and Liebes 1984; Liebes 1984; see also Ang 1985). The *Dallas* studies make use of qualitative research techniques, primarily focused interviews with groups of viewers, often in family or family-like settings. In addition, researchers recorded viewers' conversations and comments made while watching the show. Unlike much earlier American audience research, the focus of the *Dallas* studies has been viewer interpretation of the elements—plot, character, narrative—of the show.

Others in the United States as well have begun to move their studies of their audience out of the "mainstream" by using qualitative methods of study and engaging with some of the same issues and questions traditionally asked by those in the critical tradition (Lull 1987a). For some other examples of this new and exciting direction of communication research, see especially Lull (1978, 1980, 1987a, 1987b); Webster and Wakshlag (1982); Brody and Stoneman (1983); Goodman (1983); Lemish (1985, 1987); Schwartz (1986); Anderson (1987); Bryce (1987); Cantor (1987); Lindlof (1987a, 1987b); Lindlof and Meyer (1987); Messaris (1987); Schwarz and Griffin (1987); Traudt, Anderson, and Meyer (1987); Traudt and Lont (1987); Lindlof and Grodin (1989).

While my use of methodology is often similar to that employed in these studies, theoretically my project is grounded more squarely in the critical traditions I proceed to discuss (although, as I have indicated, the divisions I make here de-emphasize the considerable overlap between groupings).

2. For more extensive definitions of the term "ideology," see especially Hall (1977a, 1983); Gitlin (1980, 1983). Mannheim (1936) offers perhaps the classic sociological definition of ideology as beliefs promoted by ruling elites in order to maintain and perpetuate their position of dominance. Over the past several decades the discussion of ideology in the social sciences has evolved from an emphasis on the forcible imposition of ideas and beliefs "from the top down" to a greater recognition of the participation of those below. The translation of both Gramsci and the writings of the early Marx into English has contributed to this shift in the definition of the concept of ideology.

3. See Antonio Gramsci, *Selections from the Prison Notebooks*, ed. and trans. Quintin Hoare and Geoffrey Nowell Smith (New York: International, 1971). Gramsci's notion of hegemony has been developed more recently by Williams (1973, 1977c), and has been applied directly to contemporary media study by Gitlin (1980, 1983).

4. See Adorno (1954); Sklar (1980); Gitlin (1980, 1983, 1986); and Bagdikian (1983).

5. The definition of the term "realism" merits some discussion here. What does it mean for a television viewer to speak of a television show or character as realistic? In fact, the answer to this question is far from obvious. Viewers may vary by sex, social class, even individually as to their meaning in labeling a television program or character to be realistic. Even critics cannot agree on the meaning of the label "realism" when this is applied to a work of art or, in this case, to a product of the mass media. In general, while much used in the critical literature, the term is ill-defined and, consequently, is often used idiosyncratically by individual critics within fields and certainly by critics in different fields of analysis.

Auerbach (1953) speaks exhaustively of the vicissitudes in the attempt to define reality throughout the entire history of Western literature. While he remains reluctant to define the term "realism" itself, he limits his project instead to differences in the way "realistic subjects" have been treated from the time of classical antiquity through the modernist literature of the twentieth century. Auerbach traces the rise of subjectivism in twentieth-century writers to the decline of a widely recognized social consensus in our time as to what the real world is all about:

> As recently as the nineteenth century, and even at the beginning of the twentieth, so much clearly formulable and recognized community of thought and feeling remained in those countries that a writer engaged in representing reality had reliable criteria at hand by which to organize it. At least, within the range of contemporary movements, he could discern certain specific trends; he could delimit opposing attitudes and ways of life with a certain degree of clarity. To be sure, this had long since begun to grow increasingly difficult. . . . At the time of the first World War and after—in a Europe unsure of itself, overflowing with unsettled ideologies and ways of life, and pregnant with disaster—certain writers distinguished by instinct and insight find a method which dissolves reality into multiple and multivalent reflections of consciousness. That this method should have been developed at this time is not hard to understand. (Auerbach 1953:550–551)

Raymond Williams (1977b) echoes Auerbach's reluctance to define a specific realistic method, noting that an abstract realistic method does not exist. Rather, the question as to whether a particular work is or is not realistic must be considered within the social and political context of that work, the intentions of its authors, and the conditions of its reception. Put more simply, what is realistic in one context is not necessarily realistic in another context. While he does identify the three essential qualities of the genre of realistic literature and drama which emerged in the late nineteenth century—these are the representation of "the people" or lower classes as well as the upper classes, a movement toward setting actions in the present, and an emphasis on secular, as opposed to religious, action—Williams nevertheless maintains that these works must be contextualized in order to fully ascertain their realistic nature (Williams 1977b:63–64). In his discourse realism, as opposed to the genre of "naturalism," which also emerged at this time and signified the depiction of surface-level reality, connotes the representation of the actual reality behind the mere surface appearance of events. When one refers to a realistic work, therefore, one is not merely referring to the reflection of the world as it appears, but, drawing upon ideas that developed along with the rational scientific attitude, one is actually claiming that the work in question represents some truth about the nature of reality which transcends surface appearances (Williams 1977b: 64–65; Watt 1957:32).

Turning to the way realism is defined in discussions of the visual media, we find that what is commonly referred to by critics (although again, there is dissension) as realistic film evolved out of the conventions characterizing the nineteenth-century realistic novel and drama as described by Williams above. When applied to the use of a film camera, realism most often connotes the following conventions: the camera is a single eye, and there is no possibility of an alternative viewpoint; as Williams puts it, "the viewer has to go along or detach him or herself, he or she has no complex seeing within the action. . . . a great deal is taken for granted in knowledge and recognition of the situation" (1977b:69).

This sense that much is taken for granted, as to how the viewer will understand and contextualize the situation depicted, certainly characterizes current television entertainment programming in this country. While much is beginning to be written regarding the possible differences between film and television realism (Ellis 1982; Feuer 1986) from the critics' point of view, in this volume I have investigated the way television is received as realistic from the vantage of television viewers themselves. Whatever critics eventually decide as to the precise definition of television realism in relation to filmic realism, the programs I investigated all follow what are for my purposes very similar conventions with regard to the placement of the camera and the positioning of the spectator.

6. For discussions of the decline of the public sphere, see Habermas (1962) and, more recently, Postman's (1985) interesting discussion of the way television has come to substitute for a true public sphere in our society and the effects this has had on the nature of our public discourse. See also Meyrowitz (1985).

7. Bellah et al. (1985) challenge this assumption, studying the role of public commitment in the lives of Americans from different walks of life. They make a persuasive case for the importance of public life in the contemporary United States which in some ways undercuts the argument about television I make here.

8. See Gitlin (1983:332) for further discussion of these ideas about television

and the social world. See also Gerbner's Cultivation Project (Gerbner 1972; Gerbner and Gross 1976; Gerbner et al. 1980; and Hirsch 1981).

9. See Edmundson (1986), who notes the marked success of the television situation comedy formula over all other program formats. He theorizes that the situation comedy is a format uniquely suited to a primarily family medium.

10. Gitlin (1979) presents an excellent discussion of the primary conventions of prime-time television and of their possible effects.

11. See Metz (1982) and Mulvey (1975). Kuhn (1982) offers a good summary of the debate between feminist and Metzian film theorists, and summarizes the debate among feminists about Mulvey's thesis.

12. Fiske (1987b) discusses the tension between Althusser's influence on the work of the Birmingham School and that of Gramsci. The Gramscian emphasis on the active subject at times clashed with the Althusserian focus on ideological structures, which at times implied a more determined view of the subject. This tension in their view of the subject characterizes much of the work the CCCS produced and is in large part responsible for its richness.

13. See Press and Lembo (1989) for a review and critique of current uses of the ethnographic method in audience studies.

14. The concept of culture has been central to theorists of the school (Hall 1977a, 1980b, 1983). As in our society, culture is defined by CCCS members variably to refer in its anthropological sense to overall modes and patterns of actions and beliefs and, more narrowly, to refer to artistic products worthy of study (Williams 1976). The mass media are interesting to those who propose both definitions simultaneously, both as the center of general cultural practices and as examples of artistic consumption in our society. Members of the school have turned their attention to mass media use in both interests.

Members of the Birmingham School have produced theoretical and empirical work focusing on the cultural processes of capitalist society. The mass media have been studied by researchers associated with the school in the context of their role as repositories and disseminators of "cultural" content. Birmingham School theorists have been interested in the content the mass media produce, which they have studied as ideologically constructed texts, and in mass media as one of many institutional complexes that produce ideology. Mass media consumption and the meanings this consumption engenders have been studied as factors that interact with a group's cultural way of being in the world, as a part of the cultural fabric of life in capitalist societies.

15. See Gramsci (1971) on the role of the intellectual in the capitalist social formation. See also Konrad and Szelenyi (1979) and Bourdieu (1984).

16. In his recent work on patterns of television watching, however, Morley (1986) does use the family as the unit of analysis.

17. Willis's (1977, 1978) studies in particular sparked a reaction in the feminist community, since although he includes some infuriating sexist references indicative of the way women figure in the lives of his male subjects, he rarely addresses his informants' sexism directly and virtually omits any study or discussion of women at all.

18. See also McRobbie and Garber (1976), McRobbie and McCabe (1981), and McRobbie and Nava (1984).

19. See also Brake (1980) and McRobbie (1982).

20. There has been much debate about the status of so-called feminist methodologies in the social sciences. Although the possibility of developing a specifically feminist methodology for the study of social processes remains

tantalizing, as yet no consensus has been reached, by either feminists or their critics, as to whether this will be possible. See especially Gregg (1978), Belenky et al. (1986), Cook and Fonow (1986), Cirksena (1987), and Harding (1987) for provocative commentary on this question. Feminist theorists agree only that a feminist methodology must overtly address the inevitable power inequities between researcher and informant. See Long's (1989) discussion of Roman's (1987, 1988) interesting, innovative research for a good example of a researcher explicitly attempting to use feminist methodology, and an extremely innovative version of it, in her research.

21. See also McRobbie (1984) for a more recent, and complex, challenge to the rationalist bias of masculinist cultural studies. In two critical review essays, McRobbie (1980, 1982) spells out her criticism of British Cultural Studies more explicitly.

22. In her recent review essay, Long (1989) cites the following works as examples of feminist cultural studies research addressing the integration of class and gender: McRobbie and Garber (1976), Amos and Parmar (1981), Brundson (1981), Hobson (1981, 1982), Parmar (1982), Carter (1984), Nava (1984a, 1984b), as well as the McRobbie works already cited.

23. Here I speak particularly of Chodorow (1978) and the response her work has sparked, as well as of the more broadly popular liberal feminist tradition (Friedan 1963, 1981); see Black (1989) for a good review and history of this tradition.

24. Of course, this assumption that television viewing is primarily solitary is currently being widely challenged. See Lull (1978), Morley (1986), and Lembo (1988).

25. Holland (1975b) offers an interesting exception to this tendency. Working in the tradition of reader-response theory, Holland applies psychoanalytic theory to the analysis of five actual readers interpreting a single text, producing a fascinating document of the personal reasons that might cause readers to interpret the same text differently. Although interesting, the study was limited in its scope by its intensive focus on a few individuals; however, this sharp focus gives the study its unusual explanatory depth.

26. Reader-response criticism is a growing area of literary criticism which attempts to turn critics away from a strictly text-centered emphasis to a focus on readers as well. Those most often identified with the school include Holland (1975a, 1975b), Eco (1979), Fish (1980), Tompkins (1980), and Culler (1981). Unfortunately, few reader-response theorists propose concrete plans for audience study, which is understandable since most are rooted in a literary rather than a social-scientific tradition. The closest the tradition seems to come to actual audience study is in the work of Holland, who adopts a psychoanalytic approach. As I discussed in note 25 above, in *Five Readers Reading*, Holland traces the decodings that five different readers of a single text make to each reader's "identity theme," culled from an investigation of the reader's psychoanalytic profile with the help of interviews and projective tests. This work may be criticized for being too subjective in its explanation of the critical process. While psychoanalytic profiles may certainly be important, one must also take social, political, and economic context into account when assessing the activity of interpretation.

Radway herself mentions that, of the reader-response theorists, Fish (1980) has had the most influence on her project, particularly because of his appreciation for the social context of individual interpretation. She criticizes his ultimately text-centered, rather than reader-centered, emphasis, while noting that the primary goal of the reader-response theorists has been to integrate the two foci.

27. Radway herself mentions the patriarchal content of romances, and the possible ways this content may work against the more feminist interpretation of the act of romance reading which she offers earlier in the book. See especially Radway's concluding chapter (1984b:209–222) for a good summary of her results.

28. See Douglas (1983) for a more explicit feminist condemnation of romances, which does not even attempt to take readers' views into account (see also Douglas 1977). Douglas's work has been widely criticized by feminists; Snitow (1983) offers a reply.

29. Radway herself notes that her sample was almost exclusively middle-class.

30. See especially chapter 6 of Radway's book (1984b:186–208) for her analysis of the significance of this ambivalence toward the realism of romantic novels which she found among her informants.

31. See also Roman (1987, 1988), Rose (1989), and Amesly (1989), again all cited in Long's (1989) excellent review.

Chapter Two: Work, Family, and Social Class

1. Most empirical studies of women's images in television have used content analysis to focus somewhat narrowly on the problem of where female characters fit in with the larger overall sample of women on television. These studies compare women's images to images of men on television, noting differences and similarities between the two groups. Tedesco (1974), for example, performs content analysis which yields clear differences between male and female television characters. She notes that television women are younger, more likely to be minor than major characters, more likely to be victims of violent crimes, more likely to be married, and much less likely to hold powerful positions when compared with men on television. More recently, Lichter et al. (1986) note that some of these facts have not changed: on prime-time television, female characters are still far outnumbered by males (only one out of five characters on prime-time shows is female), and they are even more outnumbered among relatively powerful characters such as doctors, judges, lawyers, professors, and corporate executives and college graduates generally. In all of these cases, women's representation on television underrepresents their power and presence in the real world. In addition, Lichter et al. (1986) find that women on television are more concerned with sex and marriage than are men.

Studies that discuss and evaluate the specific qualities of female characters on television have been interesting, but rare. Weibel (1977) discusses generally the qualities of specific female characters in the history of television. Mendelsohn (1971) also generalizes about the qualities of television women. Adorno (1954), Gans (1966), and Sklar (1980) offer interesting discussions that focus quite distinctly on working women in television. Lemon (1978), Sklar (1980), and Gray (1986) discuss the black family. Soap opera characters have been widely reviewed, as in the works of Modleski (1979, 1982), Cantor and Pingree (1983), Intintoli (1984), Allen (1985), and Rosen (1986). Some of these studies have taken a specifically feminist perspective, but often the meaning of a feminist critical perspective vis-à-vis television analysis has been unclear.

2. One study, "Prime Time Kids: An Analysis of Children and Families on Television," was based on fifteen situation comedies that had children as continuing characters during the 1984–85 prime-time season. The study was reported in the September 2, 1985, issue of *Broadcasting*. The figures reported here are derived from this study.

3. See Andrews (1976) for a convenient summary of all of the plots of the *I Love Lucy* show.

4. See Friedan (1963) for a discussion of the housewife's invisibility as a cause of her discontent.

5. See McRobbie (1978b, 1980, 1984) for several attempts to chronicle female subcultures in Great Britain. In some respects, the female bonding depicted on *I Love Lucy* and the other shows I discuss is characterized in a way that bears some resemblance to the subcultures McRobbie describes.

6. See Rubin (1976) for a good discussion of the working-class family in the United States.

7. Frye (1957) discusses the way in which comedy often requires maintaining a strict differentiation between the sexes, as was true here.

8. See Heilbronn (1986) for a fuller discussion of childlike images of women on television situation comedies.

9. When all family shows on early television are considered, the percentage of working-class families is 29 percent of all families depicted.

10. See Komarovsky (1967) and Rubin (1976) on this point. Women's class position in the United States is discussed in more detail in the Appendix.

11. I use the terms "liberal ideology" and "dominant ideology" synonymously. By liberal ideology, I refer to the belief central to classic utilitarian liberalism, which along with some versions of republicanism underlies our legal system, that the basic unit of society and of social justice is the individual. See Eisenstein (1981) and Elshtain (1981) for a detailed discussion of the relationship between feminism and liberal thought.

12. Caputi (1989) makes this point in a recent review of Taylor (1989). Rather than emphasizing (as does Taylor) the shift toward the workplace as a displacement during the feminist period of television's family fixation, Caputi reads this as merely "a temporary relocation of traditional iconography—and its socially expedient roles and rules of paternal authority, female subordination and group loyalty—to the workplace, but only until it was safe to return to the home front" (1989:11).

13. It is interesting that when Audrey Meadows first applied to Jackie Gleason for the part of Alice on *The Honeymooners*, he found her too pretty for the character. Only when she returned for a second audition in a plain, cheap dress, her hair pulled back modestly and tied with a rag, did she get the part. There is a strong tradition on television of forgoing glamour in stereotypical portrayals of working-class women. Because working-class images are so rare on network television, however, women sans glamour are rare as well.

14. Not without some resistance by the show's producers, however. A newspaper brief reports the hiring of Jay Daniel, a "producer who specializes in handling hot-blooded talent," who was brought in to smooth relations between Roseanne Barr and the producers of her series. Reportedly, Barr wanted her character to express more anger than the producers would agree to. She had

had the show's creator and original executive producer, Matt Williams, fired, and asked to get rid of his successor, Jeff Harris (*Ann Arbor News,* January 12, 1990, p. A-10).

15. See Komarovsky (1967) and Rubin (1976) for a more complete discussion of actual working-class marital relationships. In fact, Rubin argues that communication between partners is extremely difficult in these marriages.

16. I am indebted to a personal conversation with Herman Gray for this interpretation of *Cosby* as an attempt to reclaim the black family. See Moynihan (1963, 1969) and Genovese (1974) for further explication of the debate over the actual form of the black family in the United States.

17. See Marc (1985) and Miller (1986); both offer detailed discussions of the idealized family life as portrayed on *Cosby.*

18. Taylor's perspective is somewhat different. She interprets the television narrative as "a commentary on, and resolution of, our troubles rather than a reflection of the real conditions of our lives" (1989:153). From this perspective, television can on one level be read as offering a feminist critique of male roles in the family, by giving us such atypical male figures who, with their idealized qualities, "solve," in fantasy, the problems plaguing many family women.

19. Lewin (1989) documents the obstacles female lawyers, for example, continue to face as they attempt to succeed in their profession.

Part II Introduction

1. See here especially Meyrowitz (1985) and Postman (1985).

Chapter Three: Middle-Class Women Discuss Television

1. Hochschild (1989) mentions some of these criticisms of Chodorow, but stresses the more general criticism that Chodorow's argument makes it seem as though all women develop the same attitudes toward motherhood and does not provide for individual differences among women.

2. The following texts discuss the concept of "women's culture" in further detail and from a variety of different perspectives: Welter (1966); McRobbie (1978b and 1984); Dworkin (1981); Di Leonardo (1984); Catherine Hall (1986); Peiss (1986).

3. See Bellah et al. (1985) for a fuller description of individualism as a concept central to American middle-class values.

4. Long (1986) specifically differentiates the self women readers strive for from the fragmented, decentered, postmodern notion of the "self" fashionable in current cultural theory. Her informants draw from "an older ideal of morally significant 'character' " which she feels is capable of giving readers a potentially critical perspective on the present.

5. Long cites Lyotard (1984:75) here, who labels these tendencies of cultural reception "fantasies of realism." According to Lyotard, the intention of realism in our present historical situation is "to avoid the question of reality implicated in that of art." Consequently, she notes that he would find her readers' conception of the text "an accommodationist exercise in middle-class avoidance and nostalgia."

6. Radway's data, discussed here, is based on women's answers to a question-

naire that asked them to compare the heroine's reactions and feelings with their own. Thirteen respondents saw no resemblance whatsoever, five did not answer, and twenty-two believed that the heroine's feelings "are somewhat like mine." From the same sample, twenty-two women felt that romance characters in general "were not at all similar" to people they met in real life, and twenty-three felt that the events in romances were "not at all similar" to those occurring in real life. One possible explanation for the finding that women see romance events and characters generally as unrealistic, yet see something of themselves in the heroines, is as Radway notes that the readers believe that romance heroines are more realistically portrayed than other characters. Radway explains that the romance-reading experience is therefore both "escapist," as guaranteed by the unrealistic nature of events and characters, and "affectively significant," as ensured by women's emotional identification with the central character (1984b:98).

7. Although I focus here on the speech of middle-class women, I occasionally interweave contrasting quotes from working-class women when they are necessary to illuminate the class distinctions I wish to draw. In chapter 4, which focuses on the dominant themes invoked in working-class women's discussions of television, I follow a similar strategy.

8. Rachael's use of television is similar to some of Radway's findings regarding women's use of the *act* of reading romance novels (Radway 1984b). Radway found that one primary function of romance reading for the middle-class women she studied was that the act of reading gave them time away from their duties to their husbands and children, time for themselves alone. The women Radway studied felt it was selfish to claim time for themselves alone. Like these women, Rachael feels it is selfish to claim television time for something she alone wants to watch.

Other women in my sample bring up the fact that their husbands decide what they will watch and that rather than cause disagreement, they go along, even when they would clearly prefer some other choice. This brings up the interesting issue of how families who watch television together decide which shows to watch. Unfortunately, a full discussion of this issue would require research of a slightly different nature from my own, perhaps involving more extensive participant observation of television watching as it occurs in the family setting, and of the power dynamics between family members that govern such decisions. See Morley (1986) for a good example of research which addresses this topic.

9. See Herzog (1941, 1944) for the first classic studies characterizing soap opera (in this case, radio soaps) as advice literature for female listeners.

10. See Gilligan (1982) and Gilligan et al. (1988) for a further explanation of the importance of this "self-in-relation" concept for middle-class women's sense of identity. Gilligan argues that women's conception of self is bound up with a sense of connectedness of others. Her conclusions are drawn from predominately middle-class samples of women.

11. See Dyer (1986) for an explanation of the semiotics of the "star" system in American entertainment.

12. See, for example, Marc (1985) and Miller (1986).

13. Again, one possible explanation for the working-class women's critical responses to these shows may be methodologically related. They may have been more unwilling than middle-class women to admit to a professional sociologist that female images they may now perceive as silly were ever power-

ful role models for them. I feel that this reluctance of working-class women to admit fondness for television or identification with its characters to an interviewer they may have been trying to impress was in some instances a factor that may have blocked entirely honest responses. I reiterate here, however, as I have mentioned above, that in most of my conversations with working-class women, my informants impressed me as indeed honest and that following a perhaps initially nervous period the majority seemed at ease and sincerely forthcoming in their responses.

14. As discussed in chapter 2, the *Cosby Show* depicts an intact nuclear family, which happens to be black. Like *Eight Is Enough,* the *Cosby Show* depicts a professional family, in which all the women shown have distinct career interests. Father Cliff Huxtable (Bill Cosby) is a doctor, mother Clair (Phylicia Rischaad) a lawyer, and their eldest daughter Sandra (Sabrina LeBeauf) is away at Princeton, presumably preparing for a professional career. The women's professional interests are never shown to conflict with their family roles, and many plots center on activities in which the family participates together. In one show, for example, the entire family gets together to put on an anniversary celebration for Cliff's parents. A subtheme in this show is a dialogue going on between Sandra and her boyfriend over what are proper female roles in relationships, Sandra being somewhat more "liberated" than is her slightly old-fashioned boyfriend. Cliff Huxtable is shown to be entirely liberated regarding women's roles and continually attempts to talk Sandra's friend out of his "outmoded" ideas.

Wife Clair is rarely shown at work; sometimes she is shown at home doing work from the office. More often, however, she is depicted in family-related activities, making her television persona essentially little different from that of more traditional family women. Cliff and Clair are shown to have an equal relationship, however, with the two of them often discussing their problems and solving them together.

No women really talk about Clair at great length, however, perhaps because her character is not particularly well-developed on the show, which focuses more on the father's interaction with his children. Discussion of Clair comes up in the context of the discussion of the *Cosby Show* itself, which women of different classes like for different reasons. As I discuss later, middle-class women pick up more on the family dynamics of the show, mentioning the overall ideal of the family more often than do working-class women; admiration of Clair seems only a small part of this. Working-class women, in contrast, focus more on the show's didactic aspects than do middle-class women, as I discuss in more detail in chapter 4.

15. See Hewlett (1986) and Friedan (1981).

16. See Marc (1985), Miller (1986), and Taylor (1989); all offer detailed discussions of the idealized family life as portrayed on *Cosby.*

17. The *Bob Newhart Show* depicts an unusually egalitarian marriage. Bob is a psychiatrist, Emily a teacher. Emily's character is poised, articulate, and intelligent, certainly Bob's personal equal if not equal to him in the social status and earning potential of their careers.

18. I realize that technically, given my definition of topic, my discussion should be confined to prime-time television shows, and for the most part, I remain within this stricture. Occasionally, however, given the open-ended nature of my interviews, women spoke of daytime soap operas, particularly in

connection with their discussion of prime-time soaps, and these passages in particular seemed striking to me. I beg the reader's permission to include them.

19. Another possibility, of course, is that the term "identification" itself is more familiar to middle-class women and that they are more at ease in using it. With hindsight, I suspect that in some cases there is some truth to this, and that I might have better served the respondents by using alternate terms, or by breaking down the term a bit more than I did. This problem is not a major one, however, given the extremely open-ended nature of my interviews and the fact that in most cases I must infer that identification does or does not exist, given the way women talk about characters, rather than asking them directly for information about it. In fact, after the first few interviews, I essentially stopped using the term myself, given the confusion it had generated, unless women themselves brought it up in the course of their discussions.

See Meyrowitz (1985) for more information about the dominance of male images in general on television, and for some interesting ruminations on how this fact impacts women.

Chapter Four: Working-Class Women Discuss Television

1. See Clarke et al. (1979) for further discussions of working-class culture in capitalist society. See also Thompson's (1963) classic work for more on the development of this concept.

2. Others include Radway (1988) and Grossberg (1988).

3. See also Liebes and Katz (1990).

4. According to the *Statistical Abstract of the United States,* as of February 1989 less than 13.5 percent of all people belong to the specialized professions; among blacks, the figure is less than 6.5 percent of all black males and less than 10.7 percent of all black females. The number of dual-professional families would be a small subset of this number.

5. Radway (1984b) also discusses escapism as a reason for romance reading among her informants.

6. See Meyrowitz (1985) for a fuller explication of this thesis.

7. This was pointed out to me in personal conversation with Herman Gray. See Moynihan (1963, 1969) and Genovese (1974) on the controversy concerning the black family.

8. Although there was much evidence in my interview with her that Marcie has several coworkers with whom she enjoys very close relationships—indeed, it was from a former coworker who considered herself a good friend that I received Marcie's name. Perhaps her relationships with coworkers were more similar to the coworker relationships depicted on *Alice* than her transcript indicates (unfortunately, I did not probe deeply into this issue during my interview with her, although her coworkers, some of whom I interviewed as well, did indicate that a certain amount of joking occurred between them in the work setting).

9. Again, one explanation for the working-class women's critical responses to these shows may be methodologically related. They may have been more unwilling than middle-class women to admit to a professional sociologist, given the greater social distance between us, that female images they may now

perceive as silly were ever powerful role models for them. This reluctance of working-class women to admit fondness for television or identification with its characters to an interviewer they may have been trying to impress was in some instances a factor that may have blocked entirely honest responses. I reiterate here, however, that in most of my conversations with working-class women, my informants impressed me as indeed honest, and that following a perhaps initially nervous period the majority seemed at ease and sincerely forthcoming in their responses.

10. Of course, one really cannot judge Janice's enjoyment of the show simply from her verbal responses in an interview situation. Participant observation data of her watching the show would be valuable and might indicate a disjuncture between her verbal responses and her actual watching behavior. At this point, I can only conjecture about the accuracy of her (and others') responses for describing her actual behavior.

11. My findings here bear some resemblance to Gerbner et al.'s (1980) work on "mainstreaming."

Chapter Five: Generations Remembering Television

1. My sample included six women over the age of sixty and twenty-three women age twenty-nine and under. I regret the discrepancy in these numbers. Obviously, my small numbers mandate that further research concerning generational differences in television reception will be necessary to confirm my findings.

2. Some readers might argue that the generational differences I found are due more to life-cycle differences between women of different age groups than to historical differences between the generations. For discussions of the life cycle, see Gilligan and Notman (1978), Rossi (1980), and Scarf (1980); for discussions of this issue in men, see Levinson (1978). While undoubtedly people at different stages of their life cycle differ in many ways, my study does provide evidence, I argue, that the particular differences in response to television I found are more attributable to generational differences in experiences with television than to life-cycle phenomena.

3. I chose the age of twenty-nine as my generational dividing line for younger women because this meant that, as interviews were conducted in 1985–88, those under twenty-nine had come of age roughly during and following an era of feminist activity in this country. Like feminist historians, I use the publication year of Betty Friedan's *The Feminine Mystique* (1963) as my working definition here of when this second wave of feminism, or women's liberation movement, began.

4. As discussed in chapter 2, "postfeminism" is a term feminists have begun to use to describe how our culture has adapted some of the feminist ideas of the women's liberation movement, particularly those regarding women and work, while retaining a highly traditional notion of women's position in the family.

5. I define "feminist" television images here as those that stress autonomy in portraying women. Usually, feminist television women are portrayed as single working women. Somewhat later postfeminist images of women on television retain the feminist image of women at work but seek to combine this aspect of women's lives with a fairly traditional picture of the nuclear family and of women's role within it. Postfeminist television women, then, are pictured as

having both family and work. I elaborate more on these images in chapter 2. See also Press (1989a) and Press and Strathman (1989).

6. Of course, women's opportunities have varied greatly by social class, and this accounts in part for younger women's class-differentiated responses to feminist and postfeminist television images. See Sidel (1986) on class differences in opportunity for women.

7. Current feminists have noted that, in many respects, while the rhetoric of women's work and their role in the family may have changed somewhat, our society is still structured around a traditional division of labor between the sexes. In general, workplaces in our society do not accommodate workers' family needs. A stay-at-home mother is generally assumed. School hours, the lack of a national day-care policy, spurious rights to maternity leave, and the lack of comparable pay for comparable work are all issues that attest to this. For further documentation, see Hochschild (1989) and Hewlett (1986).

8. As stated in chapter 2, in my interpretation Joyce is a feminist television image. She is depicted as the prototypical career woman in many respects. It is interesting that some viewers take issue with this interpretation, clearly seeing her as a postfeminist figure and emphasizing familial and personal qualities of her character over work qualities in their descriptions of her.

9. In fact, "splitting" female images is a common theme in psychoanalytic descriptions of how children perceive their mothers. Followers of Melanie Klein (Kleinians) in particular argue that infants cope with anger toward the mother by splitting her image into one that is entirely good and loving and another that is entirely bad (Klein 1964). Fairbairn (1952) also mentions the importance of splitting in the child's developing view of both parents. Feminists have commented that this notion of splitting the mother image into two dichotomous, good/bad parts has its origin in our cultural representations of women as extremely powerful and often evil, rather than being rooted in reality itself (Irigaray 1985a, 1985b).

10. See Tuchman et al. (1978), Press (1986), Press and Strathman (1989).

11. See Heilbronn (1986) for a complete discussion of the history of the situation comedy on television, its depiction of the family and family members, and the relationship of these changes to changing demographic characteristics of the family in American society. See also Taylor (1989) and Marc (1989).

12. The role of Dagmar was played by Iris Mann in the first year of the series, 1949 (Brooks and Marsh 1985:511).

13. For further documentation of the effects of divorce on women, see Weitzman (1985) and Arendell (1986).

14. *Little House on the Prairie,* on television from 1974–83, was set in the late 1870s in the American West. Like *The Waltons,* it was "the story of a loving family in trying times" (Brooks and Marsh 1985:485). It focused on the adventures of Charles Ingalls (Michael Landon), a homesteader in Minnesota, and his large family.

15. *Eight Is Enough* is one of the large family shows of television's feminist period, which ran from 1977–81. Plots focused on a family with eight independent children, ages 8 to 23. Their father, Tom Bradford (Dick van Patten), was a newspaper columnist for the Sacramento, California, *Register,* and Joan (Diana Hyland) was his wife of twenty-five years. Hyland's death changed the family structure, however, and the next season Tom returned as a widower who married Abby (Betty Buckley), a schoolteacher, soon afterward. Abby pursued her Ph.D. in education and began counseling work at a nearby high

school. She and the older daughters—Nancy (Dianne Kay), Susan (Susan Richardson), Joannie (Laurie Walters), and Mary (Lani O'Grady)—all were shown to be career-minded as well as socially active and popular.

Plots revolve around the social and career ups and downs of the various children in the family. One episode, for example, centers upon married daughter Susan's tiff with her husband. As it turns out, she is pregnant but reluctant to tell him until they make up. Abby and Susan's sisters all try to convince her to tell her husband, but she refuses. He shows up independently to try and make up with her, the two reconcile, and the show ends happily. Shows often focus on the apparent disarray of the large Bradford household, underneath which lies the togetherness of a loving family. In one episode, a visitor to the house views the various activities in which everyone is engaged and, dismayed, calls the vice squad because it appears that several family members are doing something illegal. It was all a misunderstanding, of course, caused by the customary confusion of such a large household. *Eight Is Enough* is essentially a 1980s version of the *Brady Bunch* or the even earlier *Leave It to Beaver* in that a very loving family is portrayed, encountering in the course of its episodes problems that are all essentially minor and can be solved summarily. Female roles, however, do pay more tribute to feminist ideas than do those found in these earlier shows, in that every woman on the show has distinct career interests. Rarely are these shown to conflict with family roles, however. In addition, almost all characters on the show are relentlessly middle class.

16. Of course, in this instance, my informant's family did not own a television during her first twelve years, and she watched comparatively little of it. Perhaps because she did not watch these shows when she was young, Terry does not have the same nostalgic reaction to them that other women who have grown up with them may exhibit.

17. See Marc (1989:217) for another discussion of the nostalgia of the *Cosby Show*.

Conclusion

1. See Habermas (1974) for an explication of both Freud and Marx on uncovering and enlightenment; Ricoeur (1970) is also useful for a discussion of the hermeneutic aspects of Freud.

2. See Gitlin (1989) and Lembo and Tucker (1990) for critical reviews illustrating how this argument has become widespread in the literature.

3. See Swidler (1986) for an interesting description of the way culture operates as a set of practical strategies.

4. "Identification," like "realism," is a concept difficult for scholars to define and use precisely. I use the term in this study to refer to cases in which women saw a part or parts of themselves in a particular television character and talked about that character in these terms. Paradoxically, while working-class women judged television to be *more* realistic than did middle-class women, they saw its character images to be *less* realistic *for themselves*—they actually identified *less* with specific characters than did middle-class women. Middle-class women, in contrast, while judging television to be less realistic overall, are much *more* able and likely to identify personally with specific characters and their problems, particularly those related to the family and situated in a family context.

5. Of course, women of both classes may be inaccurately representing how

much they like and how much they actually watch television. Some women claim to dislike television immensely, yet go on to reveal detailed knowledge of it clearly indicating that they watch it frequently and carefully.

6. I realize that both of these positions are in essence ideal types; representatives of neither hold to their position in so extreme a form without qualification. I state them here, however, because there is a tendency in the mass media literature to construe these positions in such dichotomous terms. I respond here more to this tendency than to the positions themselves.

Appendix

1. See Sudman (1976), Sudman and Bradburn (1983), and Glaser and Strauss (1967) for more general discussions of theoretical sampling and its relevance to qualitative research.

2. The reader may find the following texts useful for further theoretical discussion of this method of open-ended interviewing: Mishler (1986), Sudman (1976), Sudman and Bradburn (1983), Bradburn and Sudman (1980), and Glaser and Strauss (1967).

3. See Brooks and Marsh (1985).

4. There is a great deal of literature, most of it in anthropology, about cultural interviewing and the problems and advantages of studying those rather similar to oneself. See especially the collection by Clifford and Marcus (1986) and also Clifford (1988).

5. See Parkin (1979:3–4) for a good introduction to the Marxist and Weberian theories of class and the differences between them.

6. See Rubin (1976), Milkman (1986, 1987), and also Stacey (1987) on working-class women of Silicon Valley.

7. Rubin (1979:214–225) discusses the similar difficulties she encountered in determining the class status of women as opposed to that of families. While she attempted to define social class in terms of a combination of education and occupational factors, in the case of women, often married to—or divorced from—men of dissimilar educational background or occupational status, confusion often resulted. Rubin's baseline requirements regarding class were as follows: working-class women should have no more than a high school education and be married to a man with a similar educational background who was working at a blue-collar job; middle-class women were defined as those with a college education or more, married to a man with a like educational background who worked in one of the professions or at a managerial level in business or industry. Often, however, the backgrounds of married couples were dissimilar; in these cases, Rubin was forced to make a judgment regarding the class background of the women she interviewed which could not be traced to any inviolate, objective set of categories set up in advance, as she explains:

In some instances, a husband's status still clearly determines the wife's; in others, it clearly does not. Those are the easy ones. But that leaves the cases where there is no clarity. Then the investigator stumbles in the dark, hoping the evidence in the empirical world will be compelling enough to facilitate a reasoned and reasonable class assignment. In this research, that task was made somewhat easier by the fact that I had before me the life history of each respondent along with data about each member of the families of origin and of procreation. By examining that broader picture, it was possible to assign a respondent to a given class with some assurance that the conceptual category and the empirical world were a reasonable fit. (Rubin 1979:216–217)

My experience in this regard was similar to Rubin's. In some cases, women's class status was clear; in others, less so, and some judgment on my part was necessary. Since I also had a considerable amount of life-history material available from my interview data, I felt, like Rubin, that it was possible to make this informed judgment when necessary. I am aware that some may find this method too lacking in objectivity to constitute supposedly objective social science; to those, I apologize for the lack of objectivity in this study but point out the unavoidable lack of fit between our categories of analysis and the social world they have been created to conceptualize.

Bibliography

Acker, Joel
  1973 "Women and Social Stratification: A Case of Intellectual Sexism."
         American Journal of Sociology 78:936–945.
Adamson, Walter L.
  1980 *Hegemony and Revolution: A Study of Antonio Gramsci's Political and
         Cultural Theory.* Berkeley: University of California Press.
Adorno, Theodor
  1954 "Television and the Patterns of Mass Culture." *Quarterly of Film, Radio
         and Television* 8:213–235.
Allen, Robert C.
  1985 *Speaking of Soap Operas.* Chapel Hill: University of North Carolina
         Press.
Allen, Robert C., editor
  1986 *Channels of Discourse: Television and Contemporary Criticism.* Chapel
         Hill: University of North Carolina Press.
Althusser, Louis
  1971 *Lenin and Philosophy.* Translated by Ben Brewster. London: Monthly
         Review Press.
Altman, Rick
  1986 "Television/Sound." In *Studies in Entertainment: Critical Approaches to
         Mass Culture,* pp. 39–54. Edited by Tania Modleski. Bloomington and
         Indianapolis: Indiana University Press.
Amesly, Cassandra
  1989 "How to Watch *Star Trek.*" *Cultural Studies* 3(3):323–339.
Amos, Valerie, and Pratibha Parmar
  1981 "Resistances and Responses: The Experiences of Black Girls in Brit-
         ain." In *Feminism for Girls: An Adventure Story,* pp. 129–152. Edited by
         Angela McRobbie and Trisha McCabe. London: Routledge and
         Kegan Paul.
Anderson, James A.
  1987 "Commentary on Qualitative Research and Mediated Communica-
         tion in the Family." In *Natural Audiences,* pp. 161–174. Edited by
         Thomas R. Lindlor. Norwood, NJ: Ablex Publishing Co.
Andrews, Bart
  1976 *The Story of "I Love Lucy."* New York: Fawcett Popular Library.

Ang, Ien
  1985 *Watching Dallas: Soap Opera and the Melodramatic Imagination.* Translated by Della Couling. London and New York: Methuen.
Arbuthnot, Lucie, and Gail Seneca
  1982 "Pre-Text and Text in *Gentlemen Prefer Blondes.*" *Film Reader* 5:13–23.
Arendell, Theresa
  1986 *Mothers and Divorce: Legal, Economic, and Social Dilemmas.* Berkeley: University of California Press.
Auerbach, Erich
  1953 *Mimesis: The Representation of Reality in Western Literature.* Translated by Willard Trask. Princeton: Princeton University Press. (Originally published in 1946.)
Babcox, Deborah, and Madeline Belkin, editors
  1971 *Liberation Now! Writings from the Women's Liberation Movement.* New York: Dell Publishing Co.
Baehr, Helen, editor
  1980 *Women and Media.* Oxford: Pergamon Press.
Bagdikian, Ben
  1983 *The Media Monopoly.* Boston: Beacon Press.
Balbus, Isaac
  1980 *Marxism and Domination: A Neo-Hegelian, Feminist, Psychoanalytic Theory of Sexual, Political, and Technological Liberation.* Princeton: Princeton University Press.
Barnouw, Eric
  1975 *Tube of Plenty: The Evolution of American Television.* London: Oxford University Press.
Becker, Howard
  1963 *The Outsiders.* New York: Free Press.
Belenky, Mary Field, Blythe McVicker Clinchy, Nancy Rule Goldberger, and Jill Mattuck Tarule
  1986 *Women's Ways of Knowing: The Development of Self, Voice, and Mind.* New York: Basic Books.
Bellah, Robert, Richard Madsen, Ann Swidler, William M. Sullivan, and Steven M. Tipton
  1985 *Habits of the Heart.* Berkeley: University of California Press.
Benjamin, Jessica
  1977 "The End of Internalization: Adorno's Social Psychology." *Telos* 32:42–64.
  1978 "Authority and the Family Revisited: Or, a World Without Fathers." *New German Critique* 13:35–58.
Bernstein, Basil
  1973 *Class, Codes and Control,* vol. 1. London: Paladin.
Black, Naomi
  1989 *Social Feminism.* Ithaca and London: Cornell University Press.
Blum, Linda
  1982 "Feminism and the Mass Media: A Case Study of *The Women's Room* as Novel and Television Film." *Berkeley Journal of Sociology* 27:1–26.
  1990 *Between Feminism and Labor.* Berkeley: University of California Press.
Boggs, Carl
  1976 *Gramsci's Marxism.* London: Pluto Press.

Bottomore, Tom, editor
1983   *A Dictionary of Marxist Thought.* Cambridge: Harvard University Press.
Bourdieu, Pierre
1984   *Distinction: A Social Critique of the Judgement of Taste.* Translated by Richard Nice. Cambridge: Harvard University Press.
Bradburn, Norman M., and Seymour Sudman
1980   *Improving Interview Method and Questionnaire Design.* San Francisco: Jossey-Bass.
Brake, Mike
1980   *The Sociology of Youth Culture and Youth Subcultures.* London: Routledge and Kegan Paul.
1985   *Comparative Youth Culture: The Sociology of Youth Cultures and Youth Subcultures in America, Britain, and Canada.* London: Routledge and Kegan Paul.
Breines, Wini, Margaret Cerullo, and Judith Stacey
1978   "Social Biology, Family Studies, and Antifeminist Backlash." *Feminist Studies* 4(1):43–68.
Brody, Gene H., and Zolinda Stoneman
1983   "The Influence of Television Viewing on Family Interactions." *Journal of Family Issues* 4(2):329–348.
Brooks, Tim, and Earle Marsh
1985   *The Complete Directory to Prime Time Network Television Shows.* New York: Ballantine.
Brundson, Charlotte
1981   *"Crossroads:* Notes on Soap Opera." *Screen* 32(4):32–37.
Bryce, Jennifer W.
1987   "Family Time and Television Use." In *Natural Audiences,* pp. 121–138. Edited by Thomas R. Lindlof. Norwood, NJ: Ablex Publishing Co.
Cammett, John M.
1967   *Antonio Gramsci and the Origins of Italian Communism.* Stanford: Stanford University Press.
Cantor, Muriel G.
1987   "Commentary on Qualitative Research and Mediated Communication in Subcultures and Institutions." In *Natural Audiences,* pp. 253–262. Edited by Thomas R. Lindlof. Norwood, NJ: Ablex Publishing Co.
Cantor, Muriel, and Suzanne Pingree
1983   *The Soap Opera.* Beverly Hills: Sage.
Caputi, Jane
1989   "The American Videology: Review of *Prime-Time Families* by Ella Taylor." *Women's Review of Books* 7(2):10–11.
Carey, James
1989   *Communication as Culture.* Boston: Unwin and Hyman.
Carter, E.
1984   "Alice in the Consumer Wonderland." In *Gender and Generation,* pp. 185–214. Edited by Angela McRobbie and Mica Nava. London: Macmillan.
Chodorow, Nancy
1978   *The Reproduction of Mothering: Psychoanalysis and the Sociology of Gender.* Berkeley: University of California Press.

Cirksena, Kathryn
   1987   "Politics and Difference: Radical Feminist Epistemological Premises
         for Communication Studies." *Journal of Communication Inquiry*
         11(1):19–28.
Clarke, John, Chas Critcher, and Richard Johnson
   1978   *Working-Class Culture: Studies in History and Theory.* London: Hutchin-
         son.
Clifford, James
   1988   *The Predicament of Culture: Twentieth-Century Ethnography, Literature,
         and Art.* Cambridge: Harvard University Press.
Clifford, James, and George E. Marcus, editors
   1986   *Writing Culture: The Poetics and Politics of Ethnography.* Berkeley: Uni-
         versity of California Press.
Coffin, Thomas
   1955   "Television's Impact on Society." *American Psychologist* 10:630–641.
Cohen, Stanley
   1973   *Folk Devils and Moral Panics.* St. Albans: Paladin.
Cook, J., and M. Fonow
   1986   "Knowledge and Women's Interests: Issues of Epistemology and
         Methodology in Feminist Sociological Research." *Sociological Inquiry*
         56(1):2–29.
Culler, Jonathan
   1981   *The Pursuit of Signs: Semiotics, Literature, Deconstruction.* Ithaca: Cornell
         University Press.
Dahrendorf, Ralf
   1959   *Class and Class Conflict in Industrial Society.* Stanford: Stanford Univer-
         sity Press.
D'Amico, Debby
   1974   "To My White Working-Class Sisters." In *Marriage and the Family,* pp.
         116–121. Edited by Carolyn C. Perruci and Dena B. Targ. New York:
         David McKay Co.
Di Leonardo, Micaela
   1984   *The Varieties of Ethnic Experience: Kinship, Class, and Gender Among
         California Italian-Americans.* Ithaca: Cornell University Press.
Dinnerstein, Dorothy
   1976   *The Mermaid and the Minotaur: Sexual Arrangements and Human Mal-
         aise.* New York: Harper Colophon Books.
Douglas, Ann
   1977   *The Feminization of American Culture.* New York: Alfred A. Knopf.
   1983   "Soft-Porn Culture." *The New Republic.* 183(9):25–29.
DuBois, Ellen Carol
   1978   *Feminism and Suffrage: The Emergence of an Independent Women's Move-
         ment in America, 1848–1869.* Ithaca and London: Cornell University
         Press.
Dworkin, Andrea
   1981   *Pornography: Men Possessing Women.* New York: Perigree Books.
Dyer, Richard
   1986   *Heavenly Bodies: Film Stars and Society.* New York: St. Martin's Press.
Eco, Umberto
   1979   *The Role of the Reader: Explorations in the Semiotics of Texts.* Bloom-
         ington: Indiana University Press.

Edmundson, Mark
1986 "Father Still Knows Best." *Channels* 6(3):71–72.
Ehrenreich, Barbara
1986 "Accidental Suicide." *Atlantic* 258(4):98–100.
1989 *Fear of Falling: The Inner Life of the Middle Class.* New York: Pantheon Books.
Eisenstein, Zillah R.
1981 *The Radical Future of Liberal Feminism.* New York: Longman.
Eisenstein, Zillah R., editor
1979 *Capitalist Patriarchy and the Case for Socialist Feminism.* New York: Monthly Review.
Ellis, John
1982 *Visible Fictions: Cinema, Television, Video.* London and Boston: Routledge and Kegan Paul.
Elshtain, Jean Bethke
1981 *Public Man, Private Woman.* Princeton: Princeton University Press.
Elshtain, Jean Bethke, editor
1982 *The Family in Political Thought.* Amherst: University of Massachusetts Press.
English, Dierdre
1981 "The War Against Choice." *Mother Jones* 6(11):16–32.
Epstein, Cynthia Fuchs
1970 *Woman's Place.* Berkeley: University of California Press.
Fairbairn, W.R.D.
1952 *An Object-Relations Theory of the Personality.* New York: Basic Books.
Felson, Marcus, and David Knoke
1974 "Social Status and the Married Woman." *Journal of Marriage and the Family* 36:516–521.
Ferguson, Ann
1979 "Women as a New Revolutionary Class in the United States." In *Between Labor and Capital*, pp. 279–313. Edited by Pat Walker. Boston: South End Press.
Ferguson, Marjorie
1983 *Forever Feminine: Women's Magazines and the Cult of Femininity.* London: Heinemann Educational Books.
Ferguson, Thomas, and Joel Rogers
1986 *Right Turn: The Decline of the Democrats and the Future of American Politics.* New York: Hill and Wang.
Feuer, Jane
1983 "The Concept of Live Television: Ontology as Ideology." In *Regarding Television, Critical Approaches: An Anthology*, pp. 12–22. Edited by E. Ann Kaplan. Los Angeles: American Film Institute, Monograph Series, vol. 2. University Publications of America.
1986 "Narrative Form in American Network Television." In *High Theory/Low Culture*, pp. 101–114. Edited by Colin MacCabe. Manchester: Manchester University Press.
Fish, Stanley
1980 *Is There a Text in This Class? The Authority of Interpretive Communities.* Cambridge: Harvard University Press.
1981 "Why No One's Afraid of Wolfgang Iser." *Diacritics* 11(1):2–13.

Fiske, John
1982   *Introduction to Communication Studies.* London and New York: Methuen.
1986   "Television and Popular Culture: Reflections on British and Australian Practice." *Critical Studies in Mass Communication* 3:200–216.
1987a   *Television Culture.* New York: Methuen.
1987b   "British and American Cultural Studies." Unpublished lecture delivered to the Department of Communication, University of Michigan, Ann Arbor, Michigan, March 17, 1987.

Fiske, John, and John Hartley
1978   *Reading Television.* London: Methuen.

Flax, Jane
1983   "Political Philosophy and the Patriarchal Unconscious: A Psychoanalytic Perspective on Epistemology and Metaphysics." In *Discovering Reality,* pp. 245–282. Edited by Sandra Harding and M. B. Hintikka. Boston: D. Reidel.

Freud, Sigmund
1925   "Some Psychical Consequences of the Anatomical Distinction Between the Sexes," XIX:241–260.
1933   *New Introductory Lectures on Psychoanalysis,* XXII:1–182.

Friedan, Betty
1963   *The Feminine Mystique.* New York: W. W. Norton.
1964   "Television and the Feminine Mystique." In *Television,* pp. 267–275. Edited by Barry G. Cole. New York: Free Press.
1981   *The Second Stage.* New York: Summit Books.

Frye, Northrop
1957   *Anatomy of Criticism.* Princeton: Princeton University Press.

Galston, William A.
1985   "The Future of the Democratic Party." *Brookings Review* 3:16–24.

Gans, Herbert
1966   "Popular Culture in America: Social Problem in a Mass Society or Social Asset in a Pluralist Society." In *Social Problems: A Modern Approach.* Edited by Howard S. Becker. New York: Wiley.

Gates, Henry Louis, Jr.
1989   "TV's Black World Turns—But Stays Unreal." *The New York Times,* November 12, 1989.

Geiger, Kurt, and Robert Sokol
1959   "Social Norms in Television Watching." *American Journal of Sociology* 65:174–181.

Genovese, Eugene
1974   *Roll, Jordan, Roll: The World the Slaves Made.* New York: Pantheon Books.

Gerbner, George
1972   "Violence in Television Drama: Trends and Symbolic Functions." In *Television and Social Behavior, vol. I: Media Content and Control,* pp. 28–187. Edited by G. S. Comstock and E. A. Rubinstein. Washington, D.C.: U.S. Government Printing Office.

Gerbner, George, and Larry Gross
1976   "Living with Television: The Violence Profile." *Journal of Communication* 26(2):173–199.

Gerbner, George, Larry Gross, M. Morgan, and Nancy Signorielli
   1980   "The 'Mainstreaming' of America: Violence Profile No. 11." *Journal of Communication* 30(3):10–29.
Gerson, Kathleen
   1985   *Hard Choices: How Women Decide About Work, Career, and Motherhood.* Berkeley: University of California Press.
Giddens, Anthony
   1973   *The Class Structure of the Advanced Societies.* New York: Harper and Row.
Gilligan, Carol
   1982   *In a Different Voice: Psychological Theory and Women's Development.* Cambridge: Harvard University Press.
   1984   "The Conquistador and the Dark Continent: Reflections on the Psychology of Love." *Daedelus* 113:75–95.
Gilligan, Carol, and Malkah Notman
   1978   "Woman's Place in Man's Life Cycle." Unpublished paper presented at the Meetings of the Eastern Sociological Association, Philadelphia, March 1978.
Gilligan, Carol, Janie Victoria Ward, and Jill McLean Taylor, with
Betty Bardige, editors
   1988   *Mapping the Moral Domain.* Cambridge: Harvard University Press.
Gitlin, Todd
   1978   "Media Sociology: The Dominant Paradigm." *Theory and Society* 6(1):205–254.
   1979   "Prime Time Ideology: The Hegemonic Process in Television Entertainment." *Social Problems* 26(3):251–266.
   1980   *The Whole World Is Watching.* Berkeley: University of California Press.
   1983   *Inside Prime Time.* New York: Pantheon.
   1989   Review of *All Consuming Images* by Stuart Ewen. *Tikkun* 4(4):110–112.
Gitlin, Todd, editor
   1986   *Watching Television.* New York: Pantheon.
Glaser, Barney G., and Anselm L. Strauss
   1967   *The Discovery of Grounded Theory.* Chicago: Aldine Publishing Co.
Goodman, Irene F.
   1983   "Television's Role in Family Interaction: A Family Systems Perspective." *Journal of Family Issues* 4(2):405–424.
Gould, Christopher, Dagmar C. Stern, and Timothy Dow Adams
   1981   "TV's Distorted Vision of Poverty." *Communication Quarterly* 29(24): 309–315.
Gramsci, Antonio
   1971   *Selections from the Prison Notebooks of Antonio Gramsci.* Geoffrey Nowell-Smith and Quinton Hoare, editors. London: Lawrence and Wishart.
Gray, Herman
   1986   "Television and the New Black Man: Black Male Images in Prime-Time Situation Comedy." *Media, Culture and Society* 8:223–242.
   1988   "Television Representations of Black American Success and Failure." Presented at the Annual Meetings of the American Sociological Association, Atlanta, Georgia.
Greenberg, Bradley, and Brenda Dervin
   1970   "Mass Communication Among the Urban Poor." *Public Opinion Quarterly* 34(2):224–235.

Greer, Germaine
  1984   *Sex and Destiny: The Politics of Human Fertility.* New York: Harper and
         Row.
Gregg, Nina
  1978   "Reflections on the Feminist Critique." *Journal of Communication In-
         quiry* 11(1):8–18.
Gregg, Richard B.
  1987   "Communication Epistemology: A Study in the Language of Cogni-
         tion." *The Quarterly Journal of Speech* 73:232–242.
Gronbeck, Bruce E.
  1984   "Writing Television Criticism." In *Masscom: Modules in Mass Communi-
         cation,* pp. 1–44. Edited by Ronald L. Applebaum. Toronto: Science
         Research Associates.
Grossberg, Lawrence
  1988   "Wandering Audiences, Nomadic Critics." *Cultural Studies* 2(3):377–
         391.
Gurevitch, Michael, Tony Bennett, James Curran, and Janet Woollacott, editors
  1982   *Culture, Society and the Media.* London and New York: Methuen.
Habermas, Jürgen
  1962   *Strukturwandel der Offentlichkeit.* Berlin: Luchterhand Verlag.
  1971   *Knowledge and Human Interests.* Translated by Jeremy J. Shapiro. Bos-
         ton: Beacon Press. (Originally published in 1968.)
  1974   *Theory and Practice.* Translated by J. Viertel. London: Heinemann.
  1985   "A Philosophico-Political Profile." *New Left Review* 151:75–99.
Hacker, Helen
  1951   "Women as Minority Group." *Social Forces* 30:60–69.
Hall, Catherine
  1986   "The Tale of Samuel and Jemima: Gender and Working-Class Cul-
         ture in Early Nineteenth-Century England." In *Popular Culture and
         Social Relations,* pp. 73–93. Harmondsworth and Philadelphia: Open
         University Press.
Hall, Stuart
  1973   "Encoding and Decoding in the Television Discourse." Birmingham:
         University of Birmingham Stencilled Occasional Paper.
  1977a "Culture, the Media and the 'Ideological Effect.'" In *Mass Communi-
         cation and Society,* pp. 315–348. Edited by James Curran, Michael
         Gurevitch, and Janet Woollacott. Beverly Hills and London: Sage.
  1977b "Re-thinking the 'Base-and-Superstructure' Metaphor." In *Papers
         on Class, Hegemony and Party.* London: The Communist University.
  1978   "Debate: Psychology, Ideology and the Human Subject." *Ideology and
         Consciousness* 3:113–127.
  1980a "Cultural Studies and the Centre: Some Problematics and Prob-
         lems." In *Culture, Media, Language,* pp. 15–47. Edited by Stuart Hall
         et al. London: Hutchinson.
  1980b "Cultural Studies: Two Paradigms." *Media, Culture, and Society* 2:57–
         72.
  1980c "Popular Democratic vs. Authoritarian Populism: Two Ways of Tak-
         ing Democracy Seriously." In *Marxism and Democracy,* pp. 157–185.
         Edited by Alan Hunt. London: Lawrence and Wishart.

1980d   "Race, Articulation and Societies Structured in Dominance." In *Sociological Theories: Race and Colonization*. Paris: UNESCO Publishers.

1981   "Notes on Deconstructing 'The Popular.'" In *People's History and Socialist Theory*, pp. 227–240. Edited by Raphael Samuel. London: Routledge and Kegan Paul.

1982   "The Rediscovery of 'Ideology': Return of the Repressed in Media Studies." In *Culture, Society and the Media*, pp. 56–90. Edited by Michael Gurevitch et al. London and New York: Methuen.

1983   "The Problem of Ideology—Marxism Without Guarantees." In *Marx: A Hundred Years On*, pp. 57–86. Edited by Betty Matthews. London: Lawrence and Wishart.

Hall, Stuart, J. Clarke, T. Jefferson, and B. Roberts, eds.
1976   *Resistance Through Rituals*. London: Hutchinson.

Hall, Stuart, C. Critcher, T. Jefferson, J. Clarke, and B. Roberts
1978   *Policing the Crisis: The State and Law and Order*. London: Macmillan.

Hall, Stuart, Dorothy Hobson, Andrew Lowe, and Paul Willis, editors
1980   *Culture, Media, Language*. London: Hutchinson.

Harding, Sandra, editor
1987   *Feminism and Methodology*. Bloomington: Indiana University Press.

Hartmann, Heidi
1980   "The Family as the Locus of Gender, Class, and Political Struggle: The Example of Housework." *Signs* 6(3):366–394.

Hartmann, Heidi, and Amy Bridges
1974   "Pedagogy by the Oppressed." *Review of Radical Political Economics* 6:75–79.

1979   "The Unhappy Marriage of Marxism and Feminism: Towards a More Progressive Union." *Capital and Class* 8:1–33.

Hebdige, Dick
1979   *Subculture: The Meaning of Style*. London and New York: Methuen.

Heilbronn, Lisa
1986   *Domesticating Social Change: The Situation Comedy as Social History*. Ph.D. dissertation. Sociology Department, University of California, Berkeley, California.

Herzog, Herta
1941   "On Borrowed Experience." *Studies in Philosophy and Social Science* 9(65):65–95.

1944   "What Do We Really Know About Daytime Serial Listeners?" In *Radio Research*, pp. 3–33. Edited by Paul F. Lazarsfeld and F. N. Stanton. New York: Duell, Sloan and Pearce.

Hewlett, Sylvia Ann
1986   *A Lesser Life: The Myth of Women's Liberation in America*. New York: William Morrow and Co.

Hirsch, Paul
1980   "The 'Scary World' of the Non-Viewer and Other Anomalies: A Reanalysis of Gerbner et al.'s Findings on Cultivation Analysis." *Communication Research* 7:403–456.

1981   "On Not Learning from One's Own Mistakes: A Reanalysis of Gerbner et al.'s Findings on Cultivation Analysis, Part II." *Communication Research* 8(1):3–37.

Hirsch, Paul M., and Horace M. Newcomb
1983   "Television as a Cultural Forum: Implications for Research." *Quarterly Review of Film Studies* 8(3):45–56.
Hobson, Dorothy
1981   "Now that I'm Married . . ." In *Feminism for Girls: An Adventure Story*, pp. 101–112. Edited by Angela McRobbie and Trisha McCabe. London: Routledge and Kegan Paul.
1982   *Crossroads: The Drama of a Soap Opera.* London: Methuen.
Hochschild, Arlie Russell
1983   *The Managed Heart: Commercialization of Human Feeling.* Berkeley: University of California Press.
1989   *The Second Shift: Working Parents and the Revolution at Home.* With Anne Machung. Berkeley: University of California Press.
Hodges, Hal M., Jr.
1964   *Social Stratification in America.* Cambridge: Schenkman Publishing Co.
Holland, Norman
1975a   *The Dynamics of Literary Response.* New York: W. W. Norton.
1975b   *Five Readers Reading.* New Haven: Yale University Press.
Holub, Robert C.
1984   *Reception Theory: A Critical Introduction.* London: Methuen.
Horkheimer, Max
1949   "Authoritarianism and the Family Today." In *The Family: Its Function and Destiny*, pp. 359–374. Edited by Ruth N. Anshen. New York: Harper and Row.
1972a   "Authority and the Family." In *Critical Theory: Selected Essays.* Translated by Matthew J. O'Connell et al. New York: Seabury Press.
1972b   *Critical Theory: Selected Essays.* Translated by Matthew J. O'Connell et al. New York: Seabury Press. (Originally published in 1968.)
Horkheimer, Max, and Theodor W. Adorno
1972   *Dialectic of Enlightenment.* Translated by John Cumming. New York: Seabury Press. (Originally published in 1944.)
Horowitz, Susan
1984   "Review of *Kate and Allie.*" *Ms* 13:32–33.
Howe, Louise Kapp
1975   *Pink Collar Workers.* New York: Avon.
Intintoli, Michael James
1984   *Taking Soaps Seriously.* New York: Praeger.
Irigaray, Luce
1985a   *Speculum of the Other Woman.* Translated by Gillian C. Gill. Ithaca: Cornell University Press.
1985b   *This Sex Which Is Not One.* Translated by Catherine Porter with Carolyn Burke. Ithaca: Cornell University Press.
Iser, Wolfgang
1978   *The Act of Reading: A Theory of Aesthetic Response.* Baltimore: Johns Hopkins University Press.
Jackson-Beeck, Marilyn, and Jeff Sobal
1980   "The Social World of Heavy Television Viewers." *Journal of Broadcasting* 24:5–11.
Kaplan, Ann
1983   *Women and Film.* New York: Methuen.

Kaplan, Ann, editor
1983   *Regarding Television*. Los Angeles: The American Film Institute Monograph Series, vol. 2. University Publications of America, Inc.
Katz, Elihu
1980   "On Conceptualizing Media Effects." *Studies in Communications* 1:119–141.
Katz, Elihu, Jay G. Blumler, and Michael Gurevitch
1974   "Utilization of Mass Communication by the Individual." In *The Uses of Mass Communications*, pp. 19–34. Edited by Jay Blumler and Elihu Katz. Beverly Hills and London: Sage.
Katz, Elihu, and Paul F. Lazarsfeld
1955   *Personal Influence: The Part Played by People in the Flow of Mass Communications*. Glencoe, IL: Free Press.
Katz, Elihu, and Tamar Liebes
1984   "Once Upon a Time in Dallas." *Intermedia* 12(3):28–32.
Katznelson, Ira
1981   *City Trenches: Urban Politics and the Patterning of Class in the U.S.* Chicago: University of Chicago Press.
Kessler-Harris, Alice
1982   *Out to Work: A History of Wage-Earning Women in the U.S.* New York and Oxford: Oxford University Press.
1990   *A Woman's Wage: Historical Meanings and Social Consequences*. Lexington: University of Kentucky Press.
Klein, Ethel
1984   *Gender Politics*. Cambridge: Harvard University Press.
Klein, Melanie
1964   *Contributions to Psychoanalysis, 1921–1945*. New York: McGraw-Hill.
Komarovsky, Mirra
1967   *Blue-Collar Marriage*. New York: Random House.
Konrad, Gyorgy, and Ivan Szelenyi
1979   *The Intellectuals on the Road to Class Power*. Translated by Andrew Arato and Richard E. Allen. New York: Harcourt, Brace and Jovanovich.
Kuhn, Annette
1982   *Women's Pictures*. London: Routledge and Kegan Paul.
Lague, Louise
1984   "Real Women Make a TV Comeback Thanks to Susan Saint James and Jane Curtin in *Kate and Allie*." *People* 21(18):154–157.
Lembo, Ron
1988   "Viewing Relations in Television Culture: Toward an Ethnography of the Audience." Paper presented at the American Sociology Association, Atlanta, Georgia.
Lembo, Ronald, and Kenneth H. Tucker, Jr.
1990   "Culture, Television, and Opposition: Rethinking Cultural Studies." *Critical Studies in Mass Communication* 7(2):97–116.
Lemish, Dafna
1985   "Soap Opera Viewing in College: A Naturalistic Inquiry." *Journal of Broadcasting and Electronic Media* 29(3):275–293.
1987   "Viewers in Diapers: The Early Development of Television Viewing." In *Natural Audiences*, pp. 33–57. Edited by Tom Lindlof. Norwood, NJ: Ablex.

Lemon, Judith
1978   "Dominant or Dominated? Women on Prime-Time Television." In
       Hearth and Home, pp. 51–68. Edited by Gaye Tuchman. New York:
       Oxford University Press.
Leonard, John
1984   "Girls and Girls Together." *New York Magazine* 17:66–68.
Lesage, Julia
1982   "The Hegemonic Female Fantasy." *Film Reader* 5:83–94.
Levinson, Daniel J.
1978   *The Seasons of a Man's Life*. New York: Alfred A. Knopf.
Lewin, Tamar
1989   "Women Say They Still Face Obstacles as Lawyers." *New York Times*,
       December 4, p. A-15.
Lichter, Robert, Linda Lichter, and Stanley Rothman
1986   "The Politics of the American Dream—From Lucy to Lacey: TV's
       Dream Girls." *Public Opinion* 9(3):16–19.
Liebes, Tamar
1984   "Ethnocentricism: Israelis of Moroccan Ethnicity Negotiate the
       Meaning of *Dallas*." *Studies in Visual Communication* 10(3):46–72.
1988   "Cultural Differences in the Retellings of Television Fiction." *Critical
       Studies in Mass Communication* 5(4):277–292.
Liebes, Tamar, and Elihu Katz
1986   "Patterns of Involvement in Television Fiction: A Comparative Anal-
       ysis." *European Journal of Communication* 1:151–171.
1990   *The Export of Meaning: Cross Cultural Readings of Dallas*. Oxford and
       New York: Oxford University Press.
Lindlof, Thomas R., ed.
1987a *Natural Audiences: Qualitative Research of Media Uses and Effects*. Nor-
       wood, NJ: Ablex.
1987b "Ideology and Pragmatics of Media Access in Prison." In *Natural
       Audiences*, pp. 175–197. Edited by Thomas R. Lindlof. Norwood, NJ:
       Ablex.
Lindlof, Thomas R., and Debra Grodin
1989   "When Media Use Can't Be Observed: Problematic Aspects of the
       Researcher-Participant Relationship." Paper presented at annual
       meeting of the International Communication Association, San Fran-
       cisco, May 29, 1989.
Lindlof, Thomas R., and Timothy P. Meyer
1987   "Mediated Communication as Ways of Seeing, Acting, and Con-
       structing Culture: The Tools and Foundations of Qualitative Re-
       search." In *Natural Audiences*, pp. 1–32. Edited by Thomas R. Lindlof.
       Norwood, NJ: Ablex.
Lindlof, Thomas R., and Paul J. Traudt
1983   "Mediated Communication in Families: New Theoretical Ap-
       proaches." In *Communications in Transition*, pp. 260–278. Edited by
       Mary S. Mander. New York: Praeger.
Long, Elizabeth
1986   "Women, Reading, and Cultural Authority: Some Implications of the
       Audience Perspective in Cultural Studies." *American Quarterly*
       38:591–612.

1987   "Reading Groups and the Crisis of Cultural Authority." *Cultural Studies* 1(2):306–327.

1989   "Feminism and Cultural Studies: Britain and America." *Critical Studies in Mass Communication* 6(4):427–435.

Lovell, Terry

1980   *Pictures of Reality.* London: British Film Institute.

Lull, James

1978   "Choosing Television Programs by Family Vote." *Communication Quarterly* 26(4):53–57.

1980   "Family Communication Patterns and the Social Uses of Television." *Communication Research* 7(3):319–334.

1982   "A Rules Approach to the Study of Television and Society." *Human Communication Research* 6:197–209.

1987a   *"Critical Response:* Audience Texts and Contexts." *Critical Studies in Mass Communication* 4:318–322.

1987b   "Thrashing in the Pit: An Ethnography of San Francisco Punk Subculture." In *Natural Audiences,* pp. 225–252. Edited by Thomas R. Lindlof. Norwood, NJ: Ablex.

Lull, James, Anthony Mulac, and Shelley L. Rosen

1983   "Feminism as a Predictor of Mass Media Use." *Sex Roles* 9(2):165–177.

Lyotard, Jean-François

1984   *The Postmodern Condition: A Report on Knowledge.* Translated by Geoff Bennington and Brian Massumi. Minneapolis: University of Minnesota Press.

MacCabe, Colin

1974   "Realism and the Cinema." *Screen* 15(2):7–29.

1976   "Theory and Film: Principles of Realism and Pleasure." *Screen* 17(3):7–27.

MacCabe, Colin, editor

1986   *High Theory/Low Culture: Analyzing Popular Television and Film.* New York: St. Martin's Press.

Maccoby, Eleanor E.

1954   "Why Do Children Watch Television?" *Public Opinion Quarterly* 18:239–244.

MacKenzie, Robert

1984   "Review of *Kate and Allie." TV Guide.* September 29, p. 48.

Mannheim, Karl

1936   *Ideology and Utopia.* New York: Harcourt, Brace and Janovich.

Mansbridge, Jane J.

1986   *Why We Lost the ERA.* Chicago: University of Chicago Press.

Marc, David

1985   *Demographic Vistas.* Philadelphia: University of Pennsylvania Press.

1989   *Comic Visions: Television Comedy and American Culture.* Winchester, MA: Unwin Hyman.

Marks, Elaine, and Isabelle de Courtivron, editors

1980   *New French Feminisms: An Anthology.* Amherst: University of Massachusetts Press.

Matza, David

1964   *Delinquency and Drift.* New York: John Wiley and Sons.

McRobbie, Angela
  1978a   *Jackie: An Ideology of Adolescent Femininity*. Birmingham: The Centre
         for Contemporary Cultural Studies.
  1978b   "Working-Class Girls and the Culture of Femininity." In *Women Take
         Issue*, pp. 96–108. Edited by the Women's Studies Group. London:
         Hutchinson.
  1980   "Settling Accounts with Subcultures: A Feminist Critique." *Screen
         Education* 34:37–49.
  1981   "Just Like a *Jackie* Story." In *Feminism for Girls*, pp. 113–128. Edited by
         Angela McRobbie and Trisha McCabe. London: Routledge.
  1982   "The Politics of Feminist Research: Between Talk, Text and Action."
         Feminist Review 12:46–57.
  1984   "Dance and Social Fantasy." In *Gender and Generation*, pp. 130–162.
         Angela McRobbie and Mica Nava, editors. New York and London:
         Macmillan.
McRobbie, Angela, and Simon Frith
  1978–79 "Rock and Sexuality." *Screen Education* 29:3–19.
McRobbie, Angela, and J. Garber
  1976   "Girls and Subcultures." In *Resistance Through Rituals*, pp. 209–223.
         Edited by Stuart Hall and Tony Jefferson. London: Hutchinson.
McRobbie, Angela, and Mica Nava, editors
  1984   *Gender and Generation*. New York and London: Macmillan.
McRobbie, Angela, and Trisha McCabe, editors
  1981   *Feminism for Girls: An Adventure Story*. London: Routledge.
Mellencamp, Patricia
  1986   "Situation Comedy, Feminism, and Freud: Discourse of Gracie and
         Lucy." In *Studies in Entertainment: Critical Approaches to Mass Culture*,
         pp. 80–98. Edited by Tania Modleski. Bloomington and Indianapo-
         lis: Indiana University Press.
Mendelsohn, Harold
  1971   *The Neglected Majority: Mass Communications and the Working Person*.
         New York: Alfred P. Sloan Foundation.
Merton, Robert K., and Patricia L. Kendall
  1946   "The Focused Interview." *American Journal of Sociology* 51:541–557.
Messaris, Paul
  1987   "Mothers' Comments to Their Children About the Relationship Be-
         tween Television and Reality." In *Natural Audiences*, pp. 95–108. Ed-
         ited by Thomas R. Lindlof. Norwood, NJ: Ablex.
Metz, Christian
  1976   "The Fiction Film and Its Spectator: A Metapsychological Study."
         New Literary History 8(1):75–105.
  1982   *The Imaginary Signifier: Psychoanalysis and the Cinema*. Bloomington:
         Indiana University Press.
Meyrowitz, Joshua
  1985   *No Sense of Place: The Impact of Electronic Media on Social Behavior*.
         Oxford and New York: Oxford University Press.
Middleton, Chris
  1974   "Sexual Inequality and Stratification Theory." In *The Social Analysis of
         Class Structure*, pp. 179–203. Edited by Frank Parkin. London: Tav-
         istock.

Milkman, Ruth
  1986   "Women's History and the Sears Case." *Feminist Studies* 12:2.
  1987   *Gender at Work: The Dynamics of Job Segregation by Sex During World War II.* Chicago: University of Illinois Press.
Miller, Mark Crispin
  1986   "Deride and Conquer." In *Watching Television*, pp. 183–228. Edited by Todd Gitlin. New York: Pantheon.
  1988   *Boxed In: The Culture of TV.* Evanston, IL: Northwestern University Press.
Millett, Kate
  1971   *Sexual Politics.* New York: Avon.
Mishler, Elliot George
  1986   *Research Interviewing: Context and Narrative.* Cambridge: Harvard University Press.
Modleski, Tania
  1977   "The Search for Tomorrow in Today's Soap Operas." *Film Quarterly* 33(1):12–21.
  1982   *Loving with a Vengeance: Mass-Produced Fantasies for Women.* New York: Methuen.
Modleski, Tania, editor
  1986   *Studies in Entertainment: Critical Approaches to Mass Culture.* Bloomington: Indiana University Press.
Morgan, Michael
  1982   "Television and Adolescents' Sex Role Stereotypes: A Longitudinal Study." *Journal of Personality and Social Psychology* 43(5):947–955.
Morgan, Robin, editor
  1970   *Sisterhood Is Powerful: An Anthology of Writings from the Women's Liberation Movement.* New York: Vintage.
  1984   *Sisterhood Is Global.* New York: Anchor Press.
Morley, David
  1976   "Industrial Conflict and the Mass Media." *Sociological Review* 24(2): 245–268.
  1980   *The Nationwide Audience: Structure and Decoding.* London: British Film Institute Television Monograph, No. 11.
  1981   "The Nationwide Audience—A Critical Postscript." *Screen Education* 39:3–14.
  1983   "Cultural Transformations: The Politics of Resistance." In *Language, Image, Media*, pp. 104–117. Edited by Howard Davis and Paul Walton. New York: St. Martin's Press.
  1986   *Family Television.* London: Comedia.
Moynihan, Daniel Patrick
  1963   *Beyond the Melting Pot.* Cambridge: MIT Press.
  1969   *Perspectives on Poverty.* New York: Basic Books.
Mulvey, Laura
  1975   "Visual Pleasure and Narrative Cinema." *Screen* 16(3):6–18.
Nava, Mica
  1984a   "Drawing the Line." In *Gender and Generation*, pp. 85–111. Edited by Angela McRobbie and Mica Nava. London: Macmillan.
  1984b   "Youth Service Provision, Social Order and the Question of Girls." In *Gender and Generation*, pp. 1–30. Edited by Angela McRobbie and Mica Nava. London: Macmillan.

Newcomb, Horace, editor
1979   *Television: The Critical View.* New York: Oxford.
Newcomb, Horace, and Paul Hirsch
1985   "Television as a Cultural Forum: Implications for Research." *Quarterly Review of Film Study* 69:45–55.
Nie, Norman H., Sidney Verba, and John R. Petrocik
1976   *The Changing American Voter.* Cambridge: Harvard University Press.
Novak, Michael
1974   "Why the Working Man Hates the Media." *MORE* 4:5–26.
1981   "Television Shapes the Soul." In *Understanding Television,* pp. 19–34. Edited by Richard P. Adler. New York: Praeger.
Oakley, Ann
1974   *Woman's Work: The Housewife, Past and Present.* New York: Vintage.
Oliker, Stacey
1981   "Abortion and the Left: The Limits of a Pro-Family Politics." *Socialist Review* 56:71–95.
Ortner, Sherry, and Harriett Whitehead, editors
1981   *Sexual Meanings: The Cultural Construction of Gender and Sexuality.* Cambridge: Cambridge University Press.
Parkin, Frank
1971   *Class, Inequality and Political Order.* New York: Praeger.
1978   "Social Stratification." In *A History of Sociological Analysis,* pp. 599– 632. Ed. Tom Bottomore and Robert Nisbet. New York: Basic Books.
1979   *Marxism and Class Theory: A Bourgeois Critique.* New York: Columbia University Press.
Parmar, Pratibha
1982   "Gender, Race, and Class: Asian Women in Resistance." In *The Empire Strikes Back,* pp. 236–275. Edited by the Centre for Contemporary Cultural Studies. London: Hutchinson.
Peiss, Kathy
1986   *Cheap Amusements: Working Women and Leisure in Turn-of-the-Century New York.* Philadelphia: Temple University Press.
Postman, Neil
1985   *Amusing Ourselves to Death.* New York: Penguin Books.
Poulantzas, Nicos
1973   *Political Power and Social Classes.* London: New Left Books.
1975   *Classes in Contemporary Capitalism.* London: New Left Books.
Press, Andrea L.
1986   "Ideologies of Femininity: Film and Popular Consciousness in the Post-War Era." In *Media, Audience and Social Structure,* pp. 313–323. Ed. Muriel Cantor and Sandra Ball-Rokeach. Beverly Hills, CA: Sage.
1989a   "Class and Gender in the Hegemonic Process: Class Differences in Women's Perceptions of Realism and Identification with Television Characters." *Media, Culture and Society* 11(2):229–252.
1989b   "The Ongoing Feminist Revolution." *Critical Studies in Mass Communication* 6(2):196–202.
1990   "Class, Gender, and the Female Viewer: Women's Responses to *Dynasty.*" In *Television and Women's Culture,* pp. 158–182. Edited by Mary Ellen Brown. Beverly Hills, CA: Sage.
Press, Andrea L., and Ron Lembo
1989   "The Hegemony of the Text: A Critique of Text-Centered Concep-

tions of Television Viewing." Paper presented at the May 1989 Meetings of the International Communication Association, San Francisco, California.

Press, Andrea L., and Terry Strathman
1989   "Postfeminism as Constructed in the Mass Media." Paper presented at the August 1989 Meetings of the Society for the Study of Social Problems. Berkeley, California.

Radway, Janice
1984a   "Interpretive Communities and Variable Literacies: The Functions of Romance Reading." *Daedalus* 113(3):49–73.
1984b   *Reading the Romance: Women, Patriarchy and Popular Literature.* Chapel Hill: University of North Carolina Press.
1988   "Reception Study: Ethnography and the Problems of Dispersed Subjects." *Cultural Studies* 2(3):359–376.

Rainwater, Lee, Richard P. Coleman, and Gerald Handel
1959   *Workingman's Wife.* New York: Oceana Publications.

Rapp, Rayna
1988   "Is the Legacy of Second Wave Feminism Postfeminism?" *Socialist Review* 18(1):31–37.

Ricoeur, Paul
1970   *Freud and Philosophy: An Essay on Interpretation.* Translated by Denis Savage. New Haven: Yale University Press.

Roman, Leslie
1987   *Punk Femininity: The Formation of Young Women's Gender Identities and Class Relations in the Extramural Curriculum Within a Contemporary Subculture.* Ph.D. dissertation. Madison: University of Wisconsin–Madison.
1988   "Intimacy, Labor, and Class: Ideologies of Feminine Sexuality in the Punk Slam Dance." In *Becoming Feminine: The Politics of Popular Culture,* pp. 143–184. Edited by L. Roman, L. Christian-Smith, and E. Ellsworth. London: The Falmer Press.

Rose, Tricia
1989   "'Hit the Road Sam': Black Women Rappers and Sexual Difference." Paper delivered at the October 1989 Meetings of the American Studies Association, Toronto.

Rosen, Ruth
1986   "Search for Yesterday." In *Watching Television,* pp. 41–67. Edited by Todd Gitlin. New York: Pantheon.

Rosenfelt, Deborah, and Judith Stacey
1987   "Second Thoughts on the Second Wave." *Feminist Studies* 13(2):341–361.

Rossi, Alice S.
1977   "A Biosocial Perspective on Parenting." *Daedalus* 106(2):1–31.
1980   "Lifespan Theories and Women's Lives." *Signs* 6:4–32.
1984   "Gender and Parenthood." *American Sociological Review* 49(1):1–18.

Rubin, Lillian B.
1976   *Worlds of Pain: Life in the Working-Class Family.* New York: Basic Books.
1979   *Women of a Certain Age: The Midlife Search for Self.* New York: Harper and Row.
1983   *Intimate Strangers: Men and Women Together.* New York: Harper and Row.

Ruddick, Sarah
1980   "Maternal Thinking." *Feminist Studies* 6(2):342–367.
Ryan, Mary P.
1979   *Womanhood in America: From Colonial Times to the Present.* Second edition. New York: New Viewpoints.
Ryan, Mary P., Judith L. Newton, and Judith R. Walkowitz, editors
1983   *Sex and Class in Women's History.* London: Routledge and Kegan Paul.
Samuels, Victoria
1975   *Nowhere to be Found: A Literature Review and Annotated Bibliography on White Working Class Women.* New York: Publication of the Institute on Pluralism and Group Identity.
Scarf, Maggie
1980   *Unfinished Business: Pressure Points in the Lives of Women.* New York: Doubleday.
Schiller, Herbert I.
1985   "Breaking the West's Media Monopoly." *The Nation* 241(8):248–251.
Schlafly, Phyllis
1977   *The Power of the Positive Woman.* New Rochelle, NY: Arlington.
Schudson, Michael
1978   *Discovering the News.* New York: Basic Books.
1984   *Advertising, The Uneasy Persuasion.* New York: Basic Books.
Schwichtenberg, Cathy
1981   "Charlie's Angels (ABC-TV)." *Jump Cut* 24/25:13–15.
Schwartz, Dona
1986   "Camera Clubs and Fine Art Photography." *Urban Life* 15(2):165–195.
Schwartz, Dona, and Michael Griffin
1987   "Amateur Photography: The Organizational Maintenance of an Aesthetic Code." In *Natural Audiences,* pp. 198–224. Edited by Thomas R. Lindlof. Norwood, NJ: Ablex.
Shostak, Arthur B.
1969   *Blue-Collar Life.* New York: Random House.
Shostak, Arthur B., and William Gomberg
1964   *Blue-Collar World: Studies of the American Worker.* Englewood Cliffs, NJ: Prentice Hall.
Sidel, Ruth
1986   *Women and Children Last.* New York: Viking Press.
Simon, William, and John Gagnon
1970   "Working-Class Youth: Alienation Without an Image." In *The White Majority,* pp. 45–59. Edited by Louise Kapp Howe. New York: Random House.
Sklar, Robert
1980   *Prime-Time America: Life On and Behind the Television Screen.* Oxford: Oxford University Press.
Smith-Blau, Zena
1972   "Maternal Aspirations, Socialization, and Achievement of Boys and Girls in the White Working Class." *Journal of Youth and Adolescence* 1(1):35–57.
Smith-Rosenberg, Carroll
1975   "The Female World of Love and Ritual." *Signs* 1(1):1–29.

Snitow, Ann Barr
1983   "Mass Market Romance: Pornography for Women Is Different." In *Powers of Desire: The Politics of Sexuality,* pp. 245–263. Edited by Ann Barr Snitow, Christine Stansell, and Sharon Thompson. New York: Monthly Review Press.
Snitow, Ann Barr, Christine Stansell, and Sharon Thompson, editors
1983   *Powers of Desire: The Politics of Sexuality.* New York: Monthly Review Press.
Stacey, Judith
1983   "The New Conservative Feminism." *Feminist Studies* 9(3):559–584.
1987   "Sexism by a Subtler Name: Postindustrial Conditions and Postfeminist Consciousness in the Silicon Valley." *Socialist Review* 17(96):7–30.
Stack, Carol P.
1974   *All My Kin: Strategies for Survival in a Black Community.* New York: Harper and Row.
Sudman, Seymour
1976   *Applied Sampling.* New York: Academic Press.
Sudman, Seymour, and Norman M. Bradburn
1983   *Asking Questions: A Practical Guide to Questionnaire Design.* San Francisco: Jossey-Bass.
Swidler, Ann
1986   "Culture in Action: Symbols and Strategies." *American Sociological Review* 51:273–286.
Taylor, Ella
1989   *Prime Time Families: Television Culture in Postwar America.* Berkeley: University of California Press.
Tedesco, Nancy S.
1974   "Patterns in Prime Time." *Journal of Communication* 24(2):119–124.
Thomas, Sari, and Brian P. Callahan
1982   "Allocating Happiness: TV Families and Social Class." *Journal of Communication* 32(3):184–189.
Thompson, E. P.
1963   *The Making of the English Working Class.* New York: Vintage.
Tompkins, Jane P., editor
1980   *Reader-Response Criticism.* Baltimore: Johns Hopkins University Press.
Traudt, Paul J., James A. Anderson, and Timothy P. Meyer
1987   "Phenomenology, Empiricism, and Media Experience." *Critical Studies in Mass Communication* 4(3):302–310.
Traudt, Paul J., and Cynthia M. Lont
1987   "Media-Logic-in-Use: The Family as Locus of Study." In *Natural Audiences,* pp. 139–160. Edited by Thomas R. Lindlof. Norwood, NJ: Ablex.
Tuchman, Gaye, Arlene Kaplan Daniels, and James Benet, editors
1978   *Hearth and Home: Images of Women in the Mass Media.* New York: Oxford University Press.
U.S. Bureau of the Census
1960   *Statistical Abstract of the United States: 1960* (81st edition). Washington, D.C.: U.S. Dept. of Commerce, Government Printing Office.
1975   *Statistical Abstract of the United States: 1975* (96th edition). Washington, D.C.: U.S. Dept. of Commerce, Government Printing Office.

1987   *Statistical Abstract of the United States: 1987* (107th edition). Washington, D.C.: U.S. Dept. of Commerce, Government Printing Office.

Vaillant, George E.
1977   *Adaptation to Life.* Boston: Little, Brown.

van Zoonen, Liesbet
1988   "Rethinking Women and the News." *European Journal of Communication* 3:35–53.

Watt, Ian
1957   *The Rise of the Novel.* Berkeley: University of California Press.

Webster, James G., and Jacob J. Wakshlag
1982   "The Impact of Group Viewing on Patterns of Television Program Choice." *Journal of Broadcasting* 26(1):445–455.

Weibel, Kathryn
1977   *Mirror, Mirror.* New York: Anchor Books.

Weinbaum, Batya
1978   *The Curious Courtship of Women's Liberation and Socialism.* Boston: South End Press.

Weitzman, Lemora J.
1985   *The Divorce Revolution: The Unexpected Consequences for Women and Children.* New York: The Free Press.

West, Jackie
1972   "Women, Sex and Class." In *Feminism and Materialism*, pp. 220–253. Edited by Annette Kuhn and Anne Marie Wolpe. London: Routledge.

Williams, Raymond
1960   *Culture and Society.* New York: Columbia University Press.
1973   *The Country and the City.* New York: Oxford University Press.
1974   *Television: Technology and Cultural Form.* London: Fontana.
1976   *Keywords.* London: Fontana.
1977a   "Cultural Interpretation and Mass Communication." *Communication Research* 4:339–360.
1977b   "A Lecture on Realism." *Screen* 18(1):61–74.
1977c   *Marxism and Literature.* Oxford: Oxford University Press.

Willis, Paul
1977   *Learning to Labor: How Working-Class Kids Get Working-Class Jobs.* New York: Columbia University Press.
1978   *Profane Culture.* London: Routledge and Kegan Paul.

Women's Studies Group, University of Birmingham
1978   *Women Take Issue.* London: Hutchinson.

Wood, Peter H.
1981   "Television as Dream." In *Understanding Television*, pp. 55–72. Edited by Richard Adler. New York: Praeger.

Wright, Eric O.
1976   "Class Boundaries in Advanced Capitalist Societies." *New Left Review* 93:3–41.
1978   *Class, Crisis and the State.* London: New Left Books.

Zettl, Herbert
1981   "Television Aesthetics." In *Understanding Television*, pp. 115–141. Edited by Richard Adler. New York: Praeger.

Index

accommodation, 174
achievement ideology, 120
Acker, Joel, 183
action
   and hegemony theory, 173
   strategies of, 174
action-adventure genre, 35
actors vs. characters, 77
   middle-class women discuss, 133–34
   working-class women discuss, 133–35
Affirmative Action, 4
Alice, 37, 117–21, 128–29, 207
All My Children, 58, 88–90
alternative families, 46–47
Althusser, Louis, 19, 200
Ang, Ien, 101
audience studies, 20
Auerbach, Erich, 198
authority, in the family
   egalitarian, 34
   matriarchal, 32–34, 42
   paternal, 158
   patriarchal, 33–34
autonomy, women's, in television fiction,
   131

Bellah, Robert, 199
Bernstein, Basil, 98
Bewitched, 102–5
bias, 179
Birmingham School, 7, 19–23, 196–97,
   200
   definitions of culture, 20
   feminist criticisms of, 22–23
   See also British Cultural Studies; Cen-
tre for Contemporary Cultural
   Studies
black family 44–45, 105–6, 115–16, 206
Bob Newhart, 80, 166, 168, 169, 206
Bottomore, Tom, 182
Bourdieu, Pierre, 101
Brady Bunch, 103, 160, 162–65, 210
Breines, Wini, 195
Bridges, Amy, 184
British Cultural Studies, 15, 19–23, 26
broken homes, women from, and nostal-
   gia, 161, 163
Burns and Allen, 34

Cagney and Lacey, 37, 40, 41, 48, 146–50
capitalism, 6
capitalist society, 21
Caputi, Jane, 203
career woman
   ideal criticized by postfeminists, 5
   in television fiction,
      middle-class women discuss, 77, 79,
      112
      working-class women discuss, 79–80,
      111–12, 123
   See also professional women
Centre for Contemporary Cultural Studies (University of Birmingham),
   19, 98, 196, 200
   See also Birmingham School; British
   Cultural Studies
Cerullo, Margaret, 195
Charlie's Angels, 35–36, 148–51
Cheers, 135
children, in television fiction, 203

Chodorow, Nancy, 64, 204
class, 7, 21–22, 182
    and cultural experience, 97
    differences suppressed by mass media,
        6, 113
    feminist analyses of, 183
    and media reception, 137–39, 177
    oppression, 6
    theoretical models, 182
    women's membership, 6, 182–85, 211
    working definitions, 181–84
    See also middle class; working class
class-specific, 75, 97, 138, 176
Cohen, Stanley, 20
comedy, and social class, 125–35
comic glamour, 135, 137
commercial femininity, 39, 40
common culture, television as, 57–58,
        60, 145
conglomerate families, 156
consciousness, 20–21, 173
content analysis, 202
Cosby Show, 40, 44, 80, 84–86, 99, 105–
        11, 115–16, 134–35, 166–68,
        169–70, 206, 210
Crime Stoppers, 107
critical media studies, 197
cultural hegemony, 7
cultural space, 19
culture, as a concept, 20, 200
"culture of femininity," 22

Dallas, 70–72, 101, 105, 114, 121–22,
        197
Danny Thomas Show, The, 33, 34
December Bride, 34
de Courtivron, Isabelle, 195
Designing Women, 40, 47
Dick van Dyke Show, The, 33, 34
diegetic vs. real-world events, 132, 134–
        35
Diff'rent Strokes, 156
discrimination, 48, 63
"distance," in descriptive language, 89,
        93–94, 96, 99, 165
division of labor, 32, 64, 144, 209
divorce, 165
domesticity, doctrine of female, 183
dominant ideology, 203
domination, 21
Donna Reed Show, The, 33, 34

drama, as television genre, 34–35
DuBois, Ellen, 195
dykes, 40
Dynasty, 67–70, 73, 84, 86, 90–94, 105,
        111–14, 132

economic detail, in television fiction, 121
Edmundson, Mark, 200
effects research, 10
Eight Is Enough, 163, 206, 209, 210
Eisenstein, Zillah, 6
emotional labor, 64
empirical studies, of audience, 20
Epstein, Cynthia, 183
Equal Rights Amendment, 4
"escape," 106, 107, 128, 205, 207
essential female nature, 195
ethnic minorities, 116
ethnography, 19–20

Fairbairn, W. R. D., 209
families, 6, 18, 28
families, in television fiction
    and class, 28, 106
    conglomerate, 156
    nuclear, as nostalgic, 159
    in postfeminist television, 43–48
    in prefeminist television, 48
    pseudo-families, 36
    work families, 36–37
    See also middle-class families; working-
        class families
Family Ties, 156
"fantasies of realism," 204
fantasy, 103, 105, 119, 123, 124, 147–48
fantasy-level solutions, 28
Father Knows Best, 33, 34, 45, 158, 161–
        62
Felson, Marcus, 183
female bonding, 31, 43, 45–47
    See also women's friendship
female culture, 64
    See also women's culture
female power, 32
female solidarity, 33, 46
Feminine Mystique, The, 4, 30, 130, 208
"feminine wiles," 81, 83, 125
femininity, 22, 40
feminism, 23, 25, 37, 39
    See also women's movement
feminist

analyses of class, 183
criticisms of Birmingham School, 22–23
cultural studies, 23
methodologies, 10, 200–201
qualities of television characters, 76–79, 81, 96
television, 34–38, 77, 143, 145, 208, 209
Feuer, Jane, 132–33
film theory, 23
filmic technique, as source of meanings, 30
Fish, Stanley, 201–2
Fiske, John, 98
Freud, Sigmund, 3, 173, 210
Friedan, Betty, 4–5, 30, 38, 208
    See also Feminine Mystique, The

Gale Storm Show, The, 33
gaze, in film theory, 18
gender
    in Birmingham School analysis, 21–22
    and class as categories, 22
    identity, 3
    oppression, 6
    roles, 3
gender-specific, 65–73, 83, 97, 138, 176
generational responses to television fiction
    summarized, 167–70, 176
    See also middle-class women; older women; working-class women; younger women
generational vs. life course differences, 208
generations, women, in contemporary U.S., 142
genre, television, 34
Gerson, Kathleen, 142–43
Giddens, Anthony, 183
Gilligan, Carol, 205
Gilligan's Island, 81–83, 135–37
girl's groups, as research subjects, 22
Gitlin, Todd, 35–36, 150
glamour, in television fiction, 40, 135–37
Gold, Herbert, 155
Golden Girls, 47
Graduate, The, 87
Gramsci, Antonio, 16, 19, 98, 195, 198, 200

Gramscian-Althusserian-Marxist School, 15, 195, 200
Gray, Herman, 204, 207
Gronbeck, Bruce, 9

Hacker, Helen, 184
Hall, Stuart, 20
Happy Days, 59
Hartmann, Heidi, 6, 184, 195
Hazel, 33
hegemony, 15–17, 98, 116, 173, 177, 196
"hegemony of middle-class realism," 99, 102
    See also middle-class realism
Heilbronn, Lisa, 203, 209
Hill Street Blues, 36, 150–52
Hochschild, Arlie, 204
Holland, Norman, 201
Honeymooners, The, 31–34, 122, 156
Horatio Alger myth, 120
housework, 48, 103–4
husband-wife relationship, 45, 80

I Love Lucy, 29–34, 76–77, 83, 94–95, 104, 125–29, 133–34
I Married Joan, 34
ideal woman, in television fiction, 75–83, 96
identification, with television characters, 66
    and class differences, summarized, 95–96, 175
    as a term, 207, 210
identification processes, 18
"identify with," as conceptual description, 95
ideological hegemony, 98
ideology, 15, 20, 198
individuality, female model of, 18
intellectuals, 21
interpersonal themes, 67
interview schedule (questions), 192–93
interview subjects, 179–81
    middle-class women, 188–92
    working-class women, 185–88
interviewing techniques, 179–81
    in-depth, 20, 22
    open-ended, 180
Ironside, 94

Jackie Gleason Show, The, 55

Kate and Allie, 46–47, 123–24
Katz, Elihu, 197
Katznelson, Ira, 98, 195
Klein, Melanie, 209
Knoke, David, 183
Knot's Landing, 153–54

L.A. Law, 40, 108, 153
language, about television
  and class experience, 98
  middle- and working-class compared,
    88–96
Laverne and Shirley, 129
learning from television, 57
Leave It to Beaver, 33, 45, 162, 165, 210
lessons from television, 106
liberal ideology, 37, 203
Lichter, Robert, 202
Liebes, Tamar, 101, 197
literalism, in viewer responses, 90–92
Little House on the Prairie, 163, 209
Long, Elizabeth, 22, 25, 63, 64–65, 66,
    72, 100–101, 204
Loretta Young Show, The, 35
Love Boat, 84
Lucy (Ricardo/Lucille Ball)
  as discussed by women, 76–77, 125–
    28, 133
  as prefeminist character, 29–34, 76–77
Lyotard, Jean-François, 204

mainstream media studies, 197
Mama, 32–33, 34, 156–57
Mannheim, Karl, 198
Marks, Elaine, 195
Martha Raye Show, The, 35
Marx, Karl, 173, 198, 210
Marxism, 7, 8, 21
Mary Tyler Moore Show, The, 36–37, 77–
    80
masculinist bias, 21–22
mass media, 6, 173
matriarch, working-class, in television fic-
    tion, 32–33, 42, 156
Maude, 40
McRobbie, Angela, 20, 22, 23
media reception studies, 173–74
  See also reception
men, idealization in television fiction,
    45–46
methodology, quantitative, 20, 179–93
middle class

beliefs, 65
culture, 101
normality, 102
middle-class family, in television fiction,
    29–31, 34, 44–45
middle-class realism, 103, 105, 124, 144,
    155, 175
middle-class women
  as romance readers, 24
  as television viewers, discuss
    career women, 77–81
    interpersonal themes, 67–73
    sexiness, 81–83
    work-and-family conflict, 73–75
  expectations of realism, 66, 83–84, 86–
    87
Middleton, Chris, 184
Millet, Kate, 184
money, 31, 109–10
Monty Python, 60
moral assessments, of television charac-
    ters, 72–74, 95
morality, 73
Morgan, Robin, 195
Morley, David, 20
Murphy Brown, 40–41, 146

narrative, 18, 131
normality, middle class, 102
normative idea of reality, 124
nostalgia, 159–63, 165

Oakley, Ann, 183
object relations theory, 18
Oh, Susannah!, 33
older women, and television technology,
    53–56, 61
opportunity structures, 143
Our Miss Brooks, 33
Ozzie and Harriet, 158

parental authority, and television view-
    ing, 60
Parkin, Frank, 182–83
participant observation, 20, 208
Partridge Family, The, 160, 162
passivity, 174
paternal authority, 158
patriarchal family, Ricardo, as, 33
patriarchy, 6, 184
peer group involvement, 58–61
pleasure, and identification, 30, 31

popular culture, 196
postfeminism, 4, 5, 38–39, 43, 46, 143,
    144, 208
postfeminist
    ideology, 43, 47–49
    realism, 152–55
    television, 38–49, 80, 81, 143, 146, 176
    woman, 166
Poulantzas, Nicos, 182
practices, social, 20
prefeminist television, 77, 80, 143, 144,
    155
    and nostalgia, 159
    portrayal of women, 29
    situation comedies, 29–34
"pre-text," 30
privatization, 22
problem solving, 107–8
professional women, in television fiction,
    36, 41, 45
    discussed by women viewers, 108, 146–
    55
psychoanalytic theory, 23
public opinion, network perceptions of,
    41
public-private split, 36

race, in television fiction, 115–16
radical feminists, and class, 184
Radway, Janice, 23–26, 63–66, 69, 100–
    101, 201–2, 204–5
rationalist bias, 201
reader-response theory, 201
Reagan, Ronald, 4
realism, 37, 99, 198–99, 210
    conventions, 100–101
    as criterion for "like" or "dislike," 101
    desire for escape, 107
    ethnicity and, 101
    identification with television characters
    and, 79
    middle-class women's expectations of
        as readers, 65, 100
        as television viewers, 83–87, 99–101,
        175
    resistance and, 175
    romance readers and, 24, 65
    working-class women's expectations of,
        83–84, 99–102, 128, 174–75
"reality"
    television compared to novels, 25
    use of term, 99–104

rebellion, women's, in fiction television,
    34
reception, 25, 173, 174
"relate to" as a conceptual description, 95
relational problems, 97
Remington Steele, 152
representations, 5–6
resistance, 19–21, 159, 174, 177
    and appropriation, 98
    and femininity, 30
    in interpretation of television, 119
    male vs. female expressions of, 21
    as subtext in *I Love Lucy,* 29
    in working-class subcultures, 7
rich people, in fiction television, 112–15
role models, 91, 208
romance
    heroines, 205
    novels, 24–25, 202
    readers, 23–24, 64–65, 205
    reading, 69
Roseanne, 42–44
Rosenfelt, Deborah, 195
Rossi, Alice, 195
Rubin, Lillian, 179, 211–12
Ryan, Mary, 183, 195

sampling techniques, 179–80
self, 204
self-image, 6
self-in-relation, 205
sexuality, women's, in television fiction,
    81–83, 96, 148–51, 155
single fathers, 28
    in television fiction, 156
single mothers, 28, 117, 119–20
    in television fiction, 28, 37, 117, 119–
    20, 156
single women, in television fiction, 37,
    77–79
situation comedy, 36, 209
Smith-Blau, Zena, 183
snowball sampling, 179
soap operas, 58, 147, 148, 206
social problems, 28
social structures, 19
Socialist Feminists, 6
socializing patterns, and television, 53–
    58
spectator, 18, 199
"splitting," as interpretive strategy, 144,
    154, 155, 166, 176, 209

Stacey, Judith, 195
subcultures, 7, 21, 178
    masculinist bias in studies of, 21
    Marxist evaluations, 21
    of resistance, 30, 98
    women as, 184
subjectivity, active, 19
subtexts, 30, 31
superwoman myth, 143
symbolic annihilation, 39

Taylor, Ella, 36–37, 47, 203, 204
Tedesco, Nancy, 202
television, 8, 9, 17–19, 107, 146, 159
    audience, compared to film, 18
    characters, 71, 72, 74, 91–93, 133
        feminist qualities, 76–79, 81, 96
        See also individual program titles
    as common culture, 57–58, 60, 145
    consumption, 57, 59–61
    as cultural institution, 8, 9, 17–19, 53
    fiction narrative
        as information source, 110–11
        patriarchal values, 96
        repetitive format, 18
        and resolution of problems, 18, 72,
            107
        and romance novels, 25
        and wish-fulfillment, 122
    flow, 132
    hegemonic function, 9, 17–19, 86, 96,
        176
    as liberating force, 146
    and resistance, 9, 96
    technology, in the home, 53–56, 61
    viewers, 65–66
    viewing, 53, 55–58, 69–70
That Girl, 77–78, 129–31
thirtysomething, 48
Twilight Zone, 94

value structure, 29

Waltons, The, 158, 209
Weinbaum, Batya, 6
Who's the Boss, 120–22
Williams, Raymond, 198–99
Willis, Paul, 20–21, 200

wish-fulfillment, 30, 108–10, 122
women
    in paid labor force, 63
    as presumed audience, 18
    as readers, 64
    as separate class, 184
    in television fiction, 27–49
    work and family conflicts, 48
    See also middle-class women; working-
        class women
women's culture, 63, 64, 204
women's friendship, in television fiction,
    30, 33
"women's lib," 40
women's movement, 4, 38, 39, 141, 145,
    195
women's solidarity, 42
women's work, 183, 209
work, in television fiction, 42–44
    feminist critique of, in Roseanne, 44
work-and-family conflict, 6, 44–45, 48,
    73–75, 80–81, 130
"work families," 36–37
working class, 7, 8, 21, 98, 196
working-class families, 43, 196
    in fiction television, 31–34
working-class men, 21, 42
working-class situation comedy, 31, 33
working-class women, 34, 196
    as television viewers, discuss
        achievement and improvement,
            117–18, 120
        middle-class families, 102–11
        pre-feminist television families, 159–
            64
        rich families, 121–22
        work, 118–19
        working-class families, 116–24
    in television fiction, 32–33, 37, 42–44,
        131
working women, in television fiction
    generational responses, 145–55
Wright, Eric, 182

younger women, and television technol-
    ogy, 52–62

Zworykin, Vladimir, 9

This book was set in Baskerville and Eras typefaces. Baskerville was designed by John Baskerville at his private press in Birmingham, England, in the eighteenth century. The first typeface to depart from oldstyle typeface design, Baskerville has more variation between thick and thin strokes. In an effort to insure that the thick and thin strokes of his typeface reproduced well on paper, John Baskerville developed the first wove paper, the surface of which was much smoother than the laid paper of the time. The development of wove paper was partly responsible for the introduction of typefaces classified as modern, which have even more contrast between thick and thin strokes.

Eras was designed in 1969 by Studio Hollenstein in Paris for the Wagner Typefoundry. A contemporary script-like version of a sans-serif typeface, the letters of Eras have a monotone stroke and are slightly inclined.

Printed on acid-free paper.